"How can a preacher address the same congregation every week for over three decades with something fresh to say every Sunday? (Okay, most Sundays?) Bruce Salmon shows us how and shares 35 of those sermons with us in this helpful volume. Orally-delivered homilies in the context of worship are meant for the ears of saints in the pews. But those same sermons are just as valuable when printed for the feasting eyes of all who would read and be edified by them. Thank you, Bruce, for allowing us to eavesdrop on the sacred conversation between pastor and congregation."

—*J. Brent Walker*
Executive Director Emeritus, Baptist Joint Committee

"In an age when a pastor's average tenure is just five years, Bruce Salmon's 33-year pilgrimage with one beloved congregation is nothing short of inspiring. Full of stories and sermons that rise off the page, *Preaching for the Long Haul: A Case Study on Long-term Pastoral Ministry* is cause for celebration."

—Rev. Julie Pennington-Russell
Pastor, First Baptist Church of the City of Washington, DC

"Village Baptist Church is a wonderful embodiment of authentic Christian community. Bruce Salmon, pastor of the community for a remarkable 33 years, is an exemplary model of authentic shepherd leadership. This volume is the story, told in candid personal reflections and inclusive sermons, of how a community of parishioners and pastor over many years grew together to become an authentic reflection of the diverse oneness that is the image of God."

—Dr. Bruce T. Gourley
Historian, author, and Nurturing Faith Journal contributing editor, Bozeman, Montana

"I have known Bruce Salmon so long I can't remember when we were strangers. Our parents were good friends, we lived across the street from each other, and we played every sport we saw on television. As we got older, we stayed in touch, and I'm glad to say we're still good friends today. Bruce Salmon lives the words he writes about in this volume. He genuinely knows and cares about his family, friends, and those he has reached through his ministry. His message in the book—a great collection of sermons and personal stories—emphasizes the joys of watching a church worship, struggle, and triumph over adversity during three decades of growth. I have already learned a lot from this book. And as I read it, I'm very grateful that Bruce and I are friends…for the long haul."

—Rix Quinn
Fort Worth, Texas

"A tenure of 33 years by a pastor at one congregation today surprises almost everyone! Such a length of service forces both compassion and creativity. Dr. Salmon demonstrates these characteristics, proving that one can cross cultures while leading worship and proclaiming God's Good News. Many will wonder at his labor to preach in fresh ways as he interacted with congregational circumstances and personal challenges. His work, both in preaching and writing, invites the reader to both deeper reflection and higher praise."

—*Robert D. Cochran*
Executive Director/Minister, D. C. Baptist Convention

"This is a chronicle of living faith and leadership. Rev Bruce Salmon invites the reader's imagination onto the firm soil of an extended ministry. His narrative of one congregation's life is complemented by accompanying sermons reflecting biblical insight in the context and life moment at hand. He bundles these sermons together with a chronicler's skill and takes us through 33 years. His skill of taking us with him on this personal journey, reminds me of the movie "Boyhood," when the director returned to the same cast annually for 12 years until he had a complete and complex Oscar winning story.

Each chapter explores a transition time in ministry or a ministerial response to some clear set of changing needs. This is not a handbook of daily ministry, but a beautiful, annotated collection of shared sermons and narratives that can complement anyone's cycle of ministry and lend perspective to the professional arc of ministry in any given place."

—*Rev. Suzii Paynter*
Co-Director, Pastors for Texas Children;
former Executive Coordinator, Cooperative Baptist Fellowship (2013-2019)

"If it's possible to capture the beauty and complexity of one's life, Bruce Salmon's book, *Preaching for the Long Haul,* is it. To know the Book, you have to read lots of books about the Book. I've read oodles of religious books in my time; and written a few. A lot of them are spent elucidating the self-evident, answering questions that haven't been asked or explaining things already understood. The content is up-to-date, and utilizes a pen with language that sparkles, to jab you awake. Its truth puts you to dancing on the graves of past tradition and worn out phrases.

While staying true to the scriptures, yet offering signposts to new paths, rather than driving down stakes marking out old boundaries. Br'er Bruce even kept our proud motto: "We reserve the right to accept everybody!" The readers will be pushed out of some of their old ruts, but at the same time reminded of the good ones worth holding onto. Isn't that what we would expect of any good book?

Bruce and I go back a ways; attended the same seminary, learned from the same mentors, ministered in the same church, loved the same people—except he stayed two decades longer than me! Whew! There is irony in a guy who gets the 10-year itch writing a review of one who stayed 33 years. It takes a special form of giftedness to "stay by the stuff." Bruce has that.

Reading about a place I served from one who came after me has been like going back through home again. Over the years you forget details, but not the people, who remain seared in my memory. Some churches are the kind that drain the pastors. Village Baptist is one that makes the pastor. I commend this autobiography of a dynamic preacher baring his heart and soul, as well as his church's, that took place over 6 decades as an example of the way church oughta be.

Former Senator Hillary Clinton wrote a book of her own, "It Takes a Village—to Raise a Child," based on an African proverb. Well thanks to Bruce Salmon's long-haul tenure in Bowie, Maryland, all I gotta say is: "It Takes a Church to Raise a Village!"

—*Br'er Dan Ivins*

Former Pastor, Village Baptist Church, Bowie, Maryland (1974-1984); Former Pastor, The First Baptist Church in America, Providence, Rhode Island (2006-2014)

"Bruce Salmon genuinely lives his faith, and he has spent half his life sharing that faith with his Village Baptist Church family. These stories and sermons illustrate how good he is at making his messages memorable. Revisiting these stories and sermons reminded me of how much I admire Bruce Salmon's ability to communicate his vibrant faith in a way that anyone can understand. I know that his 33 years at Village Baptist Church have been crucial to my own journey."

—*Dave Thompson, Ph.D.*
Goddard Space Flight Center, Greenbelt, Maryland;
Member, Village Baptist Church, Bowie, Maryland

"Readers get a glimpse into what it must be like to have a caring pastor and gifted preacher stick with a congregation through many seasons of its life. Village Baptist Church is truly a special place—a diverse and open church that welcomes guest preachers including me with open arms. That beloved community didn't just happen; it was nurtured with the love and spiritual guidance of Bruce and Linda Salmon. One can witness the relationship that was built upon honest vulnerability among these Christ followers over many decades in this inspiring collection of sermons."

—*Amanda Tyler*
Executive Director, BJC

"When we were in seminary, retired seminary professor, Dr. Gaines Dobbins provided great counsel to Bruce Salmon and me. We were in our mid-20's, and he was in his late 80's. Bruce and I both took his advice to heart. He encouraged us to put down roots and stay in one place to minister for years and years. Bruce served as pastor of the Village Baptist Church for 33 years, and I served as President of Dallas Baptist University for 28 years. We were both blessed beyond measure by taking Dr. Dobbins' advice. As you read this book, you will see a pastor who loves Jesus and loves the flock he has been given to provide and care for as a shepherd."

—*Dr. Gary Cook*
Chancellor, Dallas Baptist University

BRUCE C. SALMON

Preaching for the Long Haul

A CASE STUDY ON LONG-TERM PASTORAL MINISTRY

FOREWORD BY DANIEL VESTAL

© 2019
Published in the United States by Nurturing Faith Inc., Macon GA,

www.nurturingfaith.net.

Library of Congress Cataloging-in-Publication Data is available.

ISBN: 978-1-63528-074-6

Scripture quotations (marked NRSV) are from the New Revised Standard Version Bible, copyright © 1989 the Division of Christian Education of the National Council of the Churches of Christ in the United States of America. Used by permission. All rights reserved.

Scripture quotations (marked RSV) are from the Revised Standard Version of the Bible, copyright © 1946, 1952, and 1971 National Council of the Churches of Christ in the United States of America. Used by permission. All rights reserved worldwide.

Scripture quotations marked (NIV) are taken from the Holy Bible, New International Version®, NIV®. Copyright © 1973, 1978, 1984, 2011 by Biblica, Inc.™ Used by permission of Zondervan. All rights reserved worldwide. www.zondervan.com The "NIV" and "New International Version" are trademarks registered in the United States Patent and Trademark Office by Biblica, Inc.™

Cover photo by Shaiith.

All rights reserved. Printed in the United States of America

In Loving Memory of

*James A. Langley
(1925–2018)*

*Pastor, Preacher, Poet
Mentor, Friend*

Contents

Foreword by Daniel Vestal 1
Preface 3
Introduction 5

Chapter 1 (1951–1969) 11
    The Image of God—Genesis 1:1–5, 24–28, 31 12
    A Generous Orthodoxy—Galatians 5:1, 13–14 17
    An "ISTJ" Meets Jesus—Luke 10:38–42 22

Chapter 2 (1969–1973) 27
    Filled with the Spirit—Acts 2:1–4 30
    Supernatural High—Acts 2:1–4, 12–17, 21 34
    Pentecost Power—Acts 2:1–4, 14–21 38
    The Birthday of the Church—Acts 2:1–4, 37–42 42

Chapter 3 (1973–1977) 49
    Amazing, Grace!—1 Corinthians 15:1–10 53
    Just As I Am—Mark 2:13–17 57
    All I Want for Christmas: Hope—Isaiah 9:2–7 62

Chapter 4 (1977–1984) 67
    Anatomy of a Family—Genesis 37:2–5, 18–28; 45:4–5; 50:20 69
    A Change of Plans—Matthew 1:18–25 74
    Angels in Advent: Joseph—Matthew 1:18–25 78

Chapter 5 (1985–1992) 85
    When Death Was Arrested—Revelation 21:1–7 87
    Mercies in Disguise—2 Corinthians 12:7b–9 92
    American Pie—Revelation 1:9–20 96

Chapter 6 (1993–1999) 103
    The Sign of the Fish—Mark 1:16–20 105
    Follow Me—Mark 1:16–20 109
    Making a Christian Commitment—Mark 1:14–20 112

Chapter 7 (2000–2002) **117**
    The Beginning of the Good News—Mark 1:1–8 121
    Jesus Was Baptized—Mark 1:9–15..125
    The Source of My Strength—Mark 1:32–39................................129
    Another Step in the Journey—Joshua 4:1–7................................133

Chapter 8 (2003–2010) **139**
    One in Christ Jesus—Galatians 3:27–29.......................................141
    Freedom in Christ—Galatians 3:23–29 144
    Liberty and Equality—Galatians 3:27–28; 5:1 149

Chapter 9 (2011–2017) **153**
    I Thank God for You—Philippians 1:2–6....................................156
    The Story of Village—Philippians 1:1–6......................................160
    The Fellowship of Kindred Minds—Philippians 1:1–11 167

Chapter 10 (2017–) **173**
    God's Love Made Visible—John 1:14–18 174
    Contradiction from the Start—John 1:9–14 178
    All I Want for Christmas: Love—John 1:1–5, 14, 16–18; 3:16 181
    Light in the Darkness—John 1:1–5, 14 186

Epilogue... **191**
    Balcony People—Ephesians 4:29–30...192
    Justice and Kindness—Micah 6:8 196

Bibliography.. **205**

Appendix A.. **207**
    Guest Preachers at Village Baptist Church (1985–2017)

Appendix B.. **213**
    Catalogue of Sermons at Village Baptist Church (1985–2017)

Appendix C.. **275**
    January, Winter, Summer, and Lenten Bible Studies (1986–2017)
    Pastor's Sunday School Class (2000–2017)

Foreword

By Daniel Vestal

Through the years my heroes have changed. Once I looked at esteemed theologians, social icons, or persuasive authors with unequalled admiration. Now I find inspiration and encouragement from individuals who effectively and faithfully practice Christian ministry in a local context. Of course I still draw insights from literary and spiritual masters, but at this stage in life I find myself admiring saints like Bruce Salmon, who are unnoticed except in their particular community. And that is exactly where the transforming presence of Christ's kingdom is at work—in particular communities. These are the saints, both clergy and laity, through whom God does extraordinary things.

Bruce Salmon has become one of my heroes. He has been pastor of Village Baptist Church in Bowie, Maryland, for thirty-three years. And the sermons in this collection chronicle a beautiful journey that a pastor and people have made together "for the long haul." These sermons reflect a particular time and place, which means they are incarnational. They have the taste, touch, and feel of real life, which means they are authentic. But these sermons also connect and relate beyond their time and place. The messages are timeless. The prose is compelling and at times poetic.

These sermons are real and relatable because they were born out of a pastor's relationships with God and the people of God in a specific congregation in a specific community. They are not theology in theory, but theology through personality, the personality of Bruce Salmon and Village Baptist Church. They are both biblical and narrative in the best sense of the words. They effectively communicate in relevant and delightful ways, but they point to the eternal truth revealed in Jesus Christ and recorded in Scripture. In reading them I found myself at times chuckling in amusement and then in the next moment moved to the point of prayer.

Perhaps sermons are best heard rather than read, but these sermons will bless those who are privileged to read them, just as they blessed those who were privileged to hear them. This is because they are crafted by someone who understands the gospel and also understands people. They come from one who embodies the kind of pastoral leadership that is so needed in today's church and world. Bruce leads with vision and passion, but he is humble. He loves people, but he knows how to be prophetic both in the pulpit and in the daily life of the congregation.

And he has stayed with it, in one place, with one congregation, over a long period of time. It hasn't always been easy. Tenured ministry never is. During that time he has changed, and the congregation has changed. And that longevity, along with healthy change and growth, has produced a wisdom and prudence that is reflected in this book. Now Village Baptist Church is a multicultural congregation, still committed to the gospel and its community.

All the literature I read today tells me that the future of the church must be intercultural, interracial and intergenerational if it is to embody Christ's kingdom. Village Baptist Church is a congregation anticipating that future. And much of its success is due to the pastoral preaching and leadership of Bruce Salmon. May the Spirit use these printed sermons to inspire and instruct us all, just as the Spirit used them when they were proclaimed.

Daniel Vestal, Distinguished Professor of Baptist Leadership,
Mercer University, Atlanta, Georgia

Preface

Bruce Salmon served as pastor of Village Baptist Church in Bowie, Maryland, for thirty-three years. He began his service at Village on January 1, 1985, and retired on December 31, 2017. Before that, he served as associate pastor of Montgomery Hills Baptist Church in Silver Spring, Maryland, for eight years. Thus, his entire full-time ministerial career was spent serving two congregations in suburban Maryland, just outside Washington, D.C. Both churches are members of the D.C. Baptist Convention.

A native of Fort Worth, Texas, Salmon received the bachelor of arts with a major in English from Baylor University. He received the master of divinity and the doctor of ministry from The Southern Baptist Theological Seminary in Louisville, Kentucky. He also received the master of arts in counseling psychology from Bowie State University, with a specialization in clinical pastoral counseling.

Salmon has served on several commissions of the Baptist World Alliance and several committees of the D.C. Baptist Convention. He is the author of the book *Storytelling in Preaching*. He also authored a cover feature for *Preaching* magazine, "Preaching Without a Net," which is available online.

Introduction

The year was 1975. I was a student at The Southern Baptist Theological Seminary in Louisville, Kentucky. One day in the seminary dining room, I saw my friend Gary Cook sitting at a table with an older gentleman I did not know. The man was old enough to be Gary's grandfather, maybe even Gary's great-grandfather. I thought to myself, "I wonder why Gary is having lunch with that old geezer." Well, before I could say anything, Gary saw me and invited me to join them. Gary introduced his lunch companion as Dr. Gaines Dobbins, who I later found out was eighty-nine years old.

Dr. Gaines Dobbins—somehow the name sounded vaguely familiar. Gary explained that Dr. Dobbins used to teach at the seminary. He had retired in 1956 when he reached the mandatory retirement age of seventy. After he retired from Southern Seminary, Dr. Dobbins was invited to teach at Golden Gate Baptist Theological Seminary in California, where he served as professor of church administration. He later served as a visiting professor at Baptist seminaries in Switzerland and Nigeria. He also served as chairman of the Baptist World Alliance Commission on Bible Teaching. I didn't know any of this when I sat down for lunch that day. I later learned that Dr. Dobbins was one of the most influential Baptists of the twentieth century in many areas—Christian education, church administration, missions, evangelism, and pastoral care. He was a living legend in theological education. Dr. Dobbins had returned to Southern Seminary in 1975–76 as a visiting lecturer in the Boyce Bible School, a division of the seminary for students without college degrees. Besides serving as a seminary professor, Dr. Dobbins had served as a pastor and as a chaplain during his long ministerial career. He also was a prolific writer, the author of thirty-two books and approximately 5,000 scholarly articles. To put it simply, Dr. Dobbins was a giant in theological education.

During our lunch together I was wise enough to ask questions and then listen carefully to what Dr. Dobbins had to say. He made one observation about pastoral ministry that I have never forgotten, one that greatly influenced my own ministry. Dr. Dobbins was bemoaning the fact that most pastors don't stay at a church very long. They tend to move from church to church, either for more money, or more challenges, or more prestige, or sometimes to escape from conflict at their former church. That observation is certainly true. The average pastoral tenure is just three to five years.

Dr. Dobbins made the comment that a pastor's most effective ministry occurs over time, after the pastor has been at the church long enough to establish trust and get to know the people. Then Dr. Dobbins suggested what I considered to be a radical and impractical ideal: "What if a pastor were to go to a church and stay there?"

At first hearing, that idea seemed to be almost impossible. My mind was flooded with questions. How would a pastor get a meaningful raise staying at the same church? How would a pastor enjoy the prestige of leading a larger congregation? How would a pastor be able to keep people happy over many years and avoid church conflict? How would a pastor come up with enough sermons to last an entire career at the same church? Frankly, I didn't see how it could work. Nevertheless, I was intrigued by the concept.

Well, eventually, I served as pastor of Village Baptist Church in Bowie, Maryland, for thirty-three years. It was not my entire ministerial career, but the major portion of it. Right out of seminary I served another church for eight years, so I served only two churches since I graduated from seminary in 1976. I also served part-time at a couple churches in college and was a pastoral intern at a church while in seminary.

After being pastor at Village Baptist Church for thirty-three years, I learned to appreciate the wisdom of what Dr. Dobbins was advocating. Over that time I began to answer some of my own questions about how it could be possible for a pastor to stay at the same church a long time.

Over the years I did have opportunities to leave. After my book was published, I was approached about becoming editor of a preaching magazine. A few years later, after the pastor of a former church retired, I was asked if I would be interested in returning to that church.

After serving at Village for twenty years, I came close to going to a church in Texas. It was after my father died, and my wife Linda and I had become concerned about my mother living by herself in Texas. We were thinking maybe we should consider moving closer to her. A church in Texas flew us down for a visit, and members of the pastor search committee came to Maryland to hear me preach. Linda and I really didn't want to move, but we felt we had to remain open if it were God's will for us to move. The search committee members knew we didn't want to leave Village, and they didn't call us. Shortly after that, my niece and her family moved from Chicago to live with my mother in Texas. A couple years later, my mother decided to sell her house and move into a retirement community with all levels of care available, should she ever need them. In retrospect, it was not God's will that we move, but we did have options to leave over the years.

Why did we stay at Village so long? Well, for one thing, we loved the people. Some of them are among our closest friends. One of my greatest satisfactions as a pastor was getting to know and serve people on a personal level. Our church was small enough that I could know almost everybody, if they wanted me to know them. If some people preferred to keep their distance, that was okay; I respected their privacy. But if they wanted a pastor to relate to them on a personal level, I was their man.

The second reason we stayed at Village is because the church needed us. In the early years of our ministry, the church needed someone to continue the effective ministry of the former pastors, Dr. Ken Bradshaw, Rev. John Woodall, and Dr. Dan Ivins. Ken was at Village less than a year; John served Village three years; Dan was pastor at Village ten years. When we came to Village, the church needed us to help keep it going.

Over the course of the next fifteen years, by God's grace, the church prospered and grew. Then, on a cold January day in 2000, the church building caught fire and was destroyed. After the church building burned, the church really needed us. Those thirty-four months of displacement were the toughest years of my ministry. We lost more members than we gained. We had to rent worship space from another congregation. After a while, their new pastor was anxious for us to leave. Rebuilding took a lot longer than any of us expected, with a lot more complications than I could have imagined.

Some Sundays after worship I was so discouraged that I wondered if I could keep going. Some ministerial friends knew how miserable I was, and they were eager to help me move to another church. But there was no way I was leaving when the future of Village was so precarious. After we finally entered our new building at the end of 2002, it took several more years to rebuild the congregation. I only considered leaving after our congregation was stronger than it had been before the fire.

The third reason we stayed is because of what Village became. When we came to Village in 1985, it was not a very diverse congregation. We had a couple of African-American members and their children, but the congregation was largely monochromatic. We gained a few more minority members before the fire, but the church was still not very diverse. I remember visiting

Loretta and Marion Shipman to talk with them about joining our church. Loretta remarked to me about the lack of diversity in the congregation. I invited Loretta and Marion to join us and help make it more diverse. That's exactly what they did. They joined, stuck with us during our displacement, and became key leaders after we occupied our new building. As our community became more diverse, so did our church. It was exciting to be pastor of a congregation open to all people.

This story is not just about me, but about what God has done through Village Baptist Church. I will take credit, however, for bringing two amazing women to the church. In 2011 I became acquainted with a young minister, Rev. Starlette McNeill (now Rev. Starlette Thomas), at the D.C. Baptist Convention. The more I got to know her, the more I recognized her potential. I started praying about her, and I started trying to figure out a way to get her to come to our church. Well, our congregation stepped out in faith, and she stepped out in faith, and in 2013 Pastor Star became our associate pastor. She would go on to serve as the Village interim pastor after I retired at the end of 2017.

The second amazing woman I brought to Village is my wife Linda. She has been a partner in ministry in every aspect (except for drawing a paycheck). All that she gave to Village was as a volunteer, and what a volunteer she was! Linda was a Sunday school teacher, a deacon, a commission chairperson, a children's storyteller, a worship dancer, a Vacation Bible School craft leader, a banner maker, a costume maker, a hand-bell ringer, a nursery volunteer, a meal provider for our Lenten Bible studies, a "flip flop sister," and a friend to many. Some churches might call her the "first lady," but Linda cringed when she heard that title. If anything, she was first in service.

In his letter to the Romans, the apostle Paul wrote, "For I am not ashamed of the gospel; it is the power of God for salvation to everyone who has faith" (Rom 1:16 NRSV). That's my testimony too. The only difference is that Paul wrote those words before he ever came to the church in Rome, and I was at Village thirty-three years.

In the time I served at Village, my friend Gary Cook (who introduced me to Dr. Dobbins in the seminary cafeteria) went on to bigger and better things. After seminary Gary served in churches, and then he got involved in student ministry, and then he got involved in higher education. Eventually, Dr. Gary Cook became president of Dallas Baptist University in Texas. But I wouldn't have traded places with the university president. Even though I never got a promotion or even a new title, being pastor was fine with me. (By the way, Dr. Gary Cook served as president of Dallas Baptist University for twenty-eight years [1988–2016]. He continues his service as chancellor. So maybe Gary was listening to Dr. Dobbins too.)

After I had preached my "trial sermon" at Village in fall 1984, the chair of the pastor search committee, Maury Sweetin, phoned that afternoon to say the church had voted to call me. Maury said the vote was very positive, but not quite unanimous—it was 64–1. I never knew who voted against me, but I tried to be the best pastor I could be so maybe even that one dissenter might develop a different opinion.

The biggest challenge for me of a long-term pastorate was the preaching. How does one come up with something "new" to say every Sunday? By the time I retired, some parishioners had heard me preach over 1,000 times. Dr. Dave Thompson, an astrophysicist with NASA at the Goddard Space Flight Center, had heard me preach over 2,000 times since he attended both worship services most Sunday mornings. Yes, the Bible is a vast trove of sermonic material, but the same preacher Sunday after Sunday struggles to interpret a fresh vision of biblical truth that stimulates the mind and touches the heart. Yet it is possible.

The purpose of this book is to illustrate how it is possible. It is a case study in long-term pastoral ministry. Included are sermons from thirty-three years at the same church. Over the years I preached on some biblical texts many times. Yet I never repeated a sermon in thirty-three years, except for preaching basically the same sermon at the two Sunday morning worship services during the school year. The only difference is that I preached the sermon extemporaneously from the floor for the early contemporary service, and I stood behind the pulpit (with manuscript) for the traditional second service. Thus, the sermon wasn't the same for the two services, but Dave Thompson said they were *essentially* the same.

Beyond that repetition on Sunday morning, however, no one ever came up to me and said, "I remember you preached that sermon before." For thirty-three years I preached original sermons every Sunday, except for the Sundays we had a guest preacher or choir cantata or other special event. "Preaching for the long haul" requires commitment and study and creativity and prayer, but by God's grace, it can be done.

Chapter 1

1951-1969

I never wanted to be a preacher. My childhood dream was to become a professional baseball player. Never mind that I wasn't that good at baseball. I played in neighborhood baseball games across the street from my house in Rix Quinn's spacious backyard. On the more organized level I played second base for several Little League teams during elementary school. I wasn't an outstanding player, but I loved baseball. My childhood heroes were Mickey Mantle and Willie Mayes, not Harry Emerson Fosdick or Billy Graham. In addition to playing baseball (and going to school), I went to church—a lot. I was added to the cradle roll of Broadway Baptist Church in Fort Worth, Texas, shortly after I was born. As a child, almost every Sunday, my mother took me and my sister and my brother to Sunday school and morning worship. She took us back to church on Sunday nights for Training Union and evening worship. I sang in the children's and youth choirs at church. I was a regular at Vacation Bible School. I even went to dinner and Royal Ambassadors on Wednesday nights. The church was a big part of our lives growing up. Still, I did not aspire to be a preacher.

I was good in Sunday school, however, meaning I was a willing student of the Bible. Most of my Sunday school teachers were glad to have me in their class. Often, I could answer their questions when other class members were disinterested. I found the stories in the Bible to be fascinating, even if some stretched the bounds of credulity. I learned the art of the "willing suspension of disbelief."

Sunday school teachers, youth leaders, music leaders, and eventually pastors had a big influence on my personal and spiritual development. I was shy and introverted around my more socially accomplished peers, but many adults at church helped me feel better about myself. They acted like they saw some value, some potential, in me.

My senior year in high school, I was selected to be the "pastor" during youth week at the church. I would not preach a sermon, but I would read Scripture from the pulpit on Sunday morning and give a prayer during the Wednesday evening prayer service. More significantly, I would accompany the associate pastor, Rev. Roy DeBrand, on a round of hospital visits. The idea was to give me a feel for what pastors did apart from their public appearances on Sundays. It was Rev. DeBrand who taught me to take the elevator to the highest level of the hospital and then to take the stairs down, floor by floor, visiting the church members who were patients along the way. He also demonstrated the craft of appropriate questions and prayers for those we visited.

My other mentor was Dr. J. P. Allen, the senior pastor at Broadway. Not given to small talk, Dr. Allen nevertheless took an interest in me. He coached me on proper platform decorum and speaking slowly and distinctly into the microphone. I don't know if he saw me as ministerial material or not, but at least he knew who I was in a church of several thousand members.

Sometime after youth week, the idea crossed my mind that maybe I could be a pastor for real. It seemed a little preposterous at first, since I hated being in front of people and risking embarrassment. I did not see myself as a public speaker, even though I had won second place in junior high school in an oratory contest sponsored by the Optimist Club. But the potential for humiliation in trying to deliver a sermon seemed far greater than the prospect of glory.

Nevertheless, I began to wonder if perhaps God were calling me into the ministry. I wouldn't have been the first unlikely candidate that God called into service.

The Image of God
Genesis 1:1-5, 24-28, 31 (NRSV)

In the beginning when God created the heavens and the earth, the earth was a formless void and darkness covered the face of the deep, while a wind from God swept over the face of the waters.

Then God said, "Let there be light"; and there was light. And God saw that the light was good; and God separated the light from the darkness. God called the light Day, and the darkness he called Night. And there was evening and there was morning, the first day....

And God said, "Let the earth bring forth living creatures of every kind: cattle and creeping things and wild animals of the earth of every kind." And it was so. God made the wild animals of the earth of every kind, and the cattle of every kind, and everything that creeps upon the ground of every kind. And God saw that it was good.

Then God said, "Let us make humankind in our image, according to our likeness; and let them have dominion over the fish of the sea, and over the birds of the air, and over the cattle, and over all the wild animals of the earth, and over every creeping thing that creeps upon the earth." So God created humankind in his image, in the image of God he created them; male and female he created them. God blessed them, and God said to them, "Be fruitful and multiply, and fill the earth and subdue it; and have dominion over the fish of the sea and over the birds of the air and over every living thing that moves upon the earth."…

God saw everything that he had made, and indeed, it was very good. And there was evening and there was morning, the sixth day.

I was a guest at Rix Quinn's birthday party. That was a big deal because I was only five years old at the time, and Rix was turning eight. Rix lived across the street, and despite our age difference we were friends. Rix and I used to play baseball in his backyard, along with other kids in the neighborhood. Rix's dad, Bill Quinn, now age 100, used to take me and Rix to see the Fort Worth Cats play minor league baseball. We always took our baseball gloves with us, hoping to catch a foul ball. I don't remember ever catching one, but we lived in hope that one day a ball would come our way.

Rix sent me a photo taken at his eighth birthday party. I don't recall most of the kids in the photo, except for Rix and Ridgway Scott, who also lived on our street. That's me sitting on the floor. Rix, the birthday boy, is sitting in the chair, along with two of his buddies. Ridgway is the tall boy standing next to the chair. There are some girls in the photo that I don't remember at all, despite my penchant for older women. To be honest about it, I really don't remember the birthday party. But I must have been there because I'm in the picture. And I must have been enjoying myself, judging by the look on my face.

The expression on my face in the photo suggests that there was a time in my life when I was a happy kid. I'd almost forgotten about that time. I began my sermon a few weeks ago by saying, "I was a shy and skinny kid, with a poor self-image and low self-esteem. So my childhood was not exactly what I would call joyful." But after looking again at the photo of me at Rix Quinn's birthday party, I've begun to rethink that assessment of my childhood. Yes, I was a shy and skinny kid, and yes, as I grew older, my self-image was poor, and my self-esteem was low. But there were moments during my childhood that were joyful, especially times during those early years when I was too innocent to worry about what other people might think of me.

I'm embarrassed to admit it, but sometimes I don't come across as very joyful now. That's not to say I'm unhappy. In fact, I am very happy in my life, but I don't always show it. Because I have a rather low-key personality, my true disposition is not always apparent. I'm not what you would call a "Snoopy dancer." I like to laugh, and I enjoy being with friends, but basically I'm an introvert. What I do on Sunday mornings does not come naturally to me. About the most expressive emotion you are liable to see from me is when I sink a putt on the golf course and give a little fist pump. Most of the time, I'm pretty subdued. In fact, when I was working on my master's in counseling psychology at Bowie State University, one of my supervisors told me I had a "depressive" personality. I took offense at that. I told him that just because I'm not an extrovert, that doesn't mean I'm depressive. I'll admit to being earnest and focused and serious and task-oriented, but don't call me depressive! Still, seeing my picture in that birthday party photo showed me a side of myself that I had almost forgotten. I can be mischievous and fun-loving and lighthearted too.

The passage of time and the circumstances of our lives have a way of changing us. Eventually, most of us lose some of that innocent joy that we had as children as we become burdened with the responsibilities of adulthood. The poet Wordsworth wrote, "The world is too much with us." Another poet of the English Romantic movement, William Blake, noted that as we grow older, we pass from the age of innocence to the age of experience. Children are innocent. They live for the moment. They don't worry about the future. But as they grow older, they tend to lose their innocence and enter the world of experience. And experience can dampen childlike faith; experience can suppress un-self-conscious joy. Experience can make us watchful and wary. Experience can cause us to be guarded with our emotions, to be perpetually on the defensive, to be careful not to expose our vulnerabilities. For me, as

I grew older and entered the world of experience, the innocence faded, and with it the joy of the moment and the freedom to just be who I was.

I apologize if this opening illustration sounds overly personal, but there is a connection to our scripture for this morning. The Bible begins with Genesis, and Genesis begins with the story of creation, which fundamentally is a story about who we really are. It's a story about innocence and the freedom God gave us to be authentic to ourselves. The story of creation is how out of that formless void and darkness, God created a world and all that is in it. And at the pinnacle of creation, God gave the preeminent place to people, to humankind, to us. He made us in his image. In the Bible, image is more than just a representation, like the image on a coin is a representation of a famous president or other person. In the Bible, image shares in the nature of that which it represents. We are made in God's image. That means, to put it simply, there is something of God in us. That is why God gave us dominion over the rest of creation. We are not God, but we share in the nature of God.

We can see glimpses of that nature of God, that image of God, in the joy and innocence of children. That's why Jesus said unless we become like children, we cannot enter the kingdom of God. Jesus didn't mean we should revert to childish behavior. Not every childhood trait is Godlike. Children can be mean and selfish and petty and rude and inconsiderate of others. Children may share in the nature of God, but children certainly don't always act like God. None of us do. The image of God that is within all of us has been corrupted by sin. But there are certain qualities in children that reflect the character of God. Qualities like joy and generosity and appreciation for life reflect the image of God that is in us.

Have you ever wondered why God created the world in the first place? Scientists have long wondered how the world was created. A couple weeks ago, two studies emerged from the work that is being done at the particle accelerator outside Geneva, Switzerland. The studies suggest that the Higgs boson, the so-called "God particle" that is the basis of all matter, is close to being discovered. At least it is now "hinted at." But even if they do discover the Higgs boson or some other mechanism that explains how matter came to be, that will not answer the "why" question. Why did God create the world? The Bible answers the "why" question. God created the world because it was God's generous nature to share the joy of being. And at the pinnacle of creation, God created people to be in relationship with him. The fourth-century Christian writer Augustine said, "You made us for yourself, O God, and our hearts will not rest until they rest in You." Because that image of God is within us, our hearts will not rest until we are in relationship with the one who made us.

There were a couple interesting articles in the newspaper last week. One was a story about the "hugging saint," a woman from India who travels the world blessing followers with hugs. Her nickname is "Amma." She was at the Hilton Hotel in Alexandria, Virginia, last week. Hundreds of her devotees stood in line for hours to see her and to be hugged by her. To them, her embraces convey unconditional love. She is a deity in their eyes, the very presence of the divine. One young woman said, "Her energy is so powerful, you feel like you should look at the ground, but when you do look at her, it's the energy of your mother." "You kind of feel weak at the knees and lighthearted," the woman said after the embrace. An estimated thirty million people have attended Amma's spiritual programs around the world. Many believe she has a healing touch. Some say her embrace has changed their lives. Amma is not a Christian (she comes from a Hindu background), but some have called her "the Mother Teresa of hugging." How do you explain her appeal?

Another story in the newspaper last week told about woman from Croatia who says she sees visions of the Virgin Mary on a daily basis. This woman also draws vast numbers of people to her appearances. Last week she was in a small town in Alabama, some thirty minutes south of Birmingham. Thousands of devotees, mainly Roman Catholics, flocked to see her. Supposedly she first saw an apparition of the Virgin Mary in 1981 when she was a sixteen-year old girl living in what was once called Yugoslavia. Since then she has collected a large following who believe that she can convey special blessings. The Roman Catholic Church has yet to authenticate her visions, and some Catholic leaders are skeptical that she has received private revelations, but 18,000 people came out to see her over five days in Alabama. How do you explain her appeal?

I think both stories illustrate the need that many people feel to seek a divine connection. Whether a "hugging saint" from India or a woman from Croatia who claims to see visions of the Virgin Mary, many people are attracted to someone who seems to represent God. We all have that divine image within us, and we long to connect or reconnect with the One who made us. We have this sense that we were made for better things. We have the feeling that our lives are not all that they could be. We long to reclaim our true identity and to live in a way that is authentic to who we really are. With the psalmist David we pray, "Create in me a clean heart, O God, and put a new and right spirit with me" (Ps 51:10 NRSV).

How do we get it back—that innocence, that joy, that freedom to be who we really are? How do we find that right relationship with God? For Christians we make the connection with God through our faith in Jesus Christ. Listen to what Paul wrote about Jesus in his letter to the Colossians:

> He is the image of the invisible God, the firstborn of all creation; for in him all things in heaven and on earth were created, things visible and invisible, whether thrones or dominions or rulers or powers—all things have been created through him and for him. He himself is before all things, and in him all things hold together. He is the head of the body, the church; he is the beginning, the firstborn from the dead, so that he might come to have first place in everything. For in him all the fullness of God was pleased to dwell, and through him God was pleased to reconcile to himself all things, whether on earth or in heaven, by making peace through the blood of his cross. (Col 1:15–20 NRSV)

Jesus said you must be born again to see the kingdom of God (John 3:3). Paul said if anyone is in Christ, that person is a new creation (2 Cor 5:17). We cannot go back to the way we were, but in Christ we can become the persons God created us to be.

You were made in the image of God. You can be remade in the image of his son, the firstborn of all creation, in whom all the fullness of God was pleased to dwell. Christ in you—that is the hope of glory for all who believe.

July 15, 2012

A Generous Orthodoxy
Galatians 5:1, 13-14 (NRSV)

For freedom Christ has set us free. Stand firm, therefore, and do not submit again to a yoke of slavery....

For you were called to freedom, brothers and sisters; only do not use your freedom as an opportunity for self-indulgence, but through love become slaves to one another. For the whole law is summed up in a single commandment, "You shall love your neighbor as yourself."

Up on Route 198 in Burtonsville, Maryland, there is a church that looks like a barn. The name of the church is Cedar Ridge Community Church, and its founding pastor, Brian McLaren, is one of the most influential church leaders in America. That's somewhat ironic because Brian McLaren never intended to be a pastor. He intended to teach English literature in college, and that's what he did for a number of years at the University of Maryland. He and his wife started a Bible study group in their home in College Park in 1982, and that group eventually became a nondenominational church. The church grew to the point where they were able to purchase a sixty-three-acre farm in Burtonsville and put up a church building on it—hence, the church looks like a barn. McLaren resigned last year as pastor of Cedar Ridge so he could devote himself to writing and speaking, but the church is still going under new pastoral leadership.

Brian McLaren has been identified as a leader in the "emergent" church movement, sometimes called the "postmodern" church movement. The emergent church is identified by contemporary Christian music and more informal styles of worship and a lack of denominational identity, but also by a rethinking of what the Christian faith is all about and a focus on reaching the un-churched. McLaren expresses some amazement that he is considered a church leader because he never went to seminary, his pastoral experience is limited to Cedar Ridge, and he lacks the theological credentials one might expect of a so-called expert. McLaren describes himself as a "middle-aged bald introvert without proper credentials," who nonetheless is the author, thus far, of ten highly acclaimed books on contemporary Christianity.

About three years ago Brian McLaren wrote a book titled *A Generous Orthodoxy*, which I have used for the title of this sermon. McLaren readily confesses that the phrase is not his. It was coined by a theologian from Yale University named Hans Frei. Frei used the term to describe an understanding of the Christian faith that includes elements of both liberal (generous) theology and conservative (orthodox) theology. The word *orthodoxy* means "straight thinking" or "right opinion." Most religious controversies and conflicts over the centuries have been about orthodoxy, over whose orthodoxy is correct. McLaren notes, "Most orthodoxies of the past have not displayed much generosity toward others outside their tribe." (p. 27). He observes that "a generous orthodoxy" is an oxymoron, a contradiction in terms.

Over the past four Sundays, I've been preaching a series of sermons on our basic Baptist beliefs—Baptist orthodoxy, as it were. I didn't announce the sermon series ahead of time, because if I said I was going to preach a sermon series on Baptist orthodoxy, I'm not sure how many of you would have shown up. It is only today, at the end of the series, that I explain what I have been doing. But if you've been with us the last four weeks, you might have figured out what was going on. The first sermon was about salvation by faith and believer's baptism by immersion. Baptists are not the only Christians who stress making a personal commitment to Jesus Christ, accepting him as savior and Lord, and following him as a believer in baptism. Many other evangelical Christians share our understanding of salvation and Christian commitment, but we Baptists are known for it. We are called "Baptists" because we practice believer's baptism by immersion; we don't baptize babies. And the reason we don't baptize babies comes from our understanding of salvation as a voluntary faith commitment that only a believer can experience.

The next Sunday I preached about the authority of the Bible. I said that we Baptists are "people of the book," meaning that we look to the Bible as our authority for what we believe and how we live. In that sermon I stressed that every person has the right and the responsibility to read and interpret the Bible for himself or herself. I also said that we do not read and interpret the Bible in isolation, for we have the Holy Spirit to guide us and the church community to help us. Most importantly, Jesus is the criterion by which we interpret the Bible. The life and teachings of Jesus help us to distinguish between cultural conditions and eternal truth.

Last Sunday I preached about the priesthood of all believers. Again, most Protestant churches subscribe to the priesthood of all believers, but we Baptists have accentuated it. The priesthood of all believers is expressed through our democratic form of church governance and our emphasis upon the ministry of all believers, not just the ministry of the clergy.

Today I conclude this brief series with a sermon on the autonomy of the local church. Unlike many other churches that function as local franchises of a controlling "mother church," Baptist churches are independent and autonomous. Although we choose to affiliate with other churches for purposes one church could not do alone—such as missions and education—our affiliation is completely voluntary. No larger convention or denomination can tell our church what to believe or what to do. That's different from other churches that are hard-wired into a larger denomination and controlled by it. We are autonomous—we make our own decisions, we run our own programs, we fund our own ministries, we call our own leaders. We have a freedom of worship and leadership and organization that makes some people nervous. If a Baptist church is free to do whatever it wants, what is going to keep that church orthodox and on the right path?

Baptists began 400 years ago as a freedom movement. Back then, religious orthodoxy was the primary concern of most churches. The Roman Catholic Church, the Eastern Orthodox Church, the Anglican Church, the Lutheran Church, the Reformed Church all claimed to have the orthodox interpretation of the truth. There was no such thing as "a generous orthodoxy." The orthodoxy of most churches was strict and rigid and severe and judgmental. Almost every church back then said, "It's our way or the highway," and the "highway" meant the road that led to damnation (in their view). But freedom-loving Christians chafed under the oppressive orthodoxy of established religion.

The first Baptists were English Separatists who fled religious repression and persecution and sought refuge in Holland, which was one of the most tolerant countries of the time. Based on their reading of the Bible, particularly passages like the one we read this morning from Galatians, those first Baptists dared to believe that individual Christians should be free to follow the dictates of their own consciences. Further, they dared to believe that individual churches should be free to organize and conduct themselves according to the will of the people in those churches. In other words, they dared to believe that churches should be independent and autonomous, free from coercive hierarchies and ruling bodies. When Paul wrote to the Galatians "for freedom Christ has set us free," the early Baptists took those words to heart.

If Baptist churches are not controlled by some denominational authority or outside ruler, what's to keep us in line? How do we maintain our orthodoxy? Well, we have a scriptural authority in the Bible, and we have an inside ruler, namely the Lordship of Jesus Christ ruling in our hearts. Not only that, we are answerable to one another to keep our church on the right path. Paul wrote to the Galatians, "For you were called to freedom, brothers and sisters; only do not use your freedom for self-indulgence, but through love become slaves to one another" (5:13). That is the Baptist system of checks and balances, not through some outside authority or denominational executive or church hierarchy or creed, but the mutual accountability we feel toward one another. If something in the church needs changing, we read the Bible, we talk it over with one another, we pray about it, and then we vote on it. That's the Baptist way. We might even call it "a generous orthodoxy."

Some of you may have noticed that Village is different from a lot of churches, and even different from a lot of Baptist churches. A lot of Baptist churches are orthodox, but they are not very generous. Frankly, a lot of Baptist churches are so rigid and strict and severe and judgmental that you wonder where the grace of God is in all of it. Most of the people at Village are very orthodox—we believe in Jesus, we believe in salvation by faith and believer's baptism, we believe in the Bible, we believe in the priesthood of all believers. Most of the people at Village are orthodox when it comes to the basics of our faith, but I hope we are generous too. I hope we have a heart for people who are hurting. I hope we remember all of us are sinners in need of God's forgiveness and grace. I hope we are slow to judge and quick to love. Paul told the Galatians, "The whole law is summed up in a single commandment, 'You shall love your neighbor as yourself'" (5:14).

Jesus summed it all up like this: Love God, and love your neighbor as yourself. A generous orthodoxy means not only that we believe the right things, but that we do the right things. And to do the right things means that we do everything in love. As Christ loved us, we are to love each other too.

Of course, it would be a lot simpler if we just followed the letter of the Law rather than the spirit of love. Churches that are only concerned about orthodoxy will tell you exactly what to believe and what to do in every situation. They don't have much use for freedom. But a generous church is led by the spirit of Christ.

A pastor was on a cross-country flight when the plane hit some turbulent air. The "fasten seat belts" signs were turned on, and the flight attendants told everyone to remain in their seats. The ride got rough as the plane was tossed about like a leaf in the wind. The pastor looked around at his fellow passengers and saw many of them looking fearful and some of them praying. Then he looked across the aisle at a little girl who seemed as calm as could be. She was reading a book with her legs folded up beneath her, as if she didn't have a care in the world. When the plane safely touched down, most everyone let out a big sigh of relief, but the little girl didn't seem fazed at all. The pastor leaned over and asked the little girl if she were ever afraid during the flight.

"Afraid?" the little girl said. "Why should I be afraid? My daddy's the pilot, and he's taking me home."

Life is not always easy, and sometimes even in church we find ourselves on a bumpy ride. But have no fear—our Father is the pilot, and he's taking us home.

July 29, 2007

An "ISTJ" Meets Jesus
Luke 10:38-42 (NRSV)

Now as they went on their way, he entered a certain village, where a woman named Martha welcomed him into her home. She had a sister named Mary, who sat at the Lord's feet and listened to what he was saying. But Martha was distracted by her many tasks; so she came to him and asked, "Lord, do you not care that my sister has left me to do all the work by myself? Tell her then to help me." But the Lord answered her, "Martha, Martha, you are worried and distracted by many things; there is need of only one thing. Mary has chosen the better part, which will not be taken away from her."

You've got to admit that for someone with a degree in counseling psychology, I don't subject you to "psychobabble" all that often. In my sermons I'm more likely to talk about golf than I am about psychology. But occasionally psychology can help us to understand not just human behavior but even passages of Scripture. Today's Scripture text is a case in point.

The dynamics between the two sisters, Martha and Mary, almost demand some psychological interpretation. Apparently Martha was the older of the two sisters, because Jesus was said to be visiting in her home. My first thought was to use the studies of birth order among siblings to interpret this passage. Children typically assume roles in the family according to the order in which they were born. The oldest child, the middle child, the youngest child all have unique roles. Sometimes oldest children grow up with an elevated sense of personal responsibility because they had to help take care of their younger siblings. Some oldest children are bossy, demanding, used to imposing their will on their younger family members. Conversely, youngest children find a way to make a place for themselves in the family. Younger children may learn how to manipulate their parents or please others in order to get their own way. Sometimes the youngest child is spoiled, coddled by the parents. So we could look at the relationship between Martha and Mary in terms of their birth order, the older and the younger. Martha does seem to have an elevated sense of responsibility, and Mary (at least in Martha's eyes) acts spoiled and coddled, leisurely sitting at Jesus's feet, leaving her older sister to do all the work.

Another way to look at Martha and Mary is in terms of their personality types. At first glance Martha seems like a Type A personality. That term, "Type A," became popular some years back as a result of studies into how personality type can be an indicator of susceptibility to heart attacks. A Type A person is characterized as a hard-charging go-getter, someone whose life is driven by a sense of urgency, highly competitive, always striving for perfection. Studies led researchers to believe that a Type A personality is more susceptible to having a heart attack than a Type B personality. Conversely, the Type B person is much less hurried, much more amiable, much more willing to tolerate imperfection. At first glance it looks like Martha was a Type A personality while Mary was more of a Type B personality. We see Martha running around the house, a whirlwind of activity, almost working herself into a frenzy, trying to be the perfect hostess and get things just right for Jesus. In contrast Mary doesn't seem to be in a hurry at all. While her sister is frantically rushing about, Mary is sitting passively at Jesus's feet, listening to his teachings as if she had nothing else to do. There is something of that Type A/Type B dichotomy between Martha and Mary.

Another way to understand this story is in terms of the basic orientation of the two sisters. Sometimes people are described in terms of the dominant orientation of their lives. Some people are more task-oriented, while others are more relationship-oriented. In this scenario Martha is definitely the more task-oriented of the two sisters while Mary seems to be more relationship-oriented.

Then it occurred to me that perhaps the best way to understand the two sisters might be by looking at the Myers-Briggs personality types. The Myers-Briggs is perhaps the most widely used personality inventory in the world. Based on the writings of the Swiss psychiatrist Carl Jung and developed by the mother-daughter team of Katharine Briggs and Isabel Briggs Myers, the MBTI uses four sets of indicators to help people understand their personality differences. The various combinations of these four sets of indicators identify sixteen distinct personality types. Knowing their basic personality type can help people to understand which career would best suit them, which types of people they would be most compatible with, how they learn, what is their leadership style, how they communicate, and how they are likely to react in any given situation. The Myers-Briggs personality inventory is used in business, government, the military, academic settings, career counseling, and many other areas to help people better understand themselves.

Very quickly, let me give you the four sets of indicators. As I go over them, in your own mind, see if you can decide which fits Martha and which fits Mary. Extravert or Introvert. Sensor or Intuitive. Thinker or Feeler. Judger or Perceiver. As I understand these two sisters, I conclude that Martha was an ISTJ—Introvert, Sensor, Thinker, Judger. Of the sixteen different personality types, ISTJs make up about ten percent of the American population. There are a lot of ISTJs out there. Here are some words used to describe ISTJs: serious, quiet, practical, orderly, logical, dependable, responsible, steady, literal, realistic, careful, precise, honest, hard-working, focused, meticulous, neat, thorough, conservative, organized, determined, methodical, traditional, single-minded, no-nonsense, simple, down-to-earth, super-dependable.

That was Martha—super-dependable. The consummate hostess. Trying to get everything just right. Jesus is in the living room talking with Mary and the other disciples, and Martha's in the kitchen slaving away by herself, quietly seething, until she finally explodes. Even introverts eventually can reach the frustration point when they verbalize their feelings. "Jesus, make my lazy, self-centered, spoiled, prima donna baby sister get off her duff and help me!" That's not exactly what she said, but that was the gist of it.

In many respects it looks like Mary was the opposite of Martha. Mary was an extravert, or at least certainly more interested in being with people. She was more intuitive, more of a feeler, more of a perceiver. You should know that what Mary was doing was highly unorthodox. Mary was assuming the role of a disciple, sitting at Jesus's feet. No self-respecting rabbi would allow a woman to sit at his feet and learn from him. That was a man's place. A woman's place was in the home, in the kitchen. According to normal propriety, Mary was way out of line assuming the role of a student.

It's called triangulation. Instead of dealing directly with the person you have a problem with, you try to get a third party to do it. Martha was trying to triangulate Jesus into making Mary help her get dinner ready. Her personality traits were getting the best of her. In most situations the personality traits of an ISTJ are quite admirable. But in this situation they were causing Martha to be narrow and judgmental. In this situation Martha's personality traits were getting in the way of allowing Martha to recognize what was really important. In this situation, being with Jesus was more important than making dinner. The relationship was more important than the task. And Jesus kindly, gently helped Martha to see that.

"Martha, Martha," Jesus said. He wasn't scolding her. He wasn't berating her. Jesus spoke to her with great affection and compassion, tenderly repeating her name. Don't blame your sister, Jesus said, for wanting to be here with me instead of working in the kitchen with you. Of course food is important, but some things are even more important. Man does not live by bread alone. And the most important thing in the world, Jesus said, is being with me.

You see, Jesus wasn't criticizing Martha for being an ISTJ. He wasn't telling her that her personality was all wrong while Mary's personality was all right. Jesus loved Martha just as much as he loved Mary. But because Jesus loved Martha, he had to help her see that in her obsession to do the right thing, she was missing the best thing. Martha was trying so hard to be perfect that she was missing the only one who was perfect, Jesus himself. She was trying so hard to do things for Jesus that she was missing being with Jesus.

Life is short, and we need to choose our priorities carefully. Too many of us are driven by the tyranny of the urgent rather than following the higher calling of that which is best. Billy Graham tells about his late father-in-law, Dr. Nelson Bell, a medical missionary who was the only doctor in a 400-bed hospital in China. Every morning, Dr. Bell rose at 4:30 a.m. to spend two hours in prayer and reading the Bible. Then he would begin his morning rounds in the hospital. It was only by focusing first on God that Dr. Bell was empowered to focus on the tasks at hand throughout the day.

Jesus was not against ISTJs, or Type A personalities, or task-oriented people, or the super-dependable eldest siblings who want to do everything right. He loved all those hard-driving people. But he loved them enough to tell them what was most important. We can get ourselves wound up so tight that we worry over many things, but only a few things are really important. Life has many good things—family, work, possessions, friends—but there is only one best thing. When we make God our primary focus, everything else finds its proper place. When we seek God's kingdom first, everything else will be added to it.

A little girl came home after her first day of school. Her mother asked her how things went. "Fine," the little girl said, but then she added, "I think I started something today which I'll never finish."

No, we are not finished, not by a long shot. God isn't finished with us either. Whatever our personality types, God loves us just as we are. But because God loves us, he won't leave us just as we are. He will help us to learn and to change and to grow in his likeness. He will help us to find that one thing, that best thing, which gives meaning and purpose to all the rest.

August 13, 2000

Chapter 2

1969–1973

I always knew I was going to Baylor. My grandfather was a Baylor graduate, class of 1916. My grandmother and two of her sisters went to Baylor. Once a year our Royal Ambassadors leaders at Broadway would rent a bus and take us from Fort Worth to Waco for a Baylor football game. Baylor was the only college I applied to. It was, and remains, the premier Baptist university in the world. Yet I wasn't sure what I was going to study at Baylor.

My father, a CPA with a large accounting firm, encouraged me to be a business major. Still uncertain about my calling, I followed his advice and declared a pre-business track of study. I joined the Seventh & James Baptist Church adjacent to the Baylor campus and became active in Sunday school and morning worship and the Sunday evening *Interrobang!* worship experience for students.

The summer after my freshman year a friend from my home church and I went to Washington state to do summer mission work under the auspices of the Southern Baptist Convention Home Mission Board. We served in a little Baptist church in Cheney, Washington, leading the youth program, helping with Vacation Bible School, and even landscaping the church lawn. We met the director of missions for the local Baptist association, and he found other things for us to do. Near the end of the summer, the director of missions asked me if I would be willing to preach one Sunday for a Baptist church in Medical Lake, Washington. I had never preached a sermon before, but I figured I would give it a shot. I selected a Scripture text that seemed ready-made for "three points and a poem." It was Jesus's summons: "If any man will come after me, let him deny himself, and take up his cross daily, and follow me" (Luke 9:23 KJV). The three points were (1) deny himself, (2) take up his cross daily, and (3) follow me. I've forgotten what poem I used. The sermon lasted probably no more than twelve minutes. Yet worshipers filed out after the service and thanked me for coming and even complimented me on the message. It was my first taste of the burden, and the blessing, that is preaching.

After I returned to Baylor in the fall to begin my sophomore year, I knew that a pre-business course of study was not for me. So I switched my major to "undecided." I still wasn't sure about being called into the ministry, but at least it was something to think about. Over the winter break between the fall and spring semesters, my home church had a retreat for college students at Glorieta, the Baptist conference center in New Mexico. The new pastor at Broadway, Dr. John Claypool, was the retreat leader. During the retreat I had a chance to talk with Dr. Claypool about *possibly* feeling called into the ministry. He affirmed my feeling and suggested I should come forward the following Sunday back at Broadway and publicly declare my calling. With trepidation I announced to my parents that I intended to go forward on Sunday after the sermon.

Back at Baylor for the spring semester, I met with Dr. David Matthews, the new pastor at Seventh & James, to tell him about my ministerial calling. Knowing I would soon need to declare a major, David advised me *not* to major in religion. I would get all that in seminary. Rather, he said major in something else that would broaden my perspective. David told me that he had been an English major in college. So I decided to major in English too.

The summer after my sophomore year I went to Memphis, Tennessee, to serve as youth director of a small Baptist church pastored by the father of a college classmate. The father/pastor had tasked his daughter with finding a suitable candidate among her Baylor acquaintances to come to Memphis for the summer to work in the church. For some reason the pastor's daughter identified me as the suitable candidate. I would live with the pastor's family for the summer and work to build up the youth program. It was a church in a transitional community, meaning that African Americans were moving in and many white families were moving out. The church was still predominantly white, but several African-American teens were active in the youth group.

Near the end of the summer, the pastor told me that he was going to be away for two Sundays and he wanted me to preach in his place. So I had two sermons to prepare and deliver. I don't remember the Scripture text or topic for either of the two sermons, but I do remember that the pastor's daughter was impressed. She asked me, "Where did you learn to preach like that?" I told her I guess I had learned by osmosis after listening to Dr. J. P. Allen and Dr. John Claypool and Dr. David Matthews preach.

During my junior year at Baylor, Rev. Bob Weissinger, the associate pastor at Seventh & James, asked me if I would be interested in becoming the youth minister at the church. It was a part-time position typically filled by a Baylor upperclassman. The current youth minister, Roger Paynter, was graduating, and Bob and David Matthews had identified me as a possible successor. I would begin that summer and continue into my senior year. The job involved directing youth activities and participating in worship leadership on Sunday mornings and evenings.

Well into my tenure as youth minister, David Matthews invited me to preach for an upcoming Sunday evening worship service in the chapel. I still didn't know that much about preaching, except that it was hard to do. I pumped David for all the advice that he could give me. One bit of advice he gave I used for the rest of my ministry. David said that whenever he came across a possible sermon illustration, he would tear it out or copy it down and put it in a drawer in his desk. From time to time, he would look through the stack of possible sermon illustrations in his desk drawer to see if any of them fit a message he was working on. I learned to keep a drawer of sermon illustrations too. Many of them were never used, but from time to time, one would be just what I needed to make a point.

David Matthews offered me the opportunity to officiate my first wedding. The requirement for wedding officiants back then in Texas was a license to ministry, not ordination. I called the pastor of my home church in Fort Worth, John Claypool, and asked him if Broadway could license me. He said he could put it up for a vote on a Wednesday night…no big deal. Well, it was a big deal to me. Broadway licensed me to the ministry, and I performed my first wedding in a home ceremony outside Waco.

Before I headed off to seminary, David Matthews invited me to preach on a Sunday morning at Seventh & James. It was another big deal, preaching to a congregation filled with Baylor professors, including members of the religion faculty. The only moderating factor was that I knew many of them on a personal level because they had kids in the youth group.

I still didn't know what I was doing in writing and delivering a sermon. But I was beginning to find my way. During the sermon I referenced a recent hit movie, *The Poseidon Adventure*, and a popular song from the soundtrack, "The Morning After." After the sermon one of my English professors told me that my use of the movie's plot line and the song helped him to understand the Scripture text in a new way. This was a man who had considered going into the ministry himself and whose brother was a seminary president. Apparently he got more out of the sermon than I had intended or envisioned when I wrote it. It was an inkling into the power of storytelling in preaching.

Years later, after I became an every-Sunday preacher, I discovered that there are Sundays that call for the same Scripture text every year. For example, Pentecost almost demands that the story from Acts 2 be read. After a few Pentecost Sundays, the "long-haul preacher" might struggle with finding something new to say. But with the sermon illustration drawer, and with an openness to the Spirit, even a familiar story from Holy Scripture can speak anew.

Filled with the Spirit
Acts 2:1-4 (NRSV)

When the day of Pentecost had come, they were all together in one place. And suddenly from heaven there came a sound like the rush of a violent wind, and it filled the entire house where they were sitting. Divided tongues, as of fire, appeared among them, and a tongue rested on each of them. All of them were filled with the Holy Spirit and began to speak in other languages, as the Spirit gave them ability.

I received an invitation to a reunion at my college church. The reunion will be held next week at the Seventh & James Baptist Church in Waco, Texas. I can't go because Linda and I will be traveling to Texas later next month for the General Assembly of the Cooperative Baptist Fellowship. But receiving the invitation to the reunion got me thinking about my experiences at Seventh & James some forty years ago.

I was a member at Seventh & James from 1969–1973. The church is located right next to Baylor University, but the reason I was a member wasn't just its proximity to the campus. I joined Seventh & James because there was an atmosphere, an attitude, a spirit about the church that met my spiritual needs and fit where I was in my faith journey. For one thing, the preaching was intellectually stimulating. Riley Eubank was the pastor when I was a freshman, Clyde Fant was the interim pastor my sophomore year, and David Matthews came as pastor after that. All three men were outstanding preachers. Their sermons were fresh and thought-provoking and challenging. That was important to me.

For another thing, the music program at Seventh & James was outstanding. The minister of music and the organist were professors at the Baylor music school. The director of the college choir was Charlie Brown (no, not the comic strip character). This Charlie Brown was a composer with the Christian music publisher, Word. Kurt Kaiser, the award-winning Christian songwriter and performer, was a member at Seventh & James. When I was the youth minister at Seventh & James my last year in college, two of Kurt Kaiser's kids were in the youth group.

Another thing I liked about Seventh & James was the associate pastor, Bob Weissinger. He was the de facto minister to college students. Bob was also my immediate supervisor when I was on the church staff. Bob was more than my supervisor; he was a mentor and a friend. We often had lunch together or went to play racquetball. Bob even gave me advice about some of the girls I was dating (this was before I met Linda).

The thing I liked best about Seventh & James was the accepting and affirming attitude of the people in the congregation. I got to know a number of college professors who were members of the church. Some of them had kids in the youth group. Dr. Frank Leavell was a Baylor English professor with children in the youth group. I knew him as Dr. Leavell in the classroom, but I called him Frank at church. He even went along as a chaperone for a weekend canoe trip down the Brazos River I organized for the youth. Through the church I also got to know several religion professors at Baylor: Dr. Wally Christian, Dr. Bob Patterson, and Dr. Dan McGee. I had a professional relationship with all of them as teachers but a personal friendship with them at church.

As I said, this was almost forty years ago, but I still have fond memories of the people at Seventh & James and the time I was a member there. Apparently a lot of other former members have fond memories too. That's why they are having a reunion the second week in June and people will be traveling from all over to return to Waco, Texas.

What is it that makes a church a special place like that? It could be the preaching or the music or the youth group or some other program. But for me the most important thing is the spirit of the people in the church. It's hard to put your finger on exactly what that spirit is, but you can feel it when it's there. People care about each other. People love each other. People accept the differences in each other without being critical or condescending or judgmental. A church like that is where the spirit of the Lord is. People openly share the good news of Jesus with friends and newcomers alike.

That's what happened in our scripture for this morning. It started on the day of Pentecost when people from all over the Mediterranean world had come to Jerusalem to celebrate the holy festival. They were from many different countries and cultures, speaking different languages. But on the day of Pentecost, the spirit of God filled the followers of Jesus in such a powerful way that they began to share the good news of Jesus in languages that the other people could understand.

I can't explain it, except that God's spirit gives people power to do things they otherwise could not or would not do. God's spirit breaks down barriers that separate people from one another. God's spirit brings together people from diverse backgrounds and unites them into a fellowship of love. God's spirit empowers people to reach outside their comfort zones to those who are different.

On the day of Pentecost, the disciples of Jesus, who were all Galileans, reached out to people from at least fifteen other countries or ethnic groups. They reached out by speaking in languages that these other people could understand. We illustrated that phenomenon this morning when various members of our congregation read John 3:16 in different languages. As far as we know, none of the Galilean disciples could speak those other languages before Pentecost. But after they received the Holy Spirit, they had the power to cross racial and cultural and language barriers and share the good news of Jesus. So there was diversity in the church from the very beginning.

This was one example of being filled with the Spirit, but it was not the only way that God's spirit was manifest among the followers of Jesus. Not everyone could speak another language, but God's spirit gave the followers of Jesus other gifts. God's spirit also produced "fruits" of Christian character and behavior. In Galatians 5:22 Paul identified the fruit of the Spirit as "love, joy, peace, patience, kindness, generosity, faithfulness, gentleness, and self-control." When Christians are filled with the Holy Spirit, those are the qualities that are evident in their lives. And being filled with the Spirit is not just for super-Christians. Every person who professes faith in Christ and is baptized for the forgiveness of sin is given God's spirit. We don't always act like it, because sometimes we allow our lives to be controlled by the spirit of this world rather than by the spirit of God. But the Holy Spirit is still there, always available to empower us to live faithful Christian lives.

The fallout from the Secret Service scandal in Colombia continues. There was a detailed reporting this past week in *The Washington Post* about the sequence of events last April. *The Post* identified the Secret Service agent who spent the night with a prostitute then refused to pay her the next morning, which began the unraveling of the whole episode. The man in question is forty-one years old, married, and the father of two young sons. Up until the scandal broke, he lived with his family in Severna Park, Maryland. In fact, the family was active in a Baptist church in Glen Burnie. According to the report in the newspaper, he was among several Secret Service agents who were widely known to cheat on their wives. Associates said this particular agent acted differently on his trips than he did at home. Apparently he was leading a double life—a churchgoing family man when at home and a carousing party animal when away on assignments. Rather than being controlled by the spirit of God, this particular Secret Service agent was controlled by a very different spirit when he was away on trips. Now, it is certainly not up to me to pass judgment on his spiritual condition. But any man who cheats on his wife is not being led by God's spirit. God's spirit produces the fruit of love and faithfulness and self-control.

I think the reason I have such good memories about my college church is that there were a lot of people who were filled with God's spirit. I've been blessed in the years since college to be part of other churches where people were filled with the Spirit. Colleagues frequently express amazement that I have been able to remain at this church twenty-seven years. I tell them it's because of the quality of the people here at Village. Over the years there have been many people here in this church who were filled with the Spirit. I'm not talking about the ability to speak other languages, although some have that gift. I'm talking about the fruit of the Spirit: love, joy, peace, patience, kindness, generosity, faithfulness, gentleness, and self-control. When people are filled with the Spirit and bear such fruit in their lives, the church is a wonderful place to be.

When I was at Seventh & James, there was a special song that we would often sing that seemed to capture the spirit of the church. The song was written by the gospel singer and songwriter Doris Akers, but it had been arranged by our own Kurt Kaiser, a beloved member of the church. Kurt Kaiser also wrote another song that was popular in churches back in the 1970s, "Pass It On." The song that Kurt Kaiser introduced when I was a member at Seventh & James was his arrangement of "Sweet, Sweet Spirit."

We sang it often because it reflected how we felt about the church. That's how I feel about this church. There is a "sweet, sweet spirit in this place, and I know that it's the spirit of the Lord." On this Pentecost Sunday, may we experience the presence of the Holy Spirit in our midst, and may we be revived as we leave this place.

May 27, 2012

Supernatural High
Acts 2:1-4, 12-17, 21 (NRSV)

When the day of Pentecost had come, they were all together in one place. And suddenly from heaven there came a sound like the rush of a violent wind, and it filled the entire house where they were sitting. Divided tongues, as of fire, appeared among them, and a tongue rested on each of them. All of them were filled with the Holy Spirit and began to speak in other languages, as the Spirit gave them ability....

All were amazed and perplexed, saying to one another, "What does this mean?" But others sneered and said, "They are filled with new wine." But Peter, standing with the eleven, raised his voice and addressed them, "Men of Judea and all who live in Jerusalem, let this be known to you, and listen to what I say. Indeed, these are not drunk, as you suppose, for it is only nine o'clock in the morning. No, this is what was spoken through the prophet Joel: 'In the last days it will be, God declares, that I will pour out my Spirit upon all flesh, and your sons and your daughters shall prophesy, and your young men shall see visions, and your old men shall dream dreams....

Then everyone who calls on the name of the Lord shall be saved.'"

Just about every day, around 2:30 p.m. or 3:00 p.m., I eat a banana for my afternoon snack. Bananas are pretty nutritious. The only problem is what to do with the peel after you've eaten the banana. If I'm on the golf course, I just toss the peel into the woods. If I'm at home, I put the peel into a bag and store it in the freezer until the next trash day so it doesn't stink up the house. If I'm here at the church, I will walk outside behind the building and toss the peel among the trees at the back of our church property. If those banana peels hadn't decomposed, there would be thousands of them back there by now.

One afternoon last month I was tossing away my banana peel when I came across this can on the church lawn. I picked it up and brought it inside, intending to put it into the recycle bin. But the name on the can caught my eye: "Natty Daddy, 25 ounces." I thought to myself, "What is Natty Daddy, and who would want to drink twenty-five ounces of it?"

So out of curiosity I went to my computer and Googled "Natty Daddy." As you might have guessed, Natty Daddy is an alcoholic beverage. It's a kind of a beer or malt liquor with eight percent alcohol content. I found out more about it on a website called (and I'm not making it up) "ratebeer.com." It's kind of a "Trip Advisor" website for beer drinkers. People can rate different brands of beer and give their opinions about them. I copied some of the comments about Natty Daddy.

> Ok guys just hear me out on this one. I don't know how to explain it but the Natty Daddy is one of the greatest beer achievements in history. When I was in college at Miami U these past few years I had one go-to brew; the Natty Daddy. Sold at my local Oxford, OH Speedway for $1.25 for a 25 Oz. I would grab three of these bad boys and head home for a night of boozing and debauchery. After two years of solid drinking I fell in love.
>
> This beer is definitely meant to provide a cheap buzz - it's only sold in 25-ounce cans - and it succeeds in its mission while providing a decent flavor. It's completely worth its price tag.
>
> Taste is high alcohol, metallic, and acidic. Flavor is simple in that it's malt liquor with one purpose, to get people drunk.

Now we know what a Natty Daddy is. It would be funny, except that alcohol abuse is no laughing matter. According to *The Washington Post*, (May 3, 2015, F2), "drug abuse—including and especially alcohol abuse—costs the U.S. economy billions of dollars in lost productivity each year." Even greater than the financial cost is the human cost. It's impossible to know how many lives and families have been destroyed by alcohol and drug abuse.

In government data released last month, certain industries have high percentages of employees who drink heavily or who use illicit drugs. For example, eighteen percent of miners are heavy drinkers. The study defined heavy drinkers as "drinking 5 or more drinks on the same occasion, on 5 or more days in the past month." Using that definition, seventeen percent of construction workers are heavy drinkers, and twelve percent of hotel and restaurant workers drink heavily. When it comes to drug abuse, hotel and restaurant workers are the heaviest users by far. Nineteen percent of hotel and restaurant workers used an illicit drug in the past month. Among those least likely to be heavy drinkers or to use illicit drugs are schoolteachers and government employees (members of Congress notwithstanding).

Not surprisingly, men drink heavily and do drugs more than women, and young people do drugs and drink heavily more than older people. But there are still plenty of women with substance abuse problems and many seniors who drink to excess or get high.

In our scripture for this morning, some in the crowd that day of Pentecost accused the disciples of being drunk. The followers of Jesus had been filled with the Holy Spirit, and they began to speak in other languages as the Spirit empowered them. Hearing the cacophony of dialects, some in the crowd thought that the disciples were inebriated from drinking too much wine.

Peter refuted the accusation directly. He said, "These men are not drunk, as you suppose, for it is only nine o'clock in the morning." Peter didn't say they aren't drunk because they didn't drink. He said it was too early in the day for them to be drunk. Then he explained their behavior by quoting the prophet Joel: "In the last days…God declares…I will pour out my Spirit on all flesh" (Acts 2:17). It wasn't that the disciples had poured a few drinks for breakfast. God had poured his Spirit into them. Paul used the same analogy in his letter to the Ephesians when he wrote, "Do not get drunk with wine, for that is debauchery; but be filled with the Spirit" (Eph 5:18 NRSV).

Admittedly, I live a fairly sheltered life. The strongest drink I enjoy is a Diet Cherry Dr. Pepper. The only alcohol I drink is the occasional sip of champagne at a wedding reception, just to toast the bride and groom. That's a personal choice for me, not a religious stricture. Jesus drank wine. Jesus offered wine to his disciples during the Last Supper. Jesus turned water into wine at the wedding in Cana. The idea that Christians must abstain from alcohol is not based on the Bible. It's from the temperance movement of the nineteenth and early twentieth centuries. Still, I choose not to drink alcohol for three reasons. First, my life is fine without it. I don't need a substance to get high. Second, I have seen what the abuse of alcohol can do to destroy lives. I've had alcoholics in my family. Third, I don't want to compromise my witness for Christ. I am aware of my pastoral responsibilities as a role model, and I don't want to do anything in my personal life that might lead others astray.

Now, if you choose to drink alcohol in moderation, I don't have a problem with that… unless you are underage, or unless you are pregnant, or unless you are driving a car or flying an airplane, or unless you are performing surgery, or unless you have an addiction to alcohol. Otherwise, if you want to enjoy a glass of wine with dinner, or a beer in the clubhouse, that's okay with me. Moderation is the key. The problem with some alcoholic beverages is that they are not meant to be enjoyed in moderation. Natty Daddy is a case in point.

The larger issue is not your beverage of choice but the stewardship of your health and Christian influence. Four nights a week self-help groups meet in our church building. Two Alcoholics Anonymous groups and two Chemically Dependent Anonymous groups have weekly meetings here with the goal of helping each other stay sober. It's an ongoing struggle, and I am glad our church can support their efforts to live without ingesting harmful substances into their bodies. They are learning to "get high" on life. They are learning to appreciate the gifts of family and friends and work and health and nature and all the other blessings that God gives. They are learning to trust in a higher supernatural power that can help them be free from alcohol and drug abuse.

In Galatians 5 Paul contrasted "the works of the flesh" with "the fruit of the Spirit." Among the works of the flesh are "fornication, impurity, licentiousness, idolatry, sorcery, enmities, strife, jealousy, anger, quarrels, dissensions, factions, envy, drunkenness, carousing, and things like these." Paul warned the Galatians to avoid doing such things. Then Paul listed the fruit of the Spirit: "love, joy, peace, patience, kindness, generosity, faithfulness, gentleness, and self-control" (Gal 5:19–23 NRSV).

Today we celebrate the gift of the Holy Spirit poured out on all who believe in Jesus. The gift of the Spirit is about more than what happened on the day of Pentecost. It's about the qualities of character and behavior that the Spirit gives. It's about power that God gives us every day to live faithful lives for him. Come, Holy Spirit, come.

May 24, 2015

Pentecost Power
Acts 2:1-4, 14-21 (NRSV)

When the day of Pentecost had come, they were all together in one place. And suddenly from heaven there came a sound like the rush of a violent wind, and it filled the entire house where they were sitting. Divided tongues, as of fire, appeared among them, and a tongue rested on each of them. All of them were filled with the Holy Spirit and began to speak in other languages, as the Spirit gave them ability.

But Peter, standing with the eleven, raised his voice and addressed them, "Men of Judea and all who live in Jerusalem, let this be known to you, and listen to what I say. Indeed, these are not drunk, as you suppose, for it is only nine o'clock in the morning. No, this is what was spoken through the prophet Joel: 'In the last days it will be, God declares, that I will pour out my Spirit upon all flesh, and your sons and your daughters shall prophesy, and your young men shall see visions, and your old men shall dream dreams. Even upon my slaves, both men and women, in those days I will pour out my Spirit; and they shall prophesy. And I will show portents in the heaven above and signs on the earth below, blood, and fire, and smoky mist. The sun shall be turned to darkness and the moon to blood, before the coming of the Lord's great and glorious day. Then everyone who calls on the name of the Lord shall be saved.'"

We're not sure exactly when this took place. It was the day of Pentecost, we know that much, and Pentecost was fifty days after Passover. And if we knew the year, we could calculate the actual date, but the date of Passover changes every year. We know that Pontius Pilate was governor from A.D. 26 to A.D. 36, so that narrows the time frame a bit. But the Bible doesn't say exactly how old Jesus was when he was crucified, nor does the Bible say exactly when Jesus was born. He was thirty years old when he began his public ministry, and most scholars believe it lasted three or more years, but we can't say for sure. So scholars can only speculate about exactly when these events took place.

Pentecost was roughly forty-seven days after Jesus had been raised from the dead. It was roughly seven days after he had ascended into heaven, since the resurrected Jesus appeared to his disciples for roughly forty days. You notice I keep saying "roughly," because we don't have enough information to be exact. What we do know is that Jesus died on a Friday, the day before the beginning of Passover; he was resurrected on Sunday, the day after the Sabbath; and he ascended into heaven forty days after that.

Since Pentecost was fifty days after the beginning of Passover, we can deduce that the Holy Spirit came upon the followers of Jesus about a week after he ascended to heaven. What were the disciples doing those seven weeks between Easter and Pentecost?

Apparently they spent a lot of time meeting together and in prayer. Some of them went back home. Some of them went back to work. At least 120 of them were in Jerusalem when they chose a replacement for Judas, who had killed himself. So with the addition of Matthias, the group was back up to twelve apostles, and the female followers of Jesus, and many other disciples.

On the day of Pentecost, they were all together in one place in Jerusalem. Suddenly there came a sound from heaven like the rush of a mighty wind. Divided tongues, as of fire, rested on each of them. All of them were filled with the Holy Spirit, and they began to speak in other languages, as the Spirit gave them utterance. This was the fulfillment of what Jesus had promised. Before he had ascended to heaven, Jesus told them that the Holy Spirit would come upon them and they would receive power to be his witnesses in Jerusalem and Judea and Samaria and to the ends of the earth.

And that's what happened. The Holy Spirit came upon them, and they received power to be his witnesses. They began to speak in other languages, and devout Jews from other nations who had come to Jerusalem to celebrate Pentecost heard the gospel preached in their own native tongues. Everyone who heard it was amazed and perplexed. Some asked, "What does this mean?" Others said, "They are filled with new wine," meaning they're drunk.

That's when Peter stood up to speak. He said, "No, we're not drunk. After all, it's only 9:00 a.m. Nobody is filled with new wine at this hour. No, this fulfills what was spoken through the prophet Joel." And then Peter quoted Joel 2:28–32, about what would happen when the Messiah has come. God would pour out his Spirit on men and women, young and old. And all who called on the name of the Lord would be saved. Yes, that very day, about 3,000 people called on the name of the Lord. That very day, about 3,000 of them were saved, and were baptized, and were added to the fledgling Christian movement. That's why Pentecost is sometimes called the birthday of the church. God's spirit was poured out, and the followers of Jesus were given the power to proclaim the gospel, and many more were given the power to believe and be saved.

That in itself is enough to make Pentecost a big deal. But the part of the story that fascinates me is what happened to Peter. Remember Peter, the disciple who on the night Jesus was arrested pulled out his sword to defend Jesus and then with the other disciples deserted him and fled? Remember Peter, who followed in the shadows to the courtyard of the high priest, where, when he was confronted, he denied he even knew Jesus? Remember Peter, who went out and wept bitterly over his cowardice and failure of nerve? Remember Peter, who was there when the risen Jesus appeared beside the Sea of Galilee and fixed breakfast for the disciples? Remember Peter, how Jesus kept asking him, "Do you love me? Do you love me? Do you love me?" as if to remind Peter of his threefold denials? Peter is not exactly a hero in those Gospel stories.

But on the day of Pentecost, Peter boldly stood up before the crowd and preached! What a transformation! In just a few weeks Peter went from being a cowardly denier of Jesus to becoming a courageous proclaimer of Jesus. Peter went from being timid and afraid to being daring and fearless. How do you explain it? What can change a person like that? Could it have something to do with the gift of the Holy Spirit? Just seven weeks after Jesus was crucified, Peter stood up in the midst of a vast throng in Jerusalem and publicly proclaimed that Jesus was the Messiah. Jesus was the Messiah who had ushered in the new age of God's coming kingdom. And the sign of that new age was the Holy Spirit poured out on all who would believe. The Holy Spirit gave Peter the power to courageously stand up for Jesus, just seven weeks after Peter denied he even knew Jesus. The Holy Spirit transformed Peter from a guilt-ridden failure into a powerful prophet. And it didn't just happen to Peter. A transformation happened to all of them. Power came down from heaven. The Holy Spirit was poured out on all who believe.

There is a story in the current issue of *Time* (June 9, 2014, pp. 34-37) about a scientist at the Jet Propulsion Laboratory in Pasadena, California. He heads a team of astronomers who are tracking asteroids that could potentially threaten our planet. Currently they are monitoring over 600,000 asteroids, of the several billion asteroids that are out there. You've probably heard of the giant asteroid that struck the earth off the Yucatan Peninsula sixty-five million years ago. Six miles wide, that asteroid kicked up such a cloud of dust that the earth's atmosphere cooled to the point that the dinosaurs became extinct.

That happened sixty-five million years ago, but asteroids continue to threaten our planet. Last year an asteroid exploded over Russia with the power of thirty-three atomic bombs. It damaged 7,300 buildings, and injured over 1,600 people. It's only a matter of time before another powerful asteroid hits the earth. Actually, over 100 tons of space debris come at us every day, but most of it gets incinerated in the atmosphere before it hits anything on earth. Approximately every eight months, an asteroid the size of a small car comes at us. There are hundreds of millions of asteroids that size. Over a million asteroids are the size of a yacht, and over 20,000 asteroids are the size of one of the pyramids in Egypt.

The goal of watching all those asteroids is to try to prevent another disaster. If scientists can detect the threatening asteroid far enough away, they may be able to figure out a way to avert catastrophe. Maybe we will be able to send a rocket to intercept the asteroid. The idea is to give it a strong shove to divert its trajectory so that it flies wide by the time it reaches us. We don't have the capability to do that yet, but that's one of the possible solutions. Until that capability is developed, scientists hope at least to be able to warn people that an asteroid is coming so they can get out of the way. That too is still pretty far-fetched, but it's better than just waiting to get hit. The reality is that there is tremendous destructive power from heaven that is coming our way. The only good news is that such powerful destructive asteroids don't hit the earth that often.

There is an even greater power from heaven that has come our way. The Holy Spirit has been poured out on all who believe. It's a power from heaven, not to destroy, but to make new. Peter became a new person as he was filled with the Holy Spirit. And the Holy Spirit can transform our lives too.

They call it "the miracle on the Hudson." On a cold January day in 2009, a US Airways flight took off from LaGuardia Airport. During its ascent the plane struck a flock of Canada geese. Both engines lost power, and the crippled aircraft could not make it back to the airport. With no place to land, Captain Chesley Sullenberger and First Officer Jeffrey Skiles skillfully guided the aircraft to a touchdown in the Hudson River.

On board the aircraft was a passenger named Dave Sanderson, age fifty-three. A software sales manager for Oracle, Dave flew often for his work. When the jet hit the river, Dave didn't panic. Water was pouring into the cabin, but his first thought was to help others get out of the aircraft. Dave remembered his mother saying to him as a kid, "If you do the right thing,

God will take care of you." Dave was the last passenger to exit the plane. By the time he reached an exit, the wings of the jet were partially submerged. Dave jumped into the icy river and began to swim toward a rescue boat. By the time someone pulled him into the boat, he was so cold he couldn't feel a thing. On shore two emergency medical technicians and a guy with a Red Cross blanket began to attend to him. Dave, along with the others on the aircraft, survived the crash. But even more, Dave found a new mission in life.

Dave began speaking about his experience at Red Cross fundraisers. Last year he resigned from his position at Oracle to devote himself to speaking and fundraising for the Red Cross. To date Dave has helped raise more than seven million dollars. He's also writing a book about his experiences. Dave says, "The crash changed my perspective. I started scheduling around my family rather than my job." (*AARP The Magazine*, April-May, 2014, p. 86). Dave found a different purpose in life. He's discovered new priorities. It's almost like he has experienced a spiritual rebirth.

It's not that the plane crash totally changed him. After all, he was the last passenger to get off the plane because he stayed behind to help others escape. But Dave agrees that he's a better person now. Dave says, "Everyone has tough times in life. Now I have a confidence when things get tough." Sometimes God's spirit gets hold of a good person and makes that person even better.

The bread and the cup remind us that Jesus died for us. But even more these elements remind us that Jesus is with us through the Holy Spirit. God's power came down from heaven to make us new and better people too.

June 8, 2014

The Birthday of the Church
Acts 2:1-4, 37-42 (NRSV)

When the day of Pentecost had come, they were all together in one place. And suddenly from heaven there came a sound like the rush of a violent wind, and it filled the entire house where they were sitting. Divided tongues, as of fire, appeared among them, and a tongue rested on each of them. All of them were filled with the Holy Spirit and began to speak in other languages, as the Spirit gave them ability.

Now when they heard this, they were cut to the heart and said to Peter and to the other apostles, "Brothers, what should we do?" Peter said to them, "Repent, and be baptized every one of you in the name of Jesus Christ so that your sins may be forgiven; and you will receive the gift of the Holy Spirit. For the promise is for you, for your children, and for all who are far away, everyone whom the Lord our God calls to him." And he testified with many other arguments and exhorted them, saying, "Save yourselves from this corrupt generation." So those who welcomed his message were baptized, and that day about three thousand persons were added. They devoted themselves to the apostles' teaching and fellowship, to the breaking of bread and the prayers.

Next Sunday we are going to celebrate the birthday of Village Baptist Church. Village was constituted as an autonomous church on May 23, 1971. So next Sunday marks our forty-fifth anniversary as a church.

Today we celebrate not the birthday of Village Baptist Church, but the birthday of THE church. It was on this day, on Pentecost, that the first church was formed. The disciples of Jesus were transformed by the Holy Spirit. They changed from a leaderless group into an organized church. Led by the Holy Spirit, they devoted themselves to the apostles' teaching and fellowship, to the breaking of bread and the prayers. We're not sure how long ago it was because we're not sure the exact year that Jesus was crucified and raised from the grave and ascended into heaven. Perhaps it was the year A.D. 30. That's an educated guess. We know that Jesus was born before 4 BC, because King Herod died in 4 BC, and Herod was alive when Jesus was born. We know from Luke's Gospel that Jesus began his public ministry at about age thirty. From John's Gospel we deduce his public ministry lasted at least three years, maybe more. So putting it all together, the year A.D. 30 is an educated guess about when the church began. If that's the case, then today marks the 1,986th anniversary of the church (if anyone is counting).

The Christian church has come a long way in 1,986 or so years. From a small group of followers of Jesus, it has grown into a worldwide religion numbering over two billion believers. According to some estimates, Christians comprise about a third of the world's population. Here in the United States, Christians make up about seventy percent of the population, with sixty-two percent claiming to be church members. Any way you look at it, that's a lot of people.

In our scripture for this morning, we read that about 3,000 people were baptized and were added to the church on the day of Pentecost, some 1,986 years ago. So the church grew immensely on a single day, and the church has been growing ever since. And as the church has grown, the church has changed in many ways.

I ran across a recent study published by the Alban Institute (*Alban Weekly*, Monday, April 11, 2016),, which is now affiliated with the Duke Divinity School. The study highlights six ways the church in America has changed in recent years, since the beginning of the twenty-first century. Let me briefly share those findings with you.

1. People are increasingly concentrated in very large congregations. Yet the average congregation in America is small, and getting smaller. In 1998 the median number of regular participants in a local church was eighty. That means half the churches had eighty congregants or less, and half had eighty or more. By 2012 it had dropped to seventy congregants. So many local congregations are getting smaller. At the same time, some churches are huge. There are mega-churches in most metropolitan areas. That means that while the average church is getting smaller, the average churchgoer attends a much larger congregation. About half of all churchgoers belong to the largest seven percent of congregations.

2. There is growing diversity among and within American congregations. Racial and ethnic diversity is increasing. In 1998 twenty percent of churchgoers attended all-white congregations. By 2012 that number had decreased to eleven percent. So there are a lot fewer all-white churches than there used to be. Larger congregations, and congregations with fewer senior citizens, tend to be more diverse. More churches also are accepting women in pastoral roles, although there are some notable exceptions, such as the Roman Catholic Church and the Southern Baptist Convention, which are against women in pastoral roles. Acceptance of gays and lesbians as members and lay leaders has also increased substantially, although, again, acceptance levels vary widely across denominations.

3. Many pastors are bivocational, meaning they hold another job. More than a third of solo or senior pastors are also employed outside the church. And fourteen percent of congregations are led by a volunteer or unpaid solo or senior pastor.

4. Worship services are becoming more informal and expressive. More churches are using contemporary music, while organs and choirs are becoming less prevalent, especially among historically white

Protestant congregations. Projection equipment is increasing. There is more spontaneous speaking from people in the pews. There is more applause and more saying "Amen." There is an increase in the use of drums and raising hands in praise.
5. People in smaller churches give more money to their churches than do people in larger churches. The larger the congregation, the lower the per capita contribution. Also, fewer congregations are giving money to their denominations.
6. Congregations focus more on serving the needy than on trying to effect systemic change. Most congregations (87%) engage in some form of social service. The most common type of social service is food assistance. More than half of all congregations give food to the needy, often through an organization like the Bowie Interfaith Food Pantry or Martha's Table.

We have seen some of these changes in our own congregation: increasing diversity, worship becoming more informal and expressive, focus on serving the needy. And people in our church are very generous in their giving. If our people weren't generous in our giving, I would have to be bivocational and get another job. Pastor Star is bivocational. She works here as our associate pastor, and she works for the D.C. Baptist Convention as minister to empower congregations. Our other staff members are either bivocational or semiretired.

Churches have come a long way since that first church at Pentecost. We have buildings and budgets and church staffs and organized worship and music ministries and youth ministries and children's ministries and constitutions and bylaws and business meetings and a host of other programs. Yet in some ways the nature of the church is still the same. We still follow Jesus. We still devote ourselves to the apostles' teaching, as contained in the Holy Scriptures. We still enjoy fellowship and breaking bread together and praying together. We still baptize believers in the name of the Father and the Son and the Holy Spirit. We still share the good news of Jesus with everyone we can. We still minister to the needy in Christ's name. Some things have changed a lot in churches today, but some things have not changed all that much.

The key to all the changes that have taken place is following the leading of the Holy Spirit. Our world has changed a lot in the past 1,986 years, and the church has had to change to remain relevant to our culture. But the leadership of the Holy Spirit is what keeps the church relevant to Jesus. If we fail to follow the Holy Spirit, then the church is just like any other human organization, subject to becoming worldly and unholy and self-centered and corrupt. But if we seek to follow the Holy Spirit, then the church can remain true to what Jesus would have us to be and to do.

You see, it's not about our organization, or our style of worship, or our musical preferences, or whether we applaud during worship or raise our hands. Those are all expressions of the times in which we live. The most important part of our life together is living by the Spirit, allowing the Spirit to guide us and shape us and mold us in the church to become the people that Jesus would have us to be.

Some of us are wearing red today because red is symbolic of the Holy Spirit, of the tongues as of fire that descended and rested on all the followers of Jesus on the day of Pentecost. Most of us don't wear red every day because we would soon grow weary of the monotony of that, but the Holy Spirit is with us every day. And every day we should seek the guidance of the Holy Spirit as we live our lives and seek to follow Christ.

On the day of Pentecost, some of the people who heard Peter preach were cut to the heart and asked, "What should we do?" Peter replied, "Repent, and be baptized every one of you in the name of Jesus Christ so that your sins may be forgiven, and you will receive the gift of the Holy Spirit." That is still the message of the gospel today. Repent, and be baptized so that your sins may be forgiven, and you will receive the gift of the Holy Spirit. And we invite believers to join us in this church as we devote ourselves to the apostles' teaching and fellowship, to the breaking of bread and the prayers.

If you are not a member of our church, we invite you to join us. You can join upon your profession of faith in Jesus, following him as a believer in baptism. Your sins will be forgiven, and you will receive the gift of the Holy Spirit. Or maybe you already are a Christian, but you are not yet a member of this congregation. We invite you to join us as we devote ourselves to the apostles' teaching and fellowship, to the breaking of bread and prayer. About 3,000 people made that commitment to Christ on that Pentecost long ago. What better day than Pentecost to commit your life to Christ and his church?

Churches have changed a lot over the years, and they will continue to change. This church has changed, and it will continue to change. But God's love never changes. The grace of our Lord Jesus Christ never changes. The fellowship of the Holy Spirit never changes.

Near the end of the sixth century, Gregory the Great wrote about Pentecost, "Outwardly, tongues of fire appeared; inwardly, their hearts were set ablaze; for when the disciples received God under the appearance of fire, they began to burn with a sweet love."

May 15, 2016

Chapter 3

1973-1977

I graduated from Baylor in the spring of 1973 and enrolled at The Southern Baptist Theological Seminary in Louisville, Kentucky, for the fall semester. Several Baylor friends had gone ahead of me to Southern, so it wasn't as intimidating a move as it might have been. Most of the dormitory rooms in Manly Hall were single-occupancy, but we got to know the fellow students on our floor rather quickly. Some of them—Jim Holladay, Jim McCoy, Chris Wilburn, and Doug Kellough—became good friends. We were all starting the master of divinity degree program, feeling called in some degree to Christian ministry. The two Jims and I eventually would become pastors. Chris and Doug would find their places of service as chaplains in healthcare settings. But at the beginning none of us was sure exactly where God was leading us. For a time I thought I might go into teaching, which meant that the M.Div. would be followed by a Ph.D. I had selected Southern because of its reputation as an academic institution and because I thought I needed to experience life outside of Texas. Both rationales came to fruition. Southern was outstanding academically, and my perspective was broadened by contact with faculty and students from across the country and the world. Over time I would get to know classmates from Canada, Liberia, Nigeria, New Zealand, and many other places.

My studies were interrupted, however, by an undiagnosed illness in January of 1974 that sent me to the hospital for eleven days. After being discharged, my continued fatigue forced me to drop out of seminary and return home to Texas to recuperate. The illness was some type of liver disease, akin to hepatitis. The only prescribed remedy was diet, rest, and time. I felt lousy every day for months. Besides my parents, my main encouragers were two former pastors, Dr. John Claypool and Dr. J. P. Allen. Once I was strong enough to get out of the house, Dr. Claypool picked me up and took me to lunch on a couple of occasions. One time he took me to lunch with Dr. John Killinger, who had come to Broadway for a special preaching event. It was a thrill to meet Dr. Killinger and to listen as he and Dr. Claypool interacted in the car ride and during lunch.

Once I was strong enough to venture out on my own, Dr. Allen offered me a part-time position with the Southern Baptist Radio and Television Commission, where he was a vice president. My job was to be a correspondence counselor, answering letters from listeners to the commission's popular radio show, *Powerline*. Dr. Allen would review my responses to the listeners' questions and sometimes offer suggestions. Mainly, he affirmed the work I was doing and encouraged me to continue to get stronger so that I could return to seminary.

By the fall of 1974, I did return to Southern. I was now a semester behind my friends, but I was glad to be back in the classroom. I discovered the prayer room in the main classroom/administration building. Between classes I would go into the prayer room, close the door, and lie down on the floor to regain my strength. Casual observers might have thought I was spending a lot of time in prayer.

Beyond the required classes in Greek and Hebrew, I was drawn to biblical studies and systematic theology. I was not drawn to preaching, except for the lone preaching course I took under Dr. George Buttrick. A living legend, editor of the *Interpreter's Bible* commentary series, and author of many other books, such as *God, Pain, and Evil*, Dr. Buttrick taught one preaching class each spring semester. The class consisted of Dr. Buttrick lecturing/ruminating on the topics of his choosing and answering selected questions on preaching. He required each student in the class to write a sermon, submit it for his review, and then attend a one-on-one feedback session at his apartment, where his wife plied us awestruck students with tea and cookies. There was no actual preaching involved, just writing a manuscript and receiving Dr. Buttrick's critique.

To my amazement Dr. Buttrick liked my sermon. During the one-on-one critique he told me that after reading many sermons from my classmates, in comparison my sermon was like the sun breaking through the clouds. I was ebullient on the inside but appreciative with the proper decorum on the outside. In fact, I was so energized by the positive feedback that I wrote another sermon (not required) for his critique. In that second sermon I took my primary illustration from a popular children's novel of the time, *Hope for the Flowers*, which reflected a kind of countercultural idealism. The main character of the novel is a caterpillar named Stripe, who discovers the purpose of his existence after many disillusioning experiences. I hoped Dr. Buttrick would appreciate the metaphor and praise my second sermon too.

Boy, was I wrong! He hated it. He deemed a caterpillar from a children's fable to be a trivial figure for a sermon. Without mentioning me by name, he talked about my sermon derisively in class. None of my classmates knew who had written the sermon, but I felt lower than a caterpillar upon hearing Dr. Buttrick deride my sermon publicly. I think it was because of that second sermon (optional though it was) that my final grade for the class was a "B+" instead of the "A" I deserved. I even went to the dean of the school of theology to complain about the final grade after it had been posted. He looked at my evidence and agreed that I should have received an "A" for the course. But then he said, "It's not worth it to make an issue of it." He had reviewed my academic record and equated it with his own M.Div. studies. His record had enabled him to pursue further studies, and he was sure my grades would qualify me for doctoral work. He advised me to drop the protest, which I did.

I never took another preaching course in seminary. Years later, one of the seminars in the doctor of ministry program had a preaching component, but even then there was no actual preaching involved, just submitting sermon plans and manuscripts. So the act of preaching would have to be learned another way.

During the 1975–76 academic year I accepted a position as a pastoral intern with my church in Louisville, Crescent Hill Baptist Church. Dr. John Howell was my pastor, and he became a friend and mentor too. Another student, John Upton, also served as a pastoral intern at Crescent Hill. John would go on to missionary service, pastoral service, and denominational service as executive director of the Baptist General Association of Virginia and president of the Baptist World Alliance.

Most of my friends graduated in the spring of 1976, but I still had a semester yet to go. During that spring semester I met a young widow with a three-year-old daughter. Had I not missed a semester in 1974, it is likely that I never would have met Linda and her daughter, Amy. It is also likely that I never would have been called to the church in Silver Spring, Maryland, after I did graduate. So life has a way of recompense.

During my last semester, in the fall of 1976, I spent most evenings at Linda's home, waiting for her to put Amy to bed. I did not neglect my studies, but I had bigger fish to fry. I also put my name in the hopper for preaching assignments. The seminary had an office that fielded requests from area churches seeking substitute preachers. Many Sunday mornings I traveled the back roads of Kentucky and Indiana to preach in small churches.

Finally, I was doing more than writing sermon manuscripts. I was delivering sermons in actual churches. It was just the kind of on-the-job training I needed to learn to be a preacher.

I received the master of divinity at graduation ceremonies in December 1976. Linda and Amy were there, along with my parents, who had flown up from Texas. They met Linda and Amy for the first time and were impressed. After Christmas, Linda and Amy flew to Texas to meet the rest of my family. After a family gathering at my grandmother's house, my grandmother called me into her bedroom. She handed me a box containing a ring, her engagement ring. She was offering it to me to give to Linda. The only problem was, Linda had not agreed to marry me. For some reason she thought I should have a job before we said "I do." And in the Baptist system, seminary graduates are not guaranteed a job. They must be called to a church or other ministerial position. So placing the ring on Linda's finger would have to wait.

After I returned to Louisville in January of 1977 to begin the interview process with churches, I contracted mononucleosis. For a month I had to lay low and could not go to any interviews. I feared that all the "good" jobs would go to my fellow graduates who were able to interview. I feared that both my career and my future family life were in peril. Finally, I was well enough in February to interview with churches. The seminary set up an interview with a pastor from Maryland, Rev. Donnell Harris. Rev. Harris told me that his church was dually aligned with American Baptists and Southern Baptists through the D.C. Baptist Convention. A graduate of Colgate Rochester Divinity School, Rev. Harris was an American Baptist. He had come to Southern Seminary to recruit a Southern Baptist to come to the church as associate pastor.

Following the interview, and after a series of telephone conversations, the church in Silver Spring flew me to Maryland to meet the search committee and the congregation. I was offered the position of associate pastor at Montgomery Hills Baptist Church, and I eagerly accepted. The only requirement was that I be ordained before I began at Montgomery Hills. My Crescent Hill pastor, Dr. John Howell, graciously offered to ask the church to ordain me. John recruited an ordination council comprised mostly of Crescent Hill members who happened to be seminary faculty. The ordination service took place on a Sunday evening in the Crescent Hill chapel. I was now Rev. Salmon.

My career was back on track, and soon my future family life would be too. I moved to Silver Spring and started work with the church April 15, 1977. Linda remained in Louisville to sell her house and plan the wedding. Oh, I finally did give Linda my grandmother's engagement ring. We were married in a little chapel outside Louisville on July 2, 1977. Four-year-old Amy was the flower girl, and Dr. John Howell officiated the ceremony. After the honeymoon, Linda, Amy, and I moved into our little house in Silver Spring. Life was good.

Amazing, Grace!
1 Corinthians 15:1-10 (RSV)

Now I would remind you, brethren, in what terms I preached to you the gospel, which you received, in which you stand, by which you are saved, if you hold it fast—unless you believed in vain. For I delivered to you as of first importance what I also received, that Christ died for our sins in accordance with the scriptures, that he was buried, that he was raised on the third day in accordance with the scriptures, and that he appeared to Cephas, then to the twelve. Then he appeared to more than five hundred brethren at one time, most of whom are still alive, though some have fallen asleep. Then he appeared to James, then to all the apostles. Last of all, as to one untimely born, he appeared also to me. For I am the least of the apostles, unfit to be called an apostle, because I persecuted the church of God. But by the grace of God I am what I am, and his grace toward me was not in vain. On the contrary, I worked harder than any of them, though it was not I, but the grace of God which is with me.

In my family I am famous for the way I say grace. When we were growing up, my mother would call on one of the children to say the blessing before our evening meal. Over the years I developed a brief, succinct, to-the-point prayer, which seemed to do the job in as little time as possible. When it comes time to eat, I'm ready to get on with it. So my dinner blessing as a boy was simply this: "Dear God, thank you for this food and this day. Amen." That's it: eleven words, counting the "Amen."

When we were teaching our daughter Amy how to say grace, I used that eleven-word blessing as an example. Of course, she picked it up immediately. Now, our son Marc has learned it too. Almost every night, those eleven words are our grace before the evening meal.

Of course, there is nothing wrong with simple prayers. I imagine God would prefer a simple, sincere prayer any day to some flowery, wordy, insincere prayer. And yet there is a danger that religion can become so simple and so familiar that it begins to lose its meaning.

So it is with that simple word *grace*. When Paul wrote about grace in our Scripture text, he had something more in mind than a simple blessing before a meal. Look again at verse 10: "But by the grace of God I am what I am, and his grace toward me was not in vain. On the contrary, I worked harder than any of them, though it was not I, but the grace of God which is with me." In some respects the "grace of God" is the deepest truth of our religion. The "grace of God" is the greatest promise of the Bible, and yet that word, *grace*, has been reduced to a perfunctory prayer before a meal.

Here in 1 Corinthians, the apostle Paul is writing about grace in an entirely different way. For Paul grace is the essence of what it means to be a Christian. Grace is the power of God at work in our lives to make us all that we can be. This is not some minute point of theology. Grace is not some side issue. No, Paul was preoccupied with grace. Paul used the Greek word for grace, *charis*, over 100 times in his letters. Grace, for Paul, was the very heartbeat of his life. Grace, for Paul, was a one-word summary of the gospel. Grace is what God is. Grace is what Jesus came for. Grace is what the Bible is all about. Grace is the reason for our hope, the answer to our struggles, the greatest promise we have from God.

What, then, is this grace? According to Paul, grace is the free, unmerited, undeserved, life-sustaining, spontaneous love of God for you and me! In other words, grace is what God gives us to show us that he is on our side. Grace is what God gives us to help us along through life. And yet I suspect that some of us don't fully appreciate God's grace. I suspect that some of us, in fact, don't even want God's grace most of the time, except maybe in a crisis. Some of us feel we don't need God's grace—we can make it on our own.

A pastor stopped by the hospital to visit with some of his church members. He stood at the information desk and began to thumb through the cards of new patients who had been admitted that day and were not yet listed in the computer. He came across the admitting card of one patient that caught his eye. The patient's name was listed, and where it said "religious affiliation," he had written "none," with an asterisk. Then, on the bottom of the card beside another asterisk was the notation, "in case of emergency, Methodist."

Some of us have an "emergency only" religion. Oh, we come to church. We believe in God. But when it comes to the day-to-day issues of our lives, we prefer to go it alone. We can handle things pretty well by ourselves. We value such qualities as self-reliance, independence, drive, determination, self-sufficiency. When it comes to most things, we can get along very well without God, thank you. We pride ourselves on being able to make it on our own.

Paul had a different attitude. Paul, the greatest missionary the world has ever seen, never claimed to be a self-made man. He never claimed to be able to go it alone. No, Paul attributed his successes to the grace of God. Paul said it was grace that made the difference in his life—not dedication, not hard work, not creativity or intelligence or willpower (though he certainly had all those qualities). No, it was grace that made Paul the person he was.

Whether we admit it or not, none of us has made it this far in life without God's help either. There is no such thing as a self-made man or woman. All of us have received blessings we did not earn or deserve. Not only Paul, but every one of us can say, "By the grace of God, I am who I am." It is God who made us, and God who continues to remake us, and not we ourselves.

For the past couple of weeks, our daughter, Amy, has been attending a summer camp in Carlisle, Pennsylvania. The site is not too far from Three Mile Island. I jokingly told Amy that when she comes home, we'll have to make sure she doesn't glow in the dark. Of course, nuclear radiation is no joking matter. We still don't know the full extent of the damage caused by that accident at Three Mile Island. When deadly radiation escapes into the atmosphere, the destructive force is largely imperceptible. When it happens, you can't always tell the effects. The damage is done before we realize it. Like an invisible, malevolent power, radiation set loose in the world can do unimagined harm.

What happened at Three Mile Island is a kind of antonym, an opposite analogy, of God's grace. Instead of an invisible destructive power, God's grace is an invisible positive force set loose in the world. Like a great cloud of blessing, God's grace moves over the earth to make our lives better. Like an imperceptible leakage of good, God's grace seeps into our lives to transform our personalities, to strengthen our characters, to fulfill our potentials, to give us healing and salvation. There is a spiritual power in the air, a positive spiritual force at work in our lives.

I cannot explain how it is that this grace from God works in my life or in yours. The Bible does not explain how God changes people and makes them more like Christ. But it happens. It happened to Paul, and it happens to us. We are not alone in the universe. Beneath us and above us and around us and within us there is the invisible spirit of grace. God gives us the grace to sustain and enrich and fulfill our lives.

And yet the skeptic in us wonders. How do we know? How do we know that God really is the author of all the goodness in life? How do we know that it's not just luck, or fate, or blind chance that controls us? How do we know that there is a God, and that his nature is love, and that his grace is available to us? How do we know?

In August of 1799 a French engineer in the army of Napoleon discovered a black stone slab near the village of Rosetta, along the West Delta of the Nile River in Egypt. Upon that slab was a decree, written in three languages—Greek and two forms of Egyptian writing dating back to the second century BC. Until that time, scholars had no way to translate Egyptian hieroglyphics. They had no key to understand what the various hieroglyphic symbols mean. But in 1799, for the first time, by using the Greek inscription as a guide, they were able to decipher the hieroglyphic script. Now those mysterious hieroglyphic writings could be translated and understood. That black slab is known today as the Rosetta Stone, and it is recognized as the key that unlocked ancient Egyptian culture.

How do we know that there really is a God? How do we decipher the mystery at the heart of the universe? How can we understand that there is a power at work in human life for good? Just this—we have a key. Jesus is the Rosetta Stone of God's grace.

Jesus is the key to understanding the nature of God. Because of Jesus, we know that God is our loving, heavenly Father who showers us with blessings we did not earn or deserve. Because of Jesus, we know that our lives are directed by something more than arbitrary fate or blind chance. If you want evidence of a loving God, if you want evidence of a God who will never desert us, if you want evidence of a power to change our lives for good, you need look no further than Jesus. Jesus is the Rosetta Stone of God's grace.

A story comes from Scotland about some workers blasting rock in a quarry. One day the fuse was attached to the dynamite, and the workmen pulled back to a safe place to await the explosion. As they reached their place of cover, to their horror, they saw a small child, a two-year-old boy, wander out into the blasting zone. The workmen screamed out to the boy, they frantically waved their arms, but he would not move. No one dared to run out to save him, for the explosion was only seconds away. Then, at the moment of crisis, the boy's older brother appeared. The older brother did not scream at the child or run out. Instead, he knelt down, opened wide his arms, and called for the child to come. Instantly, the boy ran toward him, and when the explosion shook the air, the boy was held safe in his brother's arms.

It is a story not just of one small boy, but of each of us. An older brother has stretched out his arms for us and called each of us to come. The cross is God's timeless gesture of grace to every generation and every person. In our moments of crisis, but even more in all the times of our lives, God is here for us.

This morning we share the bread and the cup to remember that. We take these elements because they remind us more powerfully than explosions about the love and grace of God. There's only one catch. Like any gift, in order to receive it, we must reach out and accept it. God will not force himself upon us. May God give us the faith to believe and receive his grace.

July 7, 1985

Just As I Am

Mark 2:13-17 (NRSV)

Jesus went out again beside the sea; the whole crowd gathered around him, and he taught them. As he was walking along, he saw Levi son of Alphaeus sitting at the tax booth, and he said to him, "Follow me." And he got up and followed him. And as he sat at dinner in Levi's house, many tax collectors and sinners were also sitting with Jesus and his disciples—for there were many who followed him. When the scribes of the Pharisees saw that he was eating with sinners and tax collectors, they said to his disciples, "Why does he eat with tax collectors and sinners?" When Jesus heard this, he said to them, "Those who are well have no need of a physician, but those who are sick; I have come to call not the righteous but sinners."

He said, "You're not pretty enough." That's the last thing any wife wants to hear from her husband. They were college sweethearts and got married when she was twenty-three. After a couple of years. she felt him growing more and more distant. Finally, she provoked him into a heated argument. She asked, "Why are you treating me this way?" He said, "Jen, sometimes I think you're not pretty enough for me." It was a remark that pierced her heart. Like most people, she had struggled with her self-image, especially her appearance. Who doesn't feel vulnerable about how they look? Believe it or not, even supermodels are not as confident about their self-image as they seem to be.

Linda has introduced me to a couple of reality shows on television. *Project Runway* is a competition for aspiring fashion designers. The show's host is Heidi Klum, surely one of the most beautiful women in the world. Another female-targeted reality show is *America's Next Top Model*, starring Tyra Banks, also a natural beauty. Both Heidi Klum and Tyra Banks come across on television as supremely confident and self-assured. And why wouldn't they be? They are both beautiful. Being good-looking is a definite advantage. There is a "beauty bias" in our society that can be empirically proven. Professor Daniel Hameresh, a labor economist at the University of Texas, has published studies proving the benefits of being physically attractive. Hameresh found that good-looking people are better paid, they have an easier time getting loans, and they receive milder prison sentences than people who are not so good-looking. Yet even the most stunning people don't always feel good about themselves. Heidi Klum has been through a series of broken relationships. She is twice divorced, and she has a child by yet a third man she was never married to. She is currently romantically involved with her bodyguard. Obviously, she is not as together as she seems.

Tyra Banks also has a history of broken relationships. Coincidentally, at one time she was romantically linked with the singer Seal, who was Heidi Klum's second husband. In a television interview Tyra Banks admitted being a victim of an abusive relationship. An unnamed boyfriend cheated on her and was emotionally abusive to her. Beautiful people may have some advantages over average-looking people, but life is not perfect, even for supermodels. We all want to be accepted for who we are. And we all have a fear of being undesirable and unaccepted.

In the case of the woman whose husband said, "You're not pretty enough," she later discovered that he was cheating on her with an intern at the office. Stunned by his infidelity, at age twenty-six she divorced him. For the next thirteen years she struggled to pick up the pieces of her shattered self-esteem. Finally, in 2010, she started telling her story. She found that as she told her story, many people could relate to it. She developed a website: yourenotprettyenough.com. She set up analytics and discovered that thousands of people every month were visiting her site after Googling such phrases as "Am I pretty enough?" She found it startling, thousands of people asking the internet if they were pretty enough. It sparked something within her. She had to take action. She decided to turn the website into a support and discussion group for women on self-esteem issues.

The creator of the website, Jennifer Tress, has written a book by the same title. She is now on a mission to use what she learned from her painful experience to help others. She calls herself "an accidental body-image activist." This fall she will begin a tour of 100 campuses, offering programs for college-age women struggling with their self-images.

Most of us do care what other people think about us. Am I pretty enough? Am I handsome enough? Am I smart enough? Am I successful enough? We care about what other people think about us because we want other people to like us. There is no greater psychological pain than the pain of rejection. No one wants to feel undesirable. And there is no better feeling than to feel accepted and loved for who we are.

In our scripture for this morning, Jesus met a man that most people looked down on. His name was Levi, and he was a tax collector. In the first century, tax collectors were among the most hated people in the Roman Empire. Most of them were viewed as crooks and traitors. They collaborated with the Roman government to collect exorbitant taxes, and they charged more than what was owed to keep a cut for themselves. *The HarperCollins Bible Dictionary* says, "Opportunities for theft, fraud, and corruption abounded, and tax collectors were generally despised in Greco-Roman literature, including the New Testament." (p. 900). Because Jewish tax collectors had contact with Gentiles, they were considered ritually unclean. That's why respectable people were shocked that Jesus would have anything to do with a tax collector. But Jesus didn't judge people by outward appearances. Jesus judged people by their hearts. And Jesus was willing to love and accept people that everyone else hated.

Seeing Levi sitting at his tax collection booth, Jesus said, "Follow me," and that's exactly what Levi did. He left his tax collection booth and followed Jesus. The next thing we know, Jesus was having dinner in Levi's house. This was beyond scandalous. No self-respecting rabbi would ever set foot inside the home of a tax collector, much less have dinner with him. Not only was Jesus breaking bread with Levi; many other tax collectors and "sinners" were there too. Mark tells us that many such people followed Jesus. The phrase "tax collectors and sinners" connoted a wide range of undesirables.

The "sinners" almost certainly included prostitutes as well as others whose way of life was antithetical to the will of God. That Jesus would associate with those kinds of people, especially in an intimate social setting like dinner in a private home, was outrageous. As far as the scribes and the Pharisees were concerned, righteous people simply did not mix with the unrighteous. When Jesus heard about their criticism of his dinner companions, he said, "Those who are well have no need of a physician, but those who are sick. I have come to call not the righteous but sinners."

The irony is that the self-righteous Pharisees were sinners too, but they wouldn't admit it. They thought they were better than everybody else. They saw no need for repentance and thus no need for forgiveness. Of course, they weren't into forgiveness for anyone. Their inclination was toward judgment and condemnation. Sadly, sometimes churches can be more like the Pharisees than like Jesus.

Almost forty years ago a former pastor of our church, Dan Ivins, introduced the slogan "We reserve the right to accept everybody." Dan told me that he coined that motto in reaction to signs he had seen in restaurants, growing up in the segregated society of Tennessee: "We reserve the right to refuse service to anyone." Back then, many white businesses discriminated against African Americans, and they reserved the right to refuse service to them. Many churches may not have posted the sign, but they did the same thing. They made certain people feel undesirable and unwelcome. Racial minorities, divorced people, unwed mothers, homosexuals, couples living together outside of marriage, homeless people, alcoholics, people with drug addictions, and a host of others were not welcome in those churches. Dan wanted to instill a different attitude in this church, so he introduced a slogan with a far different message: "We reserve the right to accept everybody." Dan is now pastoring his sixth church since leaving Village, and he has carried that slogan to every church where he has served. He told me that not every church has kept it, but that's what he thinks the church should be about. After I came to Village, just about every category of "undesirables" that I mentioned had come or would come to our church. We haven't always lived up to that motto, "We reserve the right to accept everybody," but that's what Jesus did.

Jesus reserved the right to accept everybody. He was accused of being "a friend of tax collectors and sinners," and there was truth in that accusation. Those the self-righteous would judge and condemn, Jesus sought to love and forgive.

The truth is that all of us can feel undesirable at times. Just as we all have physical flaws and imperfections, we all have spiritual flaws and imperfections. But Jesus calls us, just as we are, to follow him. Jesus didn't demand that Levi change his way of life before he followed Jesus. That would come later, as a result of following Jesus; it was not a prerequisite for following Jesus. The self-righteous Pharisees didn't think tax collectors and sinners were good enough to follow Jesus. The truth is that none of us are good enough, yet Jesus calls us to follow him anyway. He will make us righteous as we receive his forgiveness and acceptance and grace.

"Just as I Am" is one of the most beloved hymns in the English language. Billy Graham used it as an altar call during many of his crusades. According to the Billy Graham Evangelistic Association, millions of people have responded to his invitation to accept Jesus Christ as their personal savior. Many of them "walked the aisle" during one of his crusades. As they came forward, it was often to the strains of the hymn "Just as I Am."

It's a beloved hymn, but you may not know the story behind the song. It began as a poem written in 1834 by a young lady in England named Charlotte Elliott. For the first thirty years of her life, Charlotte seemed pretty blessed. It didn't seem like she had a care in the world; she was even known as "Carefree Charlotte." But then she was stricken with a debilitating disease that left her chronically fatigued and in constant pain. She was so exhausted that she was confined to bed most of the time. No longer "Carefree Charlotte," she grew grim and angry. She was perpetually irritable and depressed. She said that she hated God for making her a prisoner to her own bed.

One day her father invited a pastor to come to the house to talk with Charlotte. The pastor was not well received. Charlotte lashed out at him for talking about God, with whom she was so angry. But the pastor didn't take it personally. He understood where she was coming from. He said, "You have become so tired of yourself that you are holding on to hate and anger." Charlotte apologized for her ungracious attitude. She confided, "I am miserable. I want to be saved. I want to come to Jesus. I don't know how." The pastor replied, "Why not come just as you are?"

About twelve years later Charlotte was still what was called an "invalid." What a terrible term: in-valid. But that's how she felt much of the time. Confined to bed, she was unable to help when her brother organized a charitable bazaar to raise funds for a school. Feeling helpless and useless, she began to wonder again if God had rejected her. Then she remembered the words of the pastor from years before: "Come just as you are to the Lamb of God who takes away the sin of the world." Taking those words, she began to write a poem that would become the hymn: "Just as I am...O Lamb of God, I come!"

Charlotte never was cured of her illness. She never regained her physical strength. But later she learned that copies of her poem were being sold and the money donated to the school that her brother had been raising money for. In spite of her illness, she was making a difference, just as she was. Charlotte lived to the age of eighty-two. After she died, more than a thousand letters were discovered among her personal papers, written by people whose lives had been touched by her hymn.

The Lamb of God invites us to come to him just as we are. None of us is pretty enough, or smart enough, or strong enough, or good enough, but Jesus loves us anyway. And Jesus calls us, each and every one of us, just as we are, to follow him.

August 18, 2013

All I Want for Christmas: Hope
Isaiah 9:2-7 (NRSV)

The people who walked in darkness have seen a great light; those who lived in a land of deep darkness—on them light has shined. You have multiplied the nation, you have increased its joy; they rejoice before you as with joy at the harvest, as people exult when dividing plunder. For the yoke of their burden, and the bar across their shoulders, the rod of their oppressor, you have broken as on the day of Midian. For all the boots of the tramping warriors and all the garments rolled in blood shall be burned as fuel for the fire. For a child has been born for us, a son given to us; authority rests upon his shoulders; and he is named Wonderful Counselor, Mighty God, Everlasting Father, Prince of Peace. His authority shall grow continually, and there shall be endless peace for the throne of David and his kingdom. He will establish and uphold it with justice and with righteousness from this time onward and forevermore. The zeal of the LORD of hosts will do this.

The movie *The Kite Runner* is based on the novel by the same name. The film tells the story of a boy and his father who fled Afghanistan after the Soviet invasion of that country in 1979. The story actually began in 1978 with Amir, the ten-year-old son of a wealthy Afghan businessman, living a good life in a well-appointed home in an affluent neighborhood in Kabul. Amir was a bright boy with a love of literature and a gift for writing stories. He was not as athletic as his father would have liked him to be, but he did please his father with his aptitude for flying kites. Kite-flying was a major pastime for Afghan boys. They would engage in kite fights, coating their kite strings with glue and crushed glass so they could cut the strings of the other kites. At the end of a kite battle, the string of one kite would be cut so that the kite would fly away. Kite runners would chase after the unfettered kite, and anyone who found it could keep it. It was like a victory prize. Amir was a kite flyer, and his friend Hassan was the kite runner. After Amir had cut the string of a rival kite, Hassan would run after the kite and bring it back as a trophy for his friend.

Amir and Hassan were best friends, but they were not social equals. Amir was from the majority Pashtun ethnic group. Hassan was from Hazara ancestry, a minority group that comprised about ten percent of the Afghan population. Many Pashtuns looked down on the Hazaras as inferior. Amir had come to know Hassan because Hassan was the son of the servant in Amir's home. Even though they were not social equals, the boys had grown up together. But while Amir went to school, the illiterate Hassan stayed home and helped his father do the household chores.

Amir's father was a cosmopolitan businessman who was proud of his Afghan heritage but who also was open to the ways of the Western world. He hated the Communists, and he had little tolerance for the radical religious extremists in Afghanistan. When the Soviet armies entered Kabul, Amir's father fled the country, taking Amir with him. The two of them made their way to Pakistan and eventually to America. They settled in Freemont, California, joining a large Afghan population who also had fled the Soviet invasion. Amir's father, a once-prosperous and successful businessman, eked out a modest living as a cashier at a gas station while Amir went to school and then to college.

While Amir and his father were making a life in America, the Soviets were destroying lives in Afghanistan. They ravaged the country. During the ten-year Soviet occupation, over one million Afghans were killed, and millions more fled the country. An Afghan resistance movement led by the Mujahideen guerilla fighters waged warfare against the Soviet forces. The Afghan resistance took a toll on the Soviet military. Over 15,000 Soviet forces were killed, thousands more were wounded, and hundreds of thousands became ill. The Afghan resistance movement was aided by a variety of unlikely allies, including the American CIA, which supplied Stinger missiles and other sophisticated weaponry. Other allies included Arab freedom fighters, led by a wealthy Saudi businessman and religious extremist named Osama bin Laden.

After the Soviets admitted defeat and withdrew their forces from Afghanistan in 1989, the country was wracked by civil war. Emerging from the struggle was a group that promised to bring peace and stability to the country, a group that became known as the Taliban. At first the Taliban were welcomed by many Afghans as saviors of the country. But with the Taliban rule came a strict enforcement of Islamic law. The Taliban banned all Western influences in Afghan life. Men were required to wear full beards and to cover their heads. Women were required to wear burqas, which covered them from head to foot. Females suffered ever more severe restrictions. Girls could not go to school, and most women could not hold jobs. The Taliban outlawed movies, television, videos, music, dancing, and even kite-flying. Worst of all for America, the Taliban provided safe haven for Osama bin Laden and his al Qaeda terrorist training camps. That's why after 9/11, American and allied military forces invaded Afghanistan, to strike back at Osama bin Laden and al Qaeda and their Taliban allies.

In the movie *The Kite Runner* Amir returned to Afghanistan during Taliban rule. This was before 9/11. Amir saw firsthand the desolate place that his country had become. He witnessed the brutality of Taliban rule, and he reminisced about the Afghanistan of his youth. Near the end of the movie, Amir said, "I dream flowers will bloom in the streets again and kites will fly in the sky." The movie takes us on a sad journey, in the words of the director Marc Forster, "through so many dark moments and so many moments of despair." But ultimately it is a movie about hope. Amir has hope that one day flowers will bloom in the streets again and kites will fly in the sky. He dreams that one day Afghanistan will be a place where people can live in freedom and without fear.

The prophet Isaiah had that same hope about his country. Isaiah also lived in a time of many dark moments and many moments of despair. The northern kingdom of Israel had been invaded by the mighty Assyrian army. Its leading citizens had been killed or deported to other parts of the Assyrian Empire. The major cities were destroyed, and the countryside was laid waste. Not content to stop there, the Assyrians were threatening to conquer and destroy the southern kingdom of Judah too. It was during this dark and desperate time in Jewish history that Isaiah wrote this prophecy of hope: "The people who walked in darkness have seen a great light; those who live in a land of deep darkness—on them light has shined." And then Isaiah prophesied about the birth of a child who would change everything. Isaiah wrote, "For a child has been born for us, a son given to us; authority rests upon his shoulders; and he is named Wonderful Counselor, Mighty God, Everlasting Father, Prince of Peace."

Isaiah had hope that one day flowers would bloom in the streets again. He had hope that one day the darkness of his time would give way to a great light. He had hope that a child would be born who would change everything. It took a long time, but some seven centuries later, Isaiah's prophecy was fulfilled. A child was born in Bethlehem who did change everything. A light shone into the darkness, and the darkness could not overcome it. That's why on this first Sunday of Advent, our theme is hope. Life is still subject to dark and desolate moments, but we have hope, because for us a child was born, for us a son was given. That doesn't guarantee that our lives will be free from dark times, but it means we have a light that can lead us through the darkness to a better day.

Thirty years ago, Rose Schrott began a counseling service to people in this community. Rose had been working primarily with young people here in the city of Bowie, providing counseling through the Bowie Youth Counseling Services, but she had a vision of expanding her work to help people of all ages. She was especially concerned about families and how the problems of young people are really part of a larger system that includes parents and other family members. Rose began discussions with a former pastor of this church, Dr. Dan Ivins, about beginning a family enrichment center housed in the offices of Village Baptist Church. Those discussions led to a partnership between Rose and this church that has lasted almost thirty years. Village provided office space for Rose and her clients, first in the church annex on Pointer Ridge Drive in 1979, then in the first church building that was constructed on this site in 1980, then in the rebuilt church building that was completed in 2002.

Over the past thirty years, Rose has provided hope to a lot of people. She has helped people deal with family problems. She has helped people who struggled with substance abuse. She has counseled teenagers and senior citizens, people with physical disabilities, and people with emotional problems, people with troubled marriages, and people with work-related issues. Rose never claimed to be able to solve anyone's problems, but she provided hope, even when the problems would not go away.

Although not a "Christian counselor" per se, Rose is a dedicated Christian, and she sees her counseling service as a ministry that arose out of her Christian calling. When I asked Ray Brown to design a certificate that we could present to Rose, Ray replied that he would be glad to, because she provided hope to a lot of people.

When Rose was in her office, she usually would turn on the porch light at the end of the building to let her clients know that she was there. Her clients would use that far-end entrance rather than the main entrance, both to provide a measure of confidentiality and because her office was located at the end of the building. In designing the certificate Ray asked me if I thought it would be appropriate for him to do a graphic of our church building, with the porch light shining on the far end. I replied that such a graphic would be a most fitting symbol for the hope that Rose has given many people. Through the counseling ministry of Rose Schrott, many people who have walked in darkness have begun to see the light.

Today is the first Sunday in Advent, and as we begin our journey toward Christmas, we celebrate the hope that is ours in Jesus Christ. Some of you may feel like you are walking in darkness right now. Remember, a child has been born for us; a son has been given to us. May we have hope for a day when flowers will bloom and kites will fly and the light of Christ will shine into our lives.

November 30, 2008

Chapter 4

1977–1984

The year 1977 was the beginning of a new life for me—new job, new family, new home, new city, new friends, new career. I had moved from Louisville, Kentucky, to Silver Spring, Maryland, to become associate pastor of Montgomery Hills Baptist Church. I married Linda and became an instant father to her daughter, Amy. We bought a tiny, two-bedroom, one-bathroom home a couple of miles from the church, thanks to Linda selling her house in Louisville. I had a new church family to get to know and new work responsibilities to learn and try to fulfill. I had a new boss, Rev. Donnell Harris, who would be a mentor and eventually one of my best friends. Life was challenging and a bit intimidating at times, but good.

My responsibilities at the church included overseeing the education and youth programs, pastoral care, worship leadership, and some preaching. Don Harris was the senior pastor, but he was not threatened by my professional growth and development. In fact, he was extremely generous in giving me opportunities to grow and develop as a pastor. Before long, I was making hospital visits, officiating at weddings and funerals, performing baptisms and infant dedications, leading Wednesday evening prayer services, and occasionally preaching on Sunday mornings. The church had a dedicated prayer line, where people would call and listen to a recorded Scripture reading and prayer. Writing the daily prayers and recording the messages became my bailiwick. So I was much more than the youth minister, although I did meet with the youth on Sunday nights and plan youth retreats, mission trips, and other activities.

After our son, Marc, was born in 1980, I began to sense that I needed more training if I were to move beyond being an associate pastor. I started looking into doctor of ministry programs at various seminaries and divinity schools. For a couple of years, we planned our family vacations so that I could visit Yale and Harvard and the Eastern Baptist Theological Seminary (now Palmer Theological Seminary) near Philadelphia. Ultimately, I decided to return to The Southern Baptist Theological Seminary in Louisville for my D.Min. The main reason for returning to Southern was so that my family could go with me. Linda still had family in Louisville, so she and the children would have something to do when I was in school. Montgomery Hills graciously granted me leave so I could go back to Louisville for J-terms (primarily in January and June).

When it came time to propose a research project, I was drawn to preaching. I knew I needed to learn more about it, so I began to read every preaching book that looked helpful. The books that spoke to me most forcefully were those concerned with narrative preaching. From listening to sermons over many years, I discovered that the ones that stuck with me featured stories. I recalled a conversation I had with John Claypool. I asked him how he presented his sermons since he didn't seem to rely on a manuscript or notes. John told me that after writing the sermon during the week, he would re-create orally on Sunday morning what he had written. It's not that he memorized the sermon. He simply recalled the movements of the sermon and "told it" based on those movements.

John didn't call it narrative preaching, but basically he was creating a narrative every time he preached. Sometimes John told personal stories from his own life. He told me that he was careful not to make himself the "star" of the story. The point was not to exalt himself, but to use his own personal stories to speak to the personal stories of his listeners.

I did not try to mimic the style of John Claypool. He was far more eloquent than I could ever hope to be. But I did follow his lead in using personal stories (judiciously) to connect with people in the pews.

My research project for the doctor of ministry program began with reading as many books as I could about preaching. It evolved into developing my own homiletical theory, namely that preaching can be enhanced through storytelling. After completing my degree, I realized that I could turn my research project into a book, *Storytelling in Preaching*. The book was published after I became pastor of Village Baptist Church, but it was begun in concept while I was at Montgomery Hills. The sermons in the book were preached at Village, but the basic idea was conceived while I was an associate pastor trying to figure out how I could come up with a sermon every week once I became a pastor.

After almost eight years as associate pastor at Montgomery Hills Baptist Church in Silver Spring, Maryland, I was called to become pastor of Village Baptist Church in Bowie, Maryland. The executive director of the D.C. Baptist Convention, Dr. James Langley, had recommended me to the Village search committee. I knew the Village interim pastor, Dr. James Dunn, who was also the executive director of the Baptist Joint Committee for Religious Liberty. I made an appointment with James Dunn at his office at the BJC near Capitol Hill. James told me that he thought Village and I would be a good fit.

I began my ministry at Village on January 1, 1985. We sold our home in Silver Spring and moved into a bigger house in Bowie, less than two miles from the church. The biggest challenge of being a pastor was preaching every Sunday. Most of the other pastoral roles I had experienced as an associate pastor, but preaching every Sunday was something new. What would I say, week after week?

I used every device I could fathom—sermon series, preaching through books of the Bible, following the Lectionary, connecting sermons with the special Sundays of the church year. I was constantly on the lookout for sermon ideas. Sometimes my devotional reading of Scripture would prompt sermon thoughts. Sometimes unusual experiences and other life events would find translation into sermons.

I'm still amazed that I was able to come up with an original sermon every Sunday for thirty-three years. Some biblical texts I returned to again and again and still managed to say something new.

Anatomy of a Family
Genesis 37:2-5, 18-28; 45:4-5; 50:20 (NRSV)

This is the story of the family of Jacob. Joseph, being seventeen years old, was shepherding the flock with his brothers; he was a helper to the sons of Bilhah and Zilpah, his father's wives; and Joseph brought a bad report of them to their father. Now Israel loved Joseph more than any other of his children, because he was the son of his old age; and he had made him a long robe with sleeves. But when his brothers saw that their father loved him more than all his brothers, they hated him, and could not speak peaceably to him. Once Joseph had a dream, and when he told it to his brothers, they hated him even more....

They saw him from a distance, and before he came near to them, they conspired to kill him. They said to one another, "Here comes this dreamer. Come now, let us kill him and throw him into one of the pits; then we shall say that a wild animal has devoured him, and we shall see what will become of his dreams." But when Reuben heard it, he delivered him out of their hands, saying, "Let us not take his life." Reuben said to them, "Shed no blood; throw him into this pit here in the wilderness, but lay no hand on him" —that he might rescue him out of their hand and restore him to his father.

So when Joseph came to his brothers, they stripped him of his robe, the long robe with sleeves that he wore; and they took him and threw him into a pit. The pit was empty; there was no water in it. Then they sat down to eat; and looking up they saw a caravan of Ishmaelites coming from Gilead, with their camels carrying gum, balm, and resin, on their way to carry it down to Egypt. Then Judah said to his brothers, "What profit is it if we kill our brother and conceal his blood? Come, let us sell him to the Ishmaelites, and not lay our hands on him, for he is our brother, our own flesh." And his brothers agreed. When some Midianite traders passed by, they drew Joseph up, lifting him out of the pit, and sold him to the Ishmaelites for twenty pieces of silver. And they took Joseph to Egypt....

Then Joseph said to his brothers, "Come closer to me." And they came closer. He said, "I am your brother, Joseph, whom you sold into Egypt. And now do not be distressed, or angry with yourselves, because you sold me here; for God sent me before you to preserve life....

Even though you intended to do harm to me, God intended it for good, in order to preserve a numerous people, as he is doing today.

You might think what we just read is the story of Joseph, but it's more than that. It's the anatomy of a family. And like most families, this one had some problems. It was a big family—there was daddy Jacob and his wives and their sons and daughters. But the focus of the story is on the teenage son Joseph and his older brothers. Joseph was his daddy's favorite. Jacob did not hide the fact that he like Joseph best. In fact, he flaunted it. He gave Joseph a long robe with sleeves. The King James Version of the Bible calls it a "coat of many colors." Whatever kind of garment it was, the older brothers got the message. Joseph was the apple of their father's eye. And they hated him for it.

Joseph, the youngest, the favorite, was pampered by his pa, and as you might expect, he acted like a spoiled brat. While the other brothers were out sweating in their father's fields, Joseph came and went as he pleased. When any of the brothers stepped out of line, Joseph went running back to tell Daddy all about it. It's a wonder the kid lasted seventeen years the way he fanned the flames of his brothers' hatred.

To make matters worse, Joseph was a dreamer. Joseph had a dream, and he did not hesitate to tell everyone about it. He dreamed his brothers would one day bow down to him. You can guess how the brothers felt about that. Then he had another dream. This time, not only his brothers but also his father and his mother would bow down to him. The brothers couldn't take it any longer. At the first opportunity, they plotted to eliminate this arrogant little Napoleon once and for all. Some of them wanted to kill him outright, but cooler heads prevailed. They tossed Joseph into a pit, an empty cistern, while they ate their lunch. A passing caravan provided a profitable solution. They would sell him into slavery. They could get rid of this obnoxious little twerp and make a few bucks at the same time. The deed was done. Joseph was sent packing to Egypt, and the brothers concocted a story to tell their father. They dipped his favorite-son robe into goat's blood and took it back to the old man. Jacob assumed Joseph had been killed by wild animals, and the brothers chuckled to themselves at their cleverness. At least Joseph was out of their hair, and that would be the end of it, or so they thought.

When we read about such a family, we wonder what went wrong. How did things get so fouled up? It may sound like a rather unusual situation, but it's more common than we realize. In many families there is friction. If you grew up with brothers and sisters, there was probably some rivalry in your family. Children from the same family often compete with each other—in school or in sports or in social activities or in vying for the attention of their parents. A part of that has to do with the phenomenon known as birth order. The order in which children are born influences how they find their place in the family.

Last month I was involved in a family counseling course at Bowie State University. To demonstrate the influence of birth order, the professor divided the class into groups. One group was made up of older children, those who had been born first in their family. Then there were the "middlers," those of us who were neither the oldest nor the youngest. Then there was the baby group, those who were the youngest children in their families. Finally, there were the "onlies," those who were the only children and did not have brothers or sisters.

As we discussed what it was like to grow up in our families, we discovered that within each group we shared similar experiences. The oldest children talked about how special they felt being the oldest, but they also talked about how threatening it was to have a sibling come along. The technical term for that is "dethronement." The middle group related how they were always comparing themselves with their older siblings and how they felt squeezed by younger children who came along to claim their parents' attention. The younger group also had similarities. Virtually all the younger children felt special, and most admitted that they were spoiled and pampered more than the other kids. The only children also had similar experiences. Birth order does influence how we get along in the family.

So what we see in the family of Joseph is not all that unusual. Eventually, Joseph had a younger brother, Benjamin, but for a long time Joseph was the youngest, and he was spoiled and pampered like many youngest children are. In our day, not just the youngest, but many children are spoiled and pampered. We want to give our children everything because we love them so much. We have the best of intentions. We do it out of love. But the irony is that pampering our children is a detriment to their emotional development.

Psychologists have identified four types of pampering: overindulgence, overpermissiveness, overdomineering, and overprotection. Overindulgence—we give our children everything they want: toys, bicycles, cars, jewelry, stylish clothing, money, you name it. Overpermissiveness—we let our children do anything they want. Overdomineering—we let our children escape responsibility by making all their decisions for them. Overprotection—we stress the dangers of life and minimize their ability to handle them. The reason we can identify these four types of pampering is because they are so common.

The child psychologist Rudolf Dreikurs was asked, "What is better for the child's personality development—to grow up in a permissive home atmosphere or in a strict, authoritarian environment?" Dreikurs answered, "You may as well ask me what is better—to be hung or shot?" Neither an indulgent atmosphere nor an authoritarian environment is best for children.

The family of Joseph is a good example. The father Jacob was indulgent with his younger son Joseph and authoritarian with his older sons. It's tough to be a parent, to maintain the right balance between love and respect, between holding on and letting go. But it's also tough to be a child. Any birth order brings challenges to overcome. Maybe just realizing that will help us to understand each other a little better. Parents are not perfect, and children have their problems too. When it comes to the family, we're all in this together. Any individual's problem is a family problem. It doesn't do any good to blame Jacob for being indulgent, or to blame Joseph for being spoiled, or to blame the brothers for being jealous. All of them contributed to the family's problems, and all of them must contribute to finding a solution.

Things change. Thirteen years later, the fortunes of the brothers have dramatically reversed. Joseph is the vizier of Egypt, second in command to Pharaoh. The brothers and their father are still back in Canaan, suffering from a terrible drought and famine. In desperation, the brothers go down to Egypt for food. Joseph recognizes them, but they do not recognize him. What luck! What an incredible turn of events! Joseph now has them exactly where he wants them. If ever there were an opportunity to exact revenge, this is it. But Joseph does the opposite of what we might expect. Instead of paying his brothers back for what they did to him, he forgives them. Instead of having them thrown into prison or sold into slavery or killed, he offers them his help. How do you explain such mercy?

Something happened to Joseph and his brothers to change them. God was in it. Anyone else might have given up on that dysfunctional family, but God never gave up. God had a purpose for that family which far exceeded the mistakes those brothers and their father had made. Because God was in it, the evil they had done to one another was turned to good. We should not be surprised. That's the story of the Bible. No matter how badly we mess things up, God is always working to bring about good.

About a year ago I bought a lawnmower at a yard sale here at the church. I thought I was getting a good deal. I invested fifty dollars in the lawnmower and another fifty dollars in repairs to get it running. But after mowing my yard two times last fall, it quit. I could not get the mower started again. I consulted the person who had donated the mower to the yard sale in the first place, and I found out that he had experienced the same problem with it. Not wanting to waste any more money on what I perceived to be a piece of junk, I decided to accept my losses and get rid of it. But not wanting to inflict that mower on anyone else in the church, I donated it to a Boy Scout yard sale. Imagine my surprise a couple of months ago when I saw a neighbor mowing her yard with the same lawnmower. Her husband had bought the mower from the Scouts, fixed it up, and now it's running fine.

Maybe we give up on things too soon. Maybe we give up on the family too soon. When things aren't running right, our first inclination is to junk it like a broken lawnmower. But if we learn anything from this story, we learn that families can be repaired. To be sure, we'll have to invest something in it. God will not swoop down and make everything right without any effort on our part. But in partnership with God, families can be fixed. In partnership with God, even the most broken of relationships can be redeemed.

The family of Joseph was restored, reconciled, put back together, redeemed. But that's not the end of the story. There was Another One like Joseph. Another One was given up for dead, but he came back alive! Another One was abandoned, but he returned in power! Another One was put into the ground, but he sprang forth to life! Another One—Jesus Christ our Lord. Yes, the most broken of relationships can be redeemed. That's good news for families and good news for all of us. In partnership with God, we can live together in love and peace.

August 13, 1989

A Change of Plans
Matthew 1:18-25 (NRSV)

Now the birth of Jesus the Messiah took place in this way. When his mother Mary had been engaged to Joseph, but before they lived together, she was found to be with child from the Holy Spirit. Her husband Joseph, being a righteous man and unwilling to expose her to public disgrace, planned to dismiss her quietly. But just when he had resolved to do this, an angel of the Lord appeared to him in a dream and said, "Joseph, son of David, do not be afraid to take Mary as your wife, for the child conceived in her is from the Holy Spirit. She will bear a son, and you are to name him Jesus, for he will save his people from their sins." All this took place to fulfill what had been spoken by the Lord through the prophet: "Look, the virgin shall conceive and bear a son, and they shall name him Emmanuel," which means, "God is with us." When Joseph awoke from sleep, he did as the angel of the Lord commanded him; he took her as his wife, but had no marital relations with her until she had borne a son; and he named him Jesus.

Joseph is the forgotten figure of the Christmas story. Matthew says he was a righteous man. That's about all we know about him, other than he was a carpenter from Nazareth with a family history tracing back to King David. He was far removed from his noble lineage. Carpenters were working-class folk, and Nazareth was an unremarkable town in Galilee, far from the citadels of power in Jerusalem. We don't know anything about Joseph's level of education, whether he owned his own business, or his other family connections, except that he was engaged to a young woman named Mary. We don't even know how old he was.

Back then, a young woman typically was engaged to be married when she was thirteen or fourteen years of age. The man could be about the same age or older, sometimes much older. The process began with a formal engagement, usually arranged by the two families. Then for about a year the young woman would continue to live in the home of her parents, but she would be considered legally bound to her fiancé. In fact, her fiancé would be called her husband, even though they were not yet living together. After about a year, her husband would take his wife into his family's home, and at that point they would begin to live together as husband and wife. The Scripture passage that we read took place between these two steps—after Joseph and Mary were engaged and legally bound to one another but before they had begun to live together as husband and wife.

Of course, during this engagement period, the woman was expected to remain faithful to her husband even though their marriage was not yet consummated. The Mosaic Law was very clear about this—any act of unfaithfulness would be adultery and grounds for severe punishment. In fact, in Old Testament times, the punishment for adultery was death (Deut 22:23–27). By the time of the New Testament, rabbinic tradition had softened a bit, and women were not always executed for adultery, although they could be. (Remember the woman caught in the act of adultery who was brought to Jesus for judgment? Jesus said, "Let him without sin cast the first stone.") At the very least, a woman who was unfaithful to her husband, even before they were married, would be subject to divorce proceedings and public humiliation.

When Joseph found out that Mary was pregnant, he faced a real dilemma. On the one hand, because he was a righteous man, he felt obligated to follow the Jewish Law. And that Law said that an unfaithful woman should be punished for her sin. On the other hand, Joseph was a compassionate man, who genuinely cared for his fiancée, Mary. He did not want to see her publicly disgraced and humiliated. So he decided to dismiss her quietly. In other words, instead of subjecting her to the spectacle of a public divorce, he would arrange to dissolve the engagement with as little fanfare as possible.

The story gives us an insight into Joseph's character: He was a righteous man but also a compassionate man, moral but also merciful. Joseph genuinely wanted to do the right thing, even if doing the right thing meant going beyond the letter of the Law to the spirit of the Law. How many times in our ethical lives must we make decisions about what is right, and what is fair, and what is kind? Sometimes the "Christian thing to do" is not to follow the letter of the Law. Sometimes legalism must be superseded by grace. Joseph resolved to dismiss Mary quietly because he was more concerned about preserving her dignity than about standing up for his own rights as the aggrieved fiancé. How difficult is it for us to put the feelings of others ahead of our own sense of justice or entitlement?

Before Joseph could follow through on his plans to call off the marriage, he had a dream. And in that dream Joseph learned that Mary had not betrayed him after all. Joseph had felt humiliated by the news that his future bride was pregnant, but now he understood that Mary's pregnancy was from God. The Law had not been broken because Mary had not been unfaithful. There had been no adultery because the child in Mary's womb had been conceived from the Holy Spirit. Not only should Joseph go ahead with the marriage; he should become the child's earthly father and give the child a name. Joseph would name him Jesus, for he would save his people from their sins.

The name *Jesus* came from the Hebrew and Aramaic name *Joshua*, which means "God will save." Actually, Jesus was a common name at that time. The Jewish historian Josephus knew of twenty different persons named Jesus. So just as Jesus was both human and divine, his name was both common and full of meaning. His common name connected him with the people of this world, but it also signified the saving work that he would do. Jesus, *Iesou*, Joshua would save his people, and all people, from their sins.

Perhaps the most important part of the story is that Joseph did what the angel commanded him in his dream. He did take Mary as his wife, and he did name her child, their child, Jesus. Joseph already had decided what he was going to do, but he had a dream, and then he had a change of plans. He heard the word of the Lord, and he changed the total direction of his life.

Angelic visitations and annunciations are rare these days, but the Lord continues to speak to us in other ways. First, the Lord continues to speak through the words of Scripture. Mark Twain once said that the passages of Scripture that really bothered him were not the ones he didn't understand but the ones he did understand all too well. There is much in God's Holy Word that we do understand, because God continues to speak to us through the words of the Bible: Love your neighbor as you love yourself. Love your enemies. Forgive seventy times seven. Turn the other check; go the second mile. Do good to the least of these. Yes, there is much that we do understand. The Lord speaks clearly through his written Word.

The Lord also speaks to us through other people, especially other Christians. Sometimes in the words of a sermon or a Sunday school lesson, sometimes in the testimony of a fellow Christian, sometimes in a casual conversation we hear a word from the Lord. I still remember lines from sermons I heard years ago, because the Lord was using those messages to speak to me. As a preacher I don't know all that is going on in your life. But often people will tell me that a sermon spoke to a particular situation in their lives that I knew nothing about. The Lord uses other people to communicate his message.

The Lord also speaks through our consciences. That's one of the reasons why Christian education is so important. If our consciences are shaped by Christian teaching and values, the Lord is more likely to speak to us through our own inner convictions. Sometimes the Lord speaks through the circumstances of our lives. But our consciences must be attuned to recognize how God is speaking to us through those circumstances.

To me the most remarkable thing about Joseph was not just that he heard the word of the Lord, but that he acted on it. He changed his mind about Mary, and he changed his plans about calling off the wedding. He dramatically altered the course of his life because he felt the Lord was leading him in an entirely different direction. Joseph had already decided what he was going to do, but he was not so set in his ways that he closed himself off from a new direction from God.

Here's the question: What is the Lord saying to you, and what plans might you need to change in order to fulfill God's will for your life?

When a large box arrived here at the church, I had no idea what was inside. When I opened it, I found a carefully wrapped framed picture, surrounded by wadded-up balls of paper and Styrofoam packing beads and plastic bubble wrap. Attached was a letter from my sister and brother-in-law, Carol and Richard Blocker. They explained that Richard had taken a picture of our church two years ago on Christmas Eve and that my mother had the photo reprinted for her own Christmas cards last year. Richard and Carol had enlarged the photo and framed it as a gift to our church.

After I took the picture out of the box and unwrapped it, I took the box with all the packing materials out to the street so it could by collected with the rest of the trash that day. But standing at the curb, I had a thought that maybe I should check inside that large box one more time to make sure there was nothing else remaining beyond the packing materials. So I stuck my arm down in the wadded balls of paper and Styrofoam beads and plastic bubble wrap and felt around. My hand grasped a small box, and I pulled it out. The small box was secured with ribbon and a bow, and there was a tag with my sister's name on it. This wasn't part of the packing materials. This was a Christmas present that had been concealed among the packing materials. I brought the large box back inside and carefully unpacked all the materials to make sure there were no more small presents inside. All those packing materials filled up two large plastic garbage bags, but there were no more presents to be found.

Later, when my brother-in-law Richard called to make sure the framed photo had arrived, I told him about finding the tiny gift for Carol buried at the bottom of the box among all the packing materials. Richard said it must have been left over from a past Christmas, never found then, but buried among the packing materials that they had reused for mailing the framed photo. It will be fun to give Carol that long-lost present when they come for Christmas this year.

That experience is something of a parable. Most of us get the big picture at Christmastime—it's easy enough to find. But that small gift addressed personally to us might get lost among all the trappings of Christmas. God's words to each of us, God's specific message that is addressed to the individual circumstances of our lives—that's what we might easily miss. It's wonderful to have the big picture of what Christmas means, but let's not stop there. Let's not let the clutter of the Christmas season hide that small, personal gift that God wants to give. What is it that God is saying to you that you otherwise might miss? What message does God have for you personally that could change your plans and change your life?

December 19, 2004

Angels in Advent: Joseph
Matthew 1:18-25 (NRSV)

Now the birth of Jesus the Messiah took place in this way. When his mother Mary had been engaged to Joseph, but before they lived together, she was found to be with child from the Holy Spirit. Her husband Joseph, being a righteous man and unwilling to expose her to public disgrace, planned to dismiss her quietly. But just when he had resolved to do this, an angel of the Lord appeared to him in a dream and said, "Joseph, son of David, do not be afraid to take Mary as your wife, for the child conceived in her is from the Holy Spirit. She will bear a son, and you are to name him Jesus, for he will save his people from their sins." All this took place to fulfill what had been spoken by the Lord through the prophet: "Look, the virgin shall conceive and bear a son, and they shall name him Emmanuel," which means, "God is with us." When Joseph awoke from sleep, he did as the angel of the Lord commanded him; he took her as his wife, but had no marital relations with her until she had borne a son; and he named him Jesus.

Everybody dreams. Even newborn babies dream. Dreams occur during a type of sleep known as REM, which stands for "rapid eye movement." While the eyes move rapidly behind the closed eyelids, the rest of the body is usually quiet. During REM sleep, certain regions of the brain are stimulated while other regions of the brain rest. Using PET scans, medical researchers have discovered that during REM sleep, the limbic and paralimbic regions of the brain are active. These are areas that control emotion and motivation. That explains why our dreams often have an emotional component, especially fear and anger. At the same time, during REM sleep, areas of the prefrontal cortex are inactive. These are areas that sustain working memory, attention, logic, and self-monitoring. What all this means is that dreams serve an important function for our brains. We need to dream to keep our brains balanced and healthy. When we dream, certain areas of our brains are active while other areas are not. Just as sleep is essential to our physical well-being, dreams are essential to our mental well-being.

Most of us dream about five or six times every night during REM sleep. Our dreams typically last from five to twenty minutes each. On average, adults are in REM sleep about twenty to twenty-five percent of the time they are sleeping. Newborns dream more. A typical adult might spend two hours every night dreaming. That may seem like a lot, but that's because we don't remember most of our dreams. According to Dr. John Hobson of the Harvard Medical School, we forget ninety-five to ninety-nine percent of our dreams. What some have called "the evaporation of dreams" is quite normal. If a dream occurs in the first three or four hours of sleep, it probably will not be remembered at all the next morning. A few people can remember their dreams in precise detail, but most people do not. The best chance of remembering a dream is if we wake up during REM sleep, especially if it's the last dream of the night and we wake up while the dream is still going on. If a dream has special meaning to us, however, we may make ourselves remember it.

People have been fascinated by dreams, long before there was any kind of scientific understanding of dreaming. The ancient Babylonians 5,000 years ago had a goddess of dreams and a book for interpreting dreams. The ancient Egyptians, 2,000 years before Christ, also had a god of dreams and scholars who were dream interpreters. Genesis told about a Hebrew named Joseph who had a special gift to interpret dreams. In our scripture for today, another man named Joseph had a dream.

As I said, people have long believed that dreams have meaning. Sigmund Freud, the father of modern psychoanalysis, called dreams the "royal road to the unconscious." In his classic 1900 book *The Interpretation of Dreams*, Freud advanced the idea that dreams are a key to understanding what is going on in our psyches. Freud's interpretation of dreams was based more on his own theories than on scientific research, but some scientists now believe that dreams are a way for the unconscious mind to provide solutions for repressed problems.

Of course, many of our dreams don't seem like solutions to anything. A lot of our dreams feature fearful or frustrating situations. Some common dreams are falling, or being chased, or trying to finish a particular task, or finding ourselves in a situation that we can't seem to get out of. Believe it or not, I dream a lot about playing golf. Most of those dreams are really frustrating! A lot of our dreams don't seem to make much sense. Dr. William Dement, a pioneer in dream research, who is credited as designating those periods of rapid eye movement as a distinct stage of sleep, said, "Dreaming permits each and every one of us to be quietly and safely insane every night of our lives." (*Forbes* magazine, April 6, 1998). But what if our dreams do mean something? What if our dreams are a way for our unconscious minds to suggest solutions to vexing problems? What if our dreams are not just a royal road to the unconscious but a royal road to God?

Joseph had a lot on his mind. He was a carpenter from Nazareth, engaged to a young woman named Mary. Joseph's vexing problem was that his betrothed was pregnant, and he was not the father. Joseph resolved to quietly dismiss her, call off the wedding, and send her away with as little shame and publicity as possible. By all rights Joseph could have had Mary publicly condemned and humiliated, but he didn't want to do that. Apparently he genuinely cared for Mary, and he was genuinely grieved by her unfortunate condition. As yet Joseph did not understand that the child she would bear had been conceived by the Holy Spirit. But then Joseph had a dream, a dream that he remembered. In that dream an angel of the Lord appeared and explained to him that Mary had not been unfaithful but in fact had been completely faithful to God.

I don't know about you, but sometimes I dream about things that I have been thinking about. Sometimes I even compose fragments of sermons in my dreams. Sometimes in my dreams I will discover solutions to problems or at least insights to help me better deal with some issue I have been preoccupied with. I find it entirely plausible that Joseph would dream about Mary's condition. After all, it must have been a major preoccupation in his mind. And in that dream Joseph received a solution to the problem that he never would have dreamed of himself. No one would have imagined that Mary's pregnancy was from God. Yet Joseph believed what the angel in the dream told him was true. And Joseph took Mary as his wife, and after the baby was born, Joseph named him Jesus, as the angel had said.

For some reason life seldom unfolds exactly as we had planned. Read through the Bible and notice how many times an encounter with God changed people's plans and changed their lives. The birth of that baby changed the life that Joseph and Mary had envisioned for themselves. Perhaps one of the lessons of Christmas for us is to be open to the changes and new directions that God may have in store for our lives.

This Christmas is turning out to be different from the Christmas that we had planned for our family. For the past several years my parents have come up from Texas to be with us at Christmastime, and often my brother and his family from North Carolina have joined us, as well as my sister and brother-in-law from San Antonio. This year, since the death of my father, our plans are in flux. My mother feels that it would be too difficult for her to come to Maryland this year, so my sister and brother-in-law will remain in Texas to be with my mother. We're not sure whether my brother and his family will come here for Christmas or not. This Christmas will not be what we had envisioned.

It is hard for us to see what good can come of this, but ours is a God who can bring something good out of the most difficult circumstances. Joseph and Mary must have wondered what good could come out of their difficult circumstance. In a town of no more than 2,000 people, where everybody knew everybody else, the gossip must have been rampant. What could Joseph say once the word got out that Mary was with child? "Conceived by the Holy Spirit?" Sure. Right.

I realize I am walking on shaky ground when I talk about receiving messages from God in our dreams. I am not suggesting that every dream is from God or that everything that happens in a dream should be taken seriously. Some dreams are crazy. But there are times in the Bible when God did use a dream to communicate his message. There was Jacob in the Old Testament, who dreamed of a ladder between heaven and earth. There was Joseph, son of Jacob, who dreamed of a great future and who interpreted the dreams of others. Later in the Christmas story, there were wise men, who were warned in a dream not to return to King Herod. Not every dream contains a message from God, but sometimes God does use dreams to set our lives on a different course or maybe just to keep in touch with us.

I hope you won't be offended if I tell you about two dreams that I have had recently. About three weeks ago, shortly before my father died, I had a dream that made me wonder if it were a message from God. We had just come back from Texas after spending a most difficult five days with my father and mother. My father was in bad shape. He was conscious and aware of what was going on, but his physical condition was deteriorating rapidly. My reaction to watching him suffer was one of overwhelming sadness. But after returning from Texas, I had a dream where I saw my father sitting upright in a chair in their living room, wearing a three-piece suit. Not only was he well-dressed, but he looked hearty and healthy. I wasn't sure what the dream meant, but it was strangely reassuring to have seen him that way, even in my sleep.

The three-piece suit is what puzzled me. He hadn't worn a three-piece suit in years. Hardly anybody wears a suit with a vest anymore. But some years ago, three-piece suits were in fashion. In the 1970s many businessmen wore three-piece suits. Then I realized that was when my father was in his professional prime. He was the managing partner of the Fort Worth office of a major international accounting firm. It was also during that time that he served as the president of the prestigious Colonial Country Club in Fort Worth, site of an annual PGA Tour golf tournament. So seeing him in that three-piece suit in my dream was a reminder of how vigorous and vital he once had been. It reminded me that he had not always been the frail figure I had seen lying in the hospital bed in their home.

Less than two weeks ago, the night after we received word that my father had died, I had another dream, with another image of my father. In that second dream he wasn't sitting in a chair wearing a three-piece suit. Instead, he was standing, wearing a tuxedo. At first I wasn't sure what that dream meant either. It wasn't that often that my father wore a tuxedo. Usually it was a special occasion, like my sister's wedding when he gave her away to be married. My mother has pictures of my father wearing a tuxedo at the wedding. As I've been thinking about it, I've come to realize that on that occasion, the tuxedo represented the beginning of a new life. He gave my sister away to be married, to begin a new life with her husband. Seeing my father wearing a tuxedo in that dream right after he died may have been a sign that he has now begun a new life with God in heaven.

Maybe someone else would interpret those dreams differently. But for me they were a message from God in a very troubling time. The first dream helped me remember my father as he once was, and the second dream helped me to think of my father as he now is. That doesn't take away my grief or the burden I feel for my grieving mother. But it is a step on the road to dealing with our loss and finding the strength to carry on.

This Christmas will be a sad time for our family. How could it not be sad? But in a way that is difficult to explain, it will be a joyous time as well, for the message of Christmas has special meaning for us this year. Christmas is about new life. Jesus came from the Father that we might go to the Father. Jesus descended from heaven that we might ascend to heaven. Thank God we dream, and sometimes in our dreams an angel appears with a message from above. Despite the tragedies of life, despite the hardships of life, despite the sadness of life, Christmas means good news.

December 18, 2005

Chapter 5

1985–1992

I began my service as pastor of Village Baptist Church in Bowie, Maryland, on January 1, 1985. We had not yet gone to the closing for the sale of our old house and the purchase of our new house, so for the first few weeks I commuted from Silver Spring to Bowie. It was about a thirty-five-minute drive, depending on the traffic on the Beltway and Route 50, but many people in this region have even longer daily commutes to their work.

The Village congregation was small, with maybe a hundred or so worshipers on the typical Sunday morning. Because the sanctuary also was small, a hundred or so worshipers almost filled the place. There were many young families with children and youth. I made it my mission to get to know everybody if I could. The first year I tried to visit in the home of every family in the church. We also had deacon "flock" dinners in our home. Deacons were responsible for a flock of six or seven family units, maintaining contact with flock members and reporting on needs during monthly deacons' meetings. Being pastor of a "small" church gave me the opportunity to know people on a personal level.

The shadows of the former pastor and the interim pastor loomed large the first few years after I came to Village. Dr. Dan Ivins had served as pastor at Village from 1974 to 1984. Dan had led Village to move from a "house church" into a new building on Mitchellville Road. He had a gregarious and out-size personality, and he was a hard act to follow. Another hard act to follow was Dr. James Dunn, who served Village for nine months as interim pastor after Dan moved to a church in Birmingham, Alabama. James also had an out-size personality and an intellect to go with it. His day job was executive director of the Baptist Joint Committee for Religious Liberty in Washington, D.C.

Because the Village church building was less than five years old, there were needed improvements and "completions" that became apparent as time went along. One of the first enhancements for worship was the addition of pew Bibles for the sanctuary. Since every sermon was based on the Bible, I wanted congregants to have access to a Bible for the reading of the scriptures on which the sermons were based. We also had a need for more educational and fellowship space. Thanks to moveable partitions, the back of the sanctuary could be used for adult Sunday school classrooms, church dinners, and overflow seating for Sunday worship. I soon realized that to allow for congregational growth, we needed more building space. In 1986 the floor plan for a "west wing" building expansion was approved, and ground was broken for the addition the following spring. We installed lights in the parking lot. We also began Homecoming Sunday in 1986, inviting former Villagers who had moved away to come back for a kind of family reunion. In 1987 we began to hold Picnic Sunday on the church grounds. Previously it had been held in a community park. The outdoor worship service and picnic meal was a longstanding tradition, but I didn't like the idea of leaving the church building empty on a Sunday morning in case visitors showed up.

Also in 1987 I began inviting special guest preachers from time to time. Of course I recruited supply preachers for the Sundays I would be away. But occasionally on a Sunday I would be present, we had a guest preacher. Dr. Raymond Bailey, a preaching professor at Southern Seminary who had been the major professor for my D.Min. research project, led a prayer seminar at Village. In subsequent years other guest preachers would include missionaries, former pastors, and denominational leaders.

Just as I had sensed the need for more training to become a better preacher (hence the D.Min. degree), I sensed the need for more training to be a better pastor. I enrolled in a program at Bowie State University in conjunction with the Washington Pastoral Counseling Service. The program would result in the master of arts in counseling psychology with a specialization in clinical pastoral counseling, which I received in 1991. For a time I entertained the idea of doing pastoral counseling on the side, in addition to my work as a pastor. The idea was impractical on two levels. First, I didn't have time to take on another job. Being a pastor kept me plenty busy, along with being a husband and father. Second, pastoral care is not the same as pastoral counseling. Most people don't want their preacher knowing all the gritty details of their lives. I was glad I got the training, and it helped me to be a better pastor and a better preacher. But I was not going to become a pastoral counselor even after I received the degree.

In 1991 we established a twentieth anniversary fund to purchase additional pews for the back of the sanctuary and a new church sign. In 1992 we added a second Sunday morning worship service, featuring contemporary

Christian music. Starting the "early service" was not without controversy. Our choir director viewed it as competition to the traditional 11:00 a.m. service, and others feared having a second Sunday morning service would divide the congregation. But Phil Wyrick, a Navy chaplain in the congregation, and Angela Corbett, an accomplished keyboardist, were willing to lead the music as volunteers. After Phil was transferred and Angela moved, Carlynn Thompson took over leading the early service music, using her computer expertise with projected slides and midi files. The main impact for me, besides an extra hour of work on Sunday mornings, was that it would entail a new style of preaching.

At the traditional service I preached from behind the pulpit using sermon notes or even a complete manuscript. At the early service I would preach freestanding from the floor level without a lectern. That meant I would preach extemporaneously. I called it "preaching without a net." I tried to preach the same sermon I had written for the 11:00 a.m. service, but without notes the sermon for the early service would invariably come out differently. I relied on John Claypool's technique of re-creating the sermon I had written as I delivered it. Dr. Dave Thompson, the NASA scientist who operated the sound booth at both services, heard both sermons most Sunday mornings. Dave told me that although the sermons were not identical, the message was essentially the same.

"Preaching without a net" added an extra level of stress on Sunday mornings. Although I did not memorize the sermon word for word, I tried to be thoroughly familiar with it. Having a narrative framework was essential. Storytelling in preaching became even more important.

When Death Was Arrested
Revelation 21:1-7 (NRSV)

Then I saw a new heaven and a new earth; for the first heaven and the first earth had passed away, and the sea was no more. And I saw the holy city, the new Jerusalem, coming down out of heaven from God, prepared as a bride adorned for her husband. And I heard a loud voice from the throne saying, "See, the home of God is among mortals. He will dwell with them as their God; they will be his peoples, and God himself will be with them; he will wipe every tear from their eyes. Death will be no more; mourning and crying and pain will be no more, for the first things have passed away." And the one who was seated on the throne said,

"See, I am making all things new." Also he said, "Write this, for these words are trustworthy and true." Then he said to me, "It is done! I am the Alpha and the Omega, the beginning and the end. To the thirsty I will give water as a gift from the spring of the water of life. Those who conquer will inherit these things, and I will be their God and they will be my children.

Brandon Coker is the drummer for a Christian praise band called North Point InsideOut, based in Alpharetta, Georgia. A few years ago Brandon was visiting his uncle in the small town of St. Mary's, Georgia. For some reason Brandon decided to take a walk, and he found himself strolling through a graveyard. It was the Oak Grove Cemetery, laid out in 1788. Brandon was walking through the cemetery looking at the headstones when he came across the marker for a guy named Samuel Burr. Brandon read the inscription on the headstone. Then he read it again, and then he read it again. The inscription said:

> Here lies what was mortal of Samuel Burr, age 42. In search of health far from his endeared home, death arrested his progress on 2nd of April 1831. Quietly he fell asleep in the Christian hope of immortality and glory forever. Oh the vanity of man in his best estate. Traveler pause and drop a tear on a grave of one so highly worthy and so deeply lamented and learn wisdom for eternity.

Brandon had no idea who Samuel Burr was or the circumstances of his death at age forty-two. Brandon's first thought was he hoped the descendant of whoever wrote that epitaph would be around when he bites the dust. How many tombstones do you see like that? Brandon started thinking about what happened to Samuel Burr: "Death arrested his progress." That's what death does. Eventually death will arrest the progress of all of us. But then Brandon thought, "But the King of Glory arrested death." Samuel Burr died in 1831. But now, 186 years later, Samuel Burr is alive and well and restored for eternity in the presence of Jesus.

Brandon went back to Alpharetta and told his bandmates that he had an idea for a song. Brandon didn't have the words or the tune, but he had the title: "Death Was Arrested." One of his bandmates said, "That's the weirdest name of a song I've ever heard." Then Brandon told them about walking through the graveyard and reading the inscription on the tombstone.

The other members of the band started suggesting lyrics, and gradually the verses and a chorus came together, along with the melody. They recorded the song, and other Christian artists heard it and covered it. I heard the song on the new album by Laura Story, *Open Hands*. I passed the Laura Story CD along to Kasey Malatesta, and she listened to it. Kasey learned it and sang it for us this morning. Thank you, Kasey!

It's a powerful message—death was arrested. When Jesus was raised from the grave, death was arrested.

My friend Gary Javens died suddenly and unexpectedly twelve days ago. His funeral was held last Wednesday at Clifton Park Baptist Church in Silver Spring, where Gary served as pastor for thirty-one years. Gary retired from Clifton Park at the end of 2005. A former president of the D.C. Baptist Convention, Gary was a distinguished church leader in this area for over forty years.

More importantly for me, Gary was my friend. We played golf together almost every Thursday for the last fifteen years. Gary and I were riding together in the golf cart a couple of weeks ago at the Red Gate course in Rockville. Gary was doing fine. He didn't finish the round because he had to leave early to go to a Washington Nationals baseball game that night at Nats' park. When I heard that Gary had died, just five days after we had been together, it was a terrible shock. Ironically, Gary died on another golf course. He suffered a heart attack while playing in a league in northern Virginia with his son-in-law. None of us had any idea that Gary's life would end so soon.

Quite a few people in our church knew Gary—Leslie and Pete Parreco, Mark and Michele Miles, Ed Dellinger, Joel Smith, Joe Williams, Maury Sweetin, Linda Salmon. Pete and Gary were fishing buddies. Mark and I went with Gary and Jere Allen to Jere's cabin in West Virginia for an overnight golf trip. Ed and Joe and Pete and I had Gary on our team for a couple of charity golf tournaments. Joel and Gary shared roots in western Pennsylvania and a love of the Pittsburgh Steelers. Maury and Gary knew many of the old songs from the big band era, and they would sing them together on the golf course. Gary and his wife, Grace, had dinner with the Miles, Parrecos, and Salmons a few years ago. After dinner Gary and Grace showed pictures of their trip to South Africa. Their photos inspired our trip to the Baptist World Congress in South Africa in 2015. Everybody who knew Gary will miss him.

When death arrests the progress of someone we know and love, we grieve. Yet, as our scripture from the book of Revelation reminds us, death was arrested by Jesus. Death is not the end for those who believe. And when Jesus comes again, death will be no more.

This passage from Revelation 21 is John's depiction of the end of time as we know it. The idea of a new Jerusalem coming down from heaven is John's attempt to describe what it will be like when the present world comes to an end. The new Jerusalem will be the fulfillment of all our hopes and dreams for peaceful community and eternal security. God will be with us. All will be right with the world. Death will be no more. Mourning and crying will be no more. Pain and suffering will be no more. All that keeps life from being joyful will be no more. No more tears, no more crying, no more sorrow, for God will be with his people.

John is talking about not just the hope of heaven, but about the hope of heaven on earth. At the end of time, all of creation will be made new. In the meantime, however, life goes on. Eventually death will interrupt life. That's what happened last week when my friend Gary Javens died. Death interrupted Gary's life, and death interrupted our friendship. I'm still having a hard time realizing that he is gone. Yet, yet, yet, death is not the end of the story. We who believe in Jesus have the glorious hope of eternal life. This life is not all there is. This world is not all there is. We have the hope of heaven. When Jesus was raised from the grave, death was arrested.

Baptism is a powerful symbol of that. Baptism is a symbol of our Christian hope. Baptism represents dying to the old life and being raised to new life. Baptism symbolizes death and resurrection.

I've shared with you about Gary Javens's death. Now let me share with you about his life. Gary was born in Beaver Falls, Pennsylvania, in 1940. He met the love of his life, Grace, in high school. They were married in 1959 when still teenagers. Gary went to work in a steel mill, and out of their union were born two daughters, Melanie and Cheryl.

About eight years after they were married, their local Baptist church was having a revival. The pastor of the church invited Gary to go along with the visiting evangelist to call on a prospect. Gary witnessed the visiting evangelist leading a young man to faith in Christ. Gary thought to himself, "Wow. I could do that." It was the beginning of his call into the ministry at the age of twenty-seven.

In 1968 Gary and Grace and their two girls moved to West Conshohocken, Pennsylvania, where he became pastor of the Ballingomingo Baptist Church. In addition to serving the church, Gary was going to school full-time. He enrolled at Eastern Baptist College in Philadelphia, then at Eastern Baptist Theological Seminary. After he graduated from seminary in 1974, Gary and the family moved to Silver Spring, where he became pastor of Clifton Park Baptist Church. As I said, Gary served Clifton Park for thirty-one years. After he retired, Gary served another two years as interim pastor of Forest Heights Baptist Church in Oxon Hill. After that, Gary served as a substitute preacher in many churches, including preaching here at Village on several occasions.

When Gary accepted the call into the ministry, he died to his old life as a steel worker and was raised to a new life serving Christ as a pastor. Even after he retired, Gary continued to serve Christ.

One more story about Gary. One Thursday we were on the Diamond Ridge Golf Couse in Baltimore. We came to a par 3, and there was a group ahead of us on the tee box and another group on the green. It was going to be a bit of wait, so Gary went up to a fellow in the group ahead of us and started talking. Next thing I know, Gary is sitting in the golf cart talking with the guy. When the green finally cleared and it was time for the group ahead of us to tee off, Gary came back to our golf cart. I asked him, "What were you talking with that guy about?" Gary replied, "Jesus." In a five-minute conversation, sitting in a golf cart, Gary had started witnessing about his faith in Jesus to a guy he had just met on the golf course. That's what it was about for Gary—it was all about Jesus.

Now his life and his service here on earth have ended. But Gary Javens has entered a new and glorious eternal life with Christ. May his example inspire us to live every day for Jesus, in the sure and glorious hope of eternal life. As the song says:

> Our Savior displayed on a criminal's cross
> Darkness rejoiced as though heaven had lost
> But then Jesus arose with our freedom in hand
> That's when death was arrested, and [our] life began.

June 25, 2017

Mercies in Disguise

2 Corinthians 12:7b-9 (NRSV)

Therefore, to keep me from being too elated, a thorn was given me in the flesh, a messenger of Satan to torment me, to keep me from being too elated. Three times I appealed to the Lord about this, that it would leave me, but he said to me, "My grace is sufficient for you, for power is made perfect in weakness." So, I will boast all the more gladly of my weaknesses, so that the power of Christ may dwell in me.

Laura was a senior in high school when she first met Martin, who was a junior. They met at a Fellowship of Christian Athletes barbecue in August of 1994. Martin was an athlete, and Laura says she "was trying to fellowship with one." She found out later that Martin was the best player on the baseball team. Laura wasn't athletic at all. Music was her thing. She had started playing piano when she was seven, and she took up the string bass when she was ten. They dated off and on until Laura went off to college. But they didn't become a permanent couple until ten years later when they got married.

It was the summer of 2005, and they had been married about a year. They were planning to move to Savannah, Georgia, from their home in Spartanburg, South Carolina, so Martin could attend the Savannah College of Art and Design. The idea was for Martin to get a graphics design degree so he could get a job and so Laura could stay home and raise the kids they wanted to have some day. That was the plan for their perfect life.

A detour came when a friend of Martin's called and offered Laura a job at his church in Atlanta. The church was looking for a worship leader, and Laura had recently achieved a small level of fame. A song she had written, "Indescribable," had been recorded by a guy named Chris Tomlin. The song was getting a lot of play on the radio, and the church wanted someone who could write worship songs. Laura had never led a praise team at a church. Her last job had been playing bass in a bluegrass band at a Mexican restaurant. But Laura and Martin considered the offer because the Savannah College of Art and Design had recently opened a campus in Atlanta.

The only problem was Martin wasn't feeling very well. For several months he had been experiencing some unusual symptoms. He was more forgetful than usual. Some days all he wanted to do was sleep, while other days he had trouble sleeping at all. Sometimes his heart would race, and he'd get sweaty and feel sick to his stomach, like he was having a panic attack. He had been to four different doctors, and no one had been able to come up with a diagnosis.

Nevertheless, Laura and Martin moved to Atlanta so Laura could start her new job at the church and Martin could start school.

For a time, things went well. Martin's symptoms seemed to disappear. His classes were going fine. He made all A's his first semester. Things were going great for Laura at the church. She was learning to use her musical talents and her song-writing abilities to lead worship at the large church on the north side of town. But once the Christmas holidays were over, things started going downhill. Martin seemed to be perpetually tired. He started falling asleep at inappropriate times—during Bible study or worship at church, during classes at school, even during social events.

This was totally out of character for Martin. He had always been so active and full of energy. He had been an athlete and an honor student. Laura could not remember a time when he did not work hard. But the second semester, he started missing classes because he overslept. Instead of making all A's, he started failing his classes. Then he was involved in a minor auto accident. Martin told Laura, "I fell asleep and hit a guardrail." Laura wondered if perhaps he had narcolepsy. A church member said, "I think your husband might have a mental illness." Martin went to see a psychologist. The therapist said, "It sounds like something physical. You need to see a medical doctor."

Laura was away attending a worship leadership conference when she got the phone call. Martin said, "I have a brain tumor. It's pressing against my pituitary gland, which is why my hormones have been messed up. That's why I've been so sleepy. I have no adrenaline being released." Laura also learned the tumor was close to the optic nerve and that if it were to continue to grow, Martin could lose his sight. Laura was afraid and angry it had taken a year for the doctors to find out what was wrong with her husband.

Martin would need surgery—delicate surgery, dangerous surgery—to try to remove the tumor. The doctors warned Laura that it was possible Martin would not survive. Laura began praying as she had never prayed before. She prayed that God would fix it, that God would heal her husband and they could go on with their lives. Martin did survive the surgery, but he was not okay, not by a long shot. When Martin finally regained consciousness in the ICU and could speak, it became apparent that he had serious memory problems. He knew who Laura was, but he did not remember that they were married. Plus, there were vision problems, and his speech was affected. Then Martin began to experience delusions and bouts of paranoia. He made slow progress after six weeks in the ICU, but he was a long way from being well.

Finally, Martin was discharged from the hospital. Then another crisis—he began to leak spinal fluid. More surgery would be necessary to repair the graft. Then another crisis. Martin contracted meningitis, with swelling in his brain. In the ER he stopped breathing. The resident told Laura there was "no guarantee he will make it through the night or through surgery." The medical team didn't have time to move him to the surgical floor. They had to drill a hole in his head right then and there to relieve the pressure. When that didn't solve the problem, they drilled a second hole on the opposite side of his head. The surgeon told Laura, "It's touch and go. He may not survive." He was placed into a medically induced coma. The doctor said, "Even if he survives, we're still not sure if we will be able to bring him up from the sedation."

Martin did survive. After another four weeks in ICU and two weeks in a hospital room, he was released to a step-down, in-patient rehabilitation facility. He couldn't bathe himself, or dress himself, or walk on his own. He was twenty-eight years old, six feet five inches, 230 pounds, a once-vigorous college athlete, and now he couldn't do the basic things to take care of himself. Martin and Laura had been married two years, and this was their life.

Six months after Martin got out of the hospital and rehab, he still had memory problems, and vision problems, and immune system problems, and other disabilities. Martin and Laura learned that you don't just move on from a brain tumor. Martin had spent three months in the hospital and another six months of rehabilitation, but he still wasn't fixed, not by a long shot.

Laura would need to be his primary caregiver while continuing to serve in the church. Ironically, while their personal lives were in turmoil, Laura's professional life was doing well. In 2008 she released an album of worship songs (called *Great God Who Saves*). The album reached number twenty-five on the Billboard Christian albums chart, and Laura started receiving invitations to do concerts. The church was supportive and gave Laura time off. Since Martin wasn't able to stay by himself, he would go along when Laura traveled.

It was four years after Martin's surgeries that he and Laura were on a road trip for a concert in Bentonville, Arkansas. As Laura was driving the car, she reflected on the journey that they had traveled together. She recognized that in spite of all the hardships, they were still blessed. Laura asked herself, "What if there are blessings that God offers that are greater than just a pain-free life?" Laura pulled off an exit from the highway. She took a Sharpie and a gas receipt out of the cupholder and started jotting down words.

She began to write a poem that would eventually become a song. She wrote a verse and then the chorus. Laura thought it was too personal to share. So she tossed the unfinished song into her backpack and continued down the road.

After a while, Laura did finish the song. She was reluctant to show it to anyone at first. But she had been working on a new album, and the label wanted her to add another song to those she had already written. Laura thought to herself, "What if the worst thing I had to offer—my broken story—was really the best thing I had to offer?" So she showed the song to her producer, and it became the title of the album.

In February 2011 Laura Story released the song "Blessings" as a single, and the album followed in May. By June "Blessings" reached number one on the Billboard Christian songs chart. The following year Laura Story won a Grammy for the song. Every time Laura performed the song in concert, she revealed more of their story. Laura said, "'Blessings' is a song about my prayers, filled with questions I was asking in my personal life."

Today, Laura's husband, Martin Elvington, is still not well. He is disabled in many ways. Laura says she continues to pray every day that God will completely heal her husband. But so far, complete healing hasn't come. Yet Laura and Martin are still experiencing God's blessings even "when God doesn't fix it." In fact, that's the name of a book that Laura wrote last year, *When God Doesn't Fix It.*

In his second letter to the Corinthians, Paul wrote about a "thorn in the flesh." We're not sure what that "thorn in the flesh" was, but it was something so tormenting that Paul prayed for God to remove it. Perhaps it was some sort of chronic illness. Paul wrote, "Three times I appealed to the Lord about this, that it would leave me." But the thorn in the flesh was not removed. God didn't fix it. Instead, Paul heard, "My grace is sufficient for you, for power is made perfect in weakness."

Laura wrote in her song that sometimes the trials of this life are mercies in disguise. God's power is made perfect in our weakness. The problem is, we can't see the whole story of our lives. We can see only a small part. We can see only the present moment. But it is in our weakness that the power of Christ may fully dwell.

I'm one of those nerdy people who read the liners inside the CD case. The liner of the *Blessings* CD has the words to all the songs, and the credits for those who contributed to the recording, and a note of thanks from the artist. Laura begins by thanking Jesus. Then she thanks the production team at the music label. Then she thanks her church. Finally, Laura thanks her husband, Martin. She writes, "Thanks for praising God in the midst of your trials and letting me write songs about it. You truly are God's blessing to my life." The song says:

> What if Your blessings come through raindrops?
> What if Your healing comes through tears?
> What is a thousand sleepless nights are what it takes to know
>   You're near?
> What if trials of this life are Your mercies in disguise?

Life is hard. Sometimes life is very hard. But God is good. And the full story of our lives is "in the hands of the One who means us good" (Kelly Johnson). How do we know that? How do we know that God means us good? The bread, the cup—mercies in disguise.

February 7, 2016

American Pie
Revelation 1:9-20 (NRSV)

I, John, your brother who share with you in Jesus the persecution and the kingdom and the patient endurance, was on the island called Patmos because of the word of God and the testimony of Jesus. I was in the spirit on the Lord's day, and I heard behind me a loud voice like a trumpet saying, "Write in a book what you see and send it to the seven churches, to Ephesus, to Smyrna, to Pergamum, to Thyatira, to Sardis, to Philadelphia, and to Laodicea." Then I turned to see whose voice it was that spoke to me, and on turning I saw seven golden lampstands, and in the midst of the lampstands I saw one like the Son of Man, clothed with a long robe and with a golden sash across his chest. His head and his hair were white as white wool, white as snow; his eyes were like a flame of fire, his feet were like burnished bronze, refined as in a furnace, and his voice was like the sound of many waters. In his right hand he held seven stars, and from his mouth came a sharp, two-edged sword, and his face was like the sun shining with full force. When I saw him, I fell at his feet as though dead. But he placed his right hand on me, saying, "Do not be afraid; I am the first and the last, and the living one. I was dead, and see, I am alive forever and ever; and I have the keys of Death and of Hades. Now write what you have seen, what is, and what is to take place after this. As for the mystery of the seven stars that you saw in my right hand, and the seven golden lampstands: the seven stars are the angels of the seven churches, and the seven lampstands are the seven churches.

As you have probably guessed, the title for today's sermon does not refer to the hymn sing and pie social we are having tonight. Rather, it refers to a song written and sung by a folk singer named Don McLean back in the early 1970s. We've included a copy of the lyrics on an insert in the bulletin. "American Pie" was first released on an album in 1971, and it climbed to number one on the charts as a single in 1972.

The song was something of a mystery from the very beginning. People wondered what it meant. Over the years Don McLean has been reluctant to interpret the lyrics, leaving it to the listeners to try to figure out its meaning. And for the past twenty-five years listeners have offered their own interpretations. I asked Dave and Carlynn Thompson to "surf the net" to see if there was anything about the song on the world wide web. Indeed there was. It turns out there is an "American Pie" Usenet discussion that has been going on in cyberspace since 1983. Dave and Carlynn Thompson were kind enough to download a file called "The Annotated American Pie," which summarizes many of the various interpretations that have been offered of this enigmatic song.

The entire song is over seven minutes long, so we don't have time to listen to all of it this morning, but I thought you might want to hear a little bit just to get the idea of what it's all about. The song begins as a tribute to one of the first rock-and-roll singers, Buddy Holly, who tragically was killed in a plane crash in 1959. Buddy Holly was traveling in a small plane with two other prominent pop singers of the time, Richie Valens, who recorded "La Bamba," and the Big Bopper, who recorded "Chantilly Lace." Their plane went down during a snowstorm in Iowa on February 3, 1959. Because all three singers were so popular, McLean referred to the date of the plane crash as "the day the music died." McLean himself was only a teenager at the time, delivering newspapers and working on his music. With that introduction, let me let you listen to the first part of the song.

Obviously Don McLean was deeply affected by the death of Buddy Holly. Most of us had role models growing up, people we looked up to and admired and wanted to be like. Since Don McLean wanted to be a songwriter, it's not surprising that growing up in the 1950s he would admire Buddy Holly. In the song McLean wrote,

> I can't remember if I cried
> When I read about his widowed bride,
> But something touched me deep inside,
> The day the music died.

Buddy Holly's wife was at home at the time of the plane crash, expecting their first child. She suffered a miscarriage shortly afterward.

You can understand how Don McLean would have been touched by the tragic events. But the song is about more than the death of Buddy Holly. It's about a whole era of American history, when our society was undergoing vast cultural changes. Consider all that happened in the 1960s, between the death of Buddy Holly and when the song was written a decade later. An American president, a civil rights leader, and a presidential candidate were all assassinated. The conflict in Vietnam escalated into war. The drug culture and the hippie movement were in full flower, and rock music was profoundly influencing society. Racial tensions were at a fever pitch, and the Cuban missile crisis reminded us of the threat of nuclear holocaust. There was a sense of fear and pessimism that made us long for the more happy-go-lucky days of the 1950s.

Against this backdrop, the song "American Pie" reflected the anxious and despairing spirit of the age. When I first heard the song, I didn't understand all the nuances or the allusions, but I could sense the tone of the song. It said something about the era in which we were living, times fraught with feelings of disappointment, frustration, and fear.

The song was also filled with religious references. Amidst the themes of tragedy and death McLean asked,

> And do you have faith in God above,
> If the Bible tells you so?

He asked, "Can music save your mortal soul?" He talked about Satan laughing with delight, about the sacred store being silent, and about the church bells being broken. Finally, he said,

> And the three men I admire most—
> The Father, Son, and Holy Ghost—
> They caught the last train for the coast
> The day the music died.

If we had time, we could go through the entire song, line by line, and discuss the events McLean was referring to, but I think you get the idea. The song is a commentary on life, and a rather pessimistic and downcast commentary at that. Yet it spoke to a whole generation, a lost generation, of Americans. Its images reminded us of the perils of that time—the rise of Marxism, the nuclear arms race, even the "death of God" theology. The song began with images of adolescence—the death of a childhood hero, feelings of betrayal seeing a girlfriend in love with another guy, the despair that would lead a young person to drinking, drugs, even thoughts of suicide, driving his Chevy to the levee. The song ends with an apocalyptic vision of a helter-skelter world at the brink of destruction, with things out of control and no hope of redemption, even to the point of feeling abandoned by God.

Like "American Pie," the book of Revelation is also a mystery and an enigma. Although it is not a song per se, Revelation reads like an extended poem, full of images and symbols reflecting equally tumultuous times. We do not understand all the nuances and allusions of Revelation, but we can grasp enough of its meaning to sense its tone. For Revelation also talks about a world on the brink of destruction, a world in which evil seems to triumph and Satan laughs with delight. But although the song "American Pie" and the book of Revelation describe the same world, they come to opposite conclusions. The song seems to conclude that we are lost and without hope. But Revelation says that while we are indeed lost, we are not without hope.

Revelation was written by a Christian named John. He may have been John, the beloved disciple of Jesus, who also wrote the Gospel of John. Or he may have been another John who was a respected elder of the church. Either way, the inspiration for this strange and fascinating book came from a vision John received while he was imprisoned on the island of Patmos. This imprisonment probably took place under the reign of the Roman emperor Domitian, a time of intense Christian persecution during the decade of the 90s in the first century AD.

The emperor had commanded that all subjects bow down and worship him as a god, but many Christians refused to do that. As a consequence many Christians were persecuted—arrested, imprisoned, tortured, and even killed. John had been banished to the island of Patmos, a small, rocky strip of land, ten miles long and six miles wide, forty miles out to sea off the coast of Asia Minor. It was a place the Romans sent troublemakers to, and John was a troublemaker because he wouldn't stop preaching about Christ.

While he was there, John had a vision which became the book of Revelation, a vision filled with poetic images, symbolic numbers, and scriptural allusions. The book of Revelation is a special kind of writing called apocalyptic literature, which contrasts the present time with the time to come. Revelation is filled with allusions to the Old Testament. Of the 404 verses in Revelation, 275 of those verses contain references to passages in the Old Testament.

Not only did John frequently refer to the Old Testament; he used mysterious figures and metaphors and symbols and numbers to conceal his message. Had he written plainly, the imperial police never would have allowed his message to reach the churches. But the Christians of the churches in Asia Minor and beyond recognized that John was writing about them. They understood that John was calling them to remain strong in the Lord, no matter how discouraging life seemed to be. They understood from reading Revelation that in spite of the power of Rome, God was still in control and that Christ, who had died, was now alive to give them power to overcome evil with good.

There are times when we need such a message. There are times when the events of life threaten to overwhelm us, when we become disheartened or discouraged, as evil seems to triumph. We know that Christ has won the ultimate victory over sin and death, but our world too often is still in Satan's grasp.

This week there was "bad news on the doorstep" as we opened our morning papers to read about the plane crash off the coast of Long Island. Although investigators are still investigating, it is possible that the crash was the result of terrorism, another example of a world gone mad. The great fear was that there would be a terrorist attack in Atlanta during the Olympics, but perhaps the plane crash was a terrorist attack. Certainly Satan must be laughing with delight at such evil. With the state of our world getting worse and worse, we might be tempted to succumb to pessimism or cynicism or hopelessness.

Well, Revelation was written precisely to counter such feelings of despair. Revelation was written to assure us that the Father, Son, and Holy Ghost have not caught the last train to the coast. Rather, the one who died is alive forevermore, and he holds in his hands the keys to unlock the gates of death. He was there at the beginning, and he will be there at the end, and he is here with us even now, no matter what the times may be.

A long, long time ago…
I can still remember how
The Son of God was led up a hill—
His hands and feet were nailed,
And he was crucified upon a wooden cross.
You would have thought
That would be the end of it,
You would have thought
The music would have died that day.
But even though they killed him,
No, the music did not die.
For he is now alive again,
And in his love, we find life too,
And power and strength to live for him,
In this world, and beyond, forevermore.
Now, he has given us a chance
To sing with joy, to laugh, to dance,
To live abundant life within his care.
No matter what the times may be,
He'll care for you, he'll care for me
And we will live eternally, today,
For in his love, the music never dies.

July 21, 1996

Chapter 6

1993 – 1999

Eight new pews were installed in the back of the sanctuary, new NRSV Bibles and hymnals were installed in the pew racks, and a new church sign was installed out by the street. Youth, children's, women's, men's, and benevolent ministries were all thriving. Guest preachers included Rev. Tony Cupit from the Baptist World Alliance, Dr. Jere Allen from the D.C. Baptist Convention, Rev. Brent Walker and Ms. Melissa Rogers from the Baptist Joint Committee for Religious Liberty, and field personnel (missionary) Ralph Stocks from the Cooperative Baptist Fellowship. A long-range planning committee was formed, with Dr. Duncan McIntosh of the D.C. Baptist Convention as consultant. In most respects the church was as vital as it had ever been.

The early service was going strong. A men's weeknight Bible study had begun, and a women's evening Bible study had begun, in addition to the longstanding women's weekday morning Bible study. Sunday school was going well. New ministries were started, such as support for Warm Nights (a Prince George's County interfaith ministry to the homeless); "Rip, Zip, and Roll" for White Cross, Here's Life Inner City, the CBF Romany ministry, and the Pioneer Club for children. The church voted to purchase robes for the adult choir, although some worried it might convey an unwanted sense of formality to the 11:00 a.m. Sunday worship service. We also purchased a brass altar cross for the Communion table since some had wondered why there was no cross in the sanctuary. The stained-glass window over the baptistry featured a rainbow and a dove.

With our daughter, Amy, out of college and working in New York City, and with our son, Marc, in high school, and with my own degree studies completed, I felt I could focus even more intently on pastoral ministry. There was an invitation to give the invocation for the opening session of the Maryland senate. Marc went along since he was taking a course on government in school. Some weeks our Baptist ministers golf group had two foursomes for our Thursday outings. Dave and Carlynn Thompson developed Village's home page on the burgeoning world wide web. We celebrated the twenty-fifth anniversary of the church and the twentieth anniversary of our church secretary, Gloria Newton. The church was growing, and a few African-American members joined the fellowship.

There were triumphs and tragedies—baptisms, infant dedications, weddings, vow renewal ceremonies, and funerals. An FBI agent, the son-in-law of an active church member, was shot and killed while working on a case at the D.C. police headquarters. So many people were expected for the funeral that the FBI set up closed-circuit television monitors at the Catholic church next door for overflow seating. The U.S. attorney general and the director of the FBI met with me in my office before the funeral service. There were more police cars in the procession to the cemetery than I have ever seen. The agent left behind a wife and two young children. The widow remains very active in the church. Their two children, now adults, both became agents with the FBI.

Being a longtime pastor at the same church is a multigenerational ministry. Some congregants that I dedicated as infants and baptized as youth and married as young adults now have children of their own that I dedicated and baptized. For some families I conducted the funeral for four, five, six family members. In each eulogy I tried to articulate the essence of that person's life. If I didn't know the person well, I sat down the family and asked them to tell me about their loved one while I took notes. If I knew the person well, I combined the family's remembrances with my own. I considered the eulogy at the funeral as one of my most important ministries. That, and praying with persons in times of illness or grief or family crisis or other need.

Even though the church was going well, preaching on Sunday mornings remained a challenge. I sometimes followed the "What? So what? Now what?" pattern. "What?" What does the text say? "So what?" What does the text say to me/us? "Now what?" What does the text call me/us to do? Sermons served multiple purposes—spiritual formation, call to commitment, pastoral care, call to justice and mercy, community formation. Sometimes the sermon began as a text in search of a topic. Sometimes the sermon began as a topic in search of a text. Every preacher has a "canon within the canon." Not all the texts of the Bible are of equal homiletical value. I preached from the Gospels more than any other book. Somehow, in every sermon, I wanted to get back to Jesus.

I discovered the limits of "prophetic" preaching. Two themes got pushback. One Sunday I spoke about our gun-happy culture and the strong link between handguns and murder and suicide. After the service two deacons confronted me at the back of the sanctuary, near the sound booth. One deacon was in law enforcement. The other was in the military. Both took issue with my advocacy for greater gun control. One of the deacons said that if I preached on that again, he was leaving the church.

Over the years I have preached many sermons on racial injustice. After one sermon I received a letter from a deacon. She told me she didn't understand why I kept preaching on race relations. She said there was no problem with race relations in our church. In fact, she said, one of her best friends is an African American.

I continued to preach prophetically, but the feedback from those deacons was always in the back of my mind.

The Sign of the Fish
Mark 1:16-20 (NRSV)

As Jesus passed along the Sea of Galilee, he saw Simon and his brother Andrew casting a net into the sea—for they were fishermen. And Jesus said to them, "Follow me and I will make you fish for people." And immediately they left their nets and followed him. As he went a little farther, he saw James son of Zebedee and his brother John, who were in their boat mending the nets. Immediately he called them; and they left their father Zebedee in the boat with the hired men, and followed him.

During her junior year in college, Andrea Palpant decided to make some changes in her life. She took a butter knife from her mother's kitchen drawer and went outside. Andrea used the butter knife to scrape the Christian fish symbol off the back bumper of her car. The car had belonged to her older brother before he gave it to her. He was the one who had bought the decal from a Christian bookstore and stuck the Ichthys sticker on the car bumper. But that afternoon Andrea decided she didn't want a "Jesus fish" on her bumper anymore. Squatting near the tailpipe, she began to scrape the symbol with the butter knife until the fish decal disintegrated and fell in small flakes to the ground. She spent another ten minutes trying to scrape away the outline of where the fish symbol had been on the bumper. She did her best to remove it, but some of the residue remained. Andrea scraped off the decal because she had decided that she didn't want to be identified by the sign of the fish anymore. She wanted her car to be neutral territory.

It's not that Andrea had totally given up on God. She just wasn't sure what she believed anymore. Like many young people, she was going through her own identity crisis. Raised in a Christian home, Andrea had spent the early part of her childhood in Kenya, where her parents were medical missionaries. When the family returned to the States so her father could teach at a medical school, they began to attend an evangelical church in Spokane, Washington. It was there Andrea professed her faith in Jesus and was baptized. But later Andrea began to question everything she had been raised to believe.

The seed of her doubt had been planted in those early years when she lived in western Kenya, an eight-hour drive from Nairobi. There, her father had practiced medicine in a bush hospital founded by the Quakers. On any given day her father would be diagnosing sickle-cell at the hospital while her mother was praying at someone's deathbed. Attending funerals for her dad's patients was a common occurrence. Although Andrea was only six at the time, she remembers a twelve-year-old boy who was being treated for severe tuberculosis of the brain. The boy remained at the hospital for some two months, long enough for Andrea and her brother to get to know him well. One day Andrea watched as a missionary pastor carried the boy into their bathroom and baptized him in the tub. Two weeks later the boy died. Andrea saw her father carry the boy's body from the hospital to the morgue, a mud hut just forty feet from the front door of their house. Andrea's nine-year-old brother walked alongside the sad procession for his dead friend. Later the family sat at the dining room table. Her father bowed his head to say a blessing. Halfway through the prayer, he covered his face with his hands and began to weep. Her mother finished the prayer. Andrea stared with her eyes wide open the whole time. She had never seen her father cry before.

Two days after that, Andrea went with her mother and her brother to the boy's funeral. Her father couldn't go; he had to stay and attend to patients at the hospital. During the ceremony they stood by the open grave and threw some dirt onto the wooden coffin. A pastor prayed, and the children sang a song, "Jesus, I Heard You Have a Big House." Driving home, their mom talked about death. She said the boy was in heaven with Jesus. Andrea and her brother remained silent. They didn't know what to say. All Andrea knew is that a boy had died and that she felt upset about it in a strange, inarticulate way. The death of her friend became a small stone in her heart that she would carry for years before she felt its full weight. It was the beginning of her struggle with the so-called "problem of evil." It was the beginning of her doubts about God. Years after that, Andrea would write in her memoir, *Faith and Other Flat Tires: Searching for God on the Rough Road of Doubt*, "Something was profoundly wrong with the world. God allowed suffering. God let a good kid die."

By the time Andrea was in her early twenties, her doubts had grown into a full-blown crisis of faith. She stopped going to church. She began smoking cigarettes and drinking hard liquor and hanging out in bars. She had an affair with a married man who was twice her age. She got involved with a series of other "complicated" men. She was perpetually brokenhearted. Mostly, she felt lost and alone and confused. Scraping the sign of the fish off the back bumper of her car had been the start of "searching for God on the rough road of doubt." Her unmarked car was the symbol of an unmarked heart.

Long before bumper stickers, the sign of the fish was an ancient Christian symbol. Today the cross is the most universal sign of the Christian faith, but in the first centuries it was the fish. The Greek word for fish, *ichthys*, formed an acrostic for "Jesus Christ, God's Son, Savior." The early Christians used the sign of the fish to identify themselves, their places of worship, and even their burial places. There were signs of the fish etched on the walls of the catacombs beneath the streets of Rome, where Christians met in secret and buried their martyrs. The five Greek letters in the word for fish are iota, chi, theta, upsilon, and sigma. They are the first letters of the Greek words *Iesous* (Jesus), *Christos* (Christ), *Theou* (God's), *huios* (Son), *soter* (Savior). Exactly why the early Christians chose the sign of the fish as their symbol, we cannot say for sure. But it may have something to do with the scripture for this morning.

Jesus was passing by the Sea of Galilee when he saw two fishermen casting a net into the water. Jesus said to Simon and his brother Andrew, "Follow me and I will make you fish for people." Immediately, they left their nets and followed Jesus. Going on a little farther, Jesus saw another set of fishermen, brothers James and John, sons of Zebedee, mending their nets. He called them, and they left their father and hired hands and followed Jesus. They may not have understood at the time, but they were exchanging one kind of fishing for another. It was the beginning for them of a new way of life. It's not like they slapped a fish decal on the back of their boats, but eventually they would come to be identified by the sign of the fish too.

On this first Sunday in Lent, we are beginning to follow Jesus on his journey to the cross. These six weeks of Lent are meant to be a time of spiritual preparation for Easter. It's a time to examine our own faith commitments and to reflect more deeply upon what it means to follow Jesus. That's why there is a fish symbol taped to the back of each bulletin. The idea is for you to take the fish token off the bulletin and keep it with you during Lent. Maybe you will put it on your key ring or in your change purse. Maybe you will keep it in your pocket or place it on the kitchen table or in your car as a reminder that you too have been called to follow Jesus. The idea is to use these six weeks of Lent as a time to consider what following Jesus means for you.

I suspect that when Simon and Andrew, James and John began to follow Jesus, they had no idea what they were getting into. We don't even know why they left behind their boats and nets to follow Jesus. The Bible doesn't explain their motivations. Maybe they were just curious. Maybe they felt the tug of God upon their hearts. Maybe they sensed that Jesus offered them a greater purpose in life. It's not that they gave up fishing altogether. They would return time and again to their boats and their nets. But after he called them, following Jesus became the greatest priority in their lives. It was a "higher calling," if you will.

When Andrea Palpant walked away from the church at age twenty-three, she had no idea if she would ever come back. After college, Andrea returned to Kenya, where she volunteered in an orphanage for children with AIDS. She said she saw there "the paradox of Christian compassion: on the one hand, children who seemed forsaken by God, and, on the other hand, Catholic nuns acting out the call of God to bless the forsaken." For a long time, she could not reconcile the two sides of the paradox.

After she returned to the United States, for some reason that even she did not fully understand, Andrea decided to give church a try once again. At first she wondered if she was ready to be back in worship. But then she remembered what a college professor had told her after his wife and daughter had been killed in an auto accident. The professor said, "After the accident, I went to church again, but I couldn't bring myself to sing the hymns. I let other people sing for me. I let them carry me."

That's what Andrea decided she would do. She would let others sing for her. She would let others carry her. Even in her ambivalence, Andrea could feel in her heart a longing for God. She started attending a Bible study class led by a young man just a little older than she. The teacher seemed so much more certain of his faith than she was of hers. After the class she sat with him during the worship service. They shared a hymnal, which according to a friend of hers was a form of Christian flirting. After the service the young man invited Andrea to go with him to visit an elderly woman in an adult-care facility. That's what he did every Sunday afternoon. Seeing the young man's kindness toward the old woman touched Andrea deeply. After all her years of railing against God for the problem of suffering, she now saw God's love made visible in the care of one person for another person.

Andrea came to understand that following Jesus doesn't mean that we have answers for all of life's problems and questions. It simply means that when we follow Jesus, we find a deeper meaning and a higher purpose for our lives. When we serve others in Christ's name, our questions and doubts don't seem so important anymore. In following Jesus we learn to walk in the way of love.

In his novel *Les Misérables* Victor Hugo wrote, "To love another person is to see the face of God." Jesus came to love us and to show us God's face. When we follow in his footsteps and love others as he loved us, we see the face of God too.

March 9, 2014

Follow Me
Mark 1:16-20 (NRSV)

As Jesus passed along the Sea of Galilee, he saw Simon and his brother Andrew casting a net into the sea—for they were fishermen. And Jesus said to them, "Follow me and I will make you fish for people." And immediately they left their nets and followed him. As he went a little farther, he saw James son of Zebedee and his brother John, who were in their boat mending the nets. Immediately he called them; and they left their father Zebedee in the boat with the hired men, and followed him.

I was eleven years old when I decided to follow Jesus. To be honest about it, there was never a time when I did not consider myself to be a follower of Jesus. I had gone to church from the time I was a baby. But at the age of eleven, I reached the conclusion that I wanted to follow Jesus, not because my parents wanted me to be a Christian, but because I wanted to be a Christian.

I'll never forget how nervous I was going to the pastor's study that Sunday morning during Sunday school to tell him I wanted to be baptized. I was nervous walking up to the front of the sanctuary during the last hymn that Sunday to make a public profession of my faith in Christ. And I was nervous being baptized on a Sunday after that. The whole experience was nerve-wracking. Part of it was my self-consciousness. But the bigger part was I knew it was very important. I knew that my decision to follow Jesus was the most important decision I would ever make—more important than what I would study in school, or where I would go to college, or what kind of job I would have as an adult, or even who I would marry. My decision to follow Jesus was the most important decision of my life, because it would determine not just my future happiness on earth, but my eternal security in heaven. So I did not take that decision lightly, even at the age of eleven.

Looking back, I didn't know everything I was getting into when I decided to follow Jesus at the age of eleven. I didn't have an adult understanding of the Christian faith. That's one reason why persons who become Christians later in life may have a deeper sense of commitment, because they probably have a deeper understanding of what the Christian life is all about. Sometimes I will advise a young child to wait a little while before being baptized, to have a fuller understanding of what that commitment means. But I never want to discourage anyone from following Jesus. It's the most important decision any of us can make.

Simon and Andrew, James and John made the decision to follow Jesus, and their lives were never the same. They discovered a higher calling in life, a calling to join Jesus in his mission for the world. Now, there's nothing wrong with earning an honest living. But there is more to life than making money. There is more to life than advancing in a career. God has work for us that goes beyond earning a living. God wants us to fish for people. God wants us to join in casting out the net of Jesus's love and drawing people back to himself. Jesus called Simon and Andrew, James and John to follow him for two reasons. First, he wanted to be with them. He wanted to know them and to love them, to develop a deep and lasting relationship with them. He wanted them to be his friends, his brothers, his family. But there was a second reason that Jesus called Simon and Andrew, James and John to follow him. He wanted them to join in the work he had come to do. He wanted them to be partners in his fishing enterprise of drawing people back to God.

The call to Christian discipleship is the same for us today. Jesus calls us to follow him so he can know us and love us and have a relationship with us. But Jesus also calls us to follow him so we can join in his mission of drawing people back to God. And like those first disciples, the invitation to us is the same. Jesus says to us in the midst of whatever we are doing with our lives, "Come, follow me."

The movie *The Cider House Rules* is the story of an orphanage in the remote town of St. Cloud, Maine, during the Second World War. It's hard for us to imagine what orphanages were like then because there are no such orphanages today. Now there are more parents who want to adopt children than there are children available for adoption. Of course, there are still children with special needs who grow up in foster homes, but the warehousing of orphaned children is largely a thing of the past. Yet back then, some otherwise healthy children grew up in orphanages, never to be adopted.

The movie depicts what life was like in such an orphanage and the longing of those children to "find a family" and to have a home. In one heart-rending scene, prospective adoptive parents come to the orphanage to select a child to adopt. All the children know they are on display, and they try to put on their best appearance and behavior, hoping that they might be the lucky ones to be chosen for adoption. So desperate are they for love and a place of belonging that they almost throw themselves at the visitors. One shaggy-haired, gap-toothed little boy named Curly says, without a hint of arrogance, "I'm the best one," hoping the prospective parents will see in him something that makes him worthy to be chosen.

In a sense that is our deepest need too: to find a place of love and belonging, to find a family. But the good news is that God already has chosen each of us to be his sons and daughters. God already has chosen us to find our place in his family of faith. God sent his son Jesus to tell us that we are the best ones. No matter how shaggy-haired or gap-toothed we may be, we are all the best ones.

And so we follow Jesus. But it's not enough just to follow. We live like Jesus. We join Jesus in his grand enterprise of expanding the family of God. Jesus wants to make all of us "fishers of people" who cast wide the net of God's redeeming love and draw all people to himself. Jesus said, "Follow me, and I will lead you home."

January 30, 2000

Making a Christian Commitment
Mark 1:14-20 (RSV)

Now after John was arrested, Jesus came into Galilee, preaching the gospel of God, and saying, "The time is fulfilled, and the kingdom of God is at hand; repent, and believe in the gospel."

And passing along by the Sea of Galilee, he saw Simon and Andrew the brother of Simon casting a net in the sea; for they were fishermen. And Jesus said to them, "Follow me and I will make you become fishers of men." And immediately they left their nets and followed him. And going on a little farther, he saw James the son of Zebedee and John his brother, who were in their boat mending the nets. And immediately he called them; and they left their father Zebedee in the boat with the hired servants, and followed him.

I don't know about you, but I am very deliberate when it comes to making a commitment. I usually take my time and think long and hard before I commit myself to anything. For example, I have a personal policy not to make any commitments over the telephone. The phone usually rings at our house around dinnertime. I am careful to be courteous, because it might be someone from the church calling. But nine times out of ten, it is someone trying to sell me something: storm windows, insulation, lawn service, newspaper subscription, financial investments, you name it. It's become quite a racket. Fraudulent telephone sales schemes are rampant. According to an article in the current issue of *Newsweek*, con artists are using the telephone to push travel scams, vitamin-pill rip-offs, false art, grandfather clocks, cellular-telephone franchises, even cures for AIDS.

But it's not just a matter of not buying things over the telephone. I am a cautious person in most areas of my life. I am slow to commit myself to anything that might require my money or my time or my energies. Most of us, I would imagine, are rather hesitant to make commitments. That's why our Scripture text seems so unusual.

In the text that we just read, four men were very quick to commit themselves to following Jesus. Simon and Andrew, James and John, two sets of brothers, were fishermen on the Sea of Galilee. From what we can tell, they made a decent living at it. In the case of James and John, not only did they work with their father, Zebedee, but they had hired servants in the business. Apparently it was a thriving concern. We can assume that they had more than enough to fill their time. They had careers, families, social responsibilities. They had property to keep up, fishing boats and nets and other equipment. They were probably homeowners. We know that Simon owned a house in Capernaum, which later became a base of operations for Jesus.

When we read between the lines, we see that these men were just as busy as we are; they were just as occupied with work and family and other responsibilities as any of us. And yet they made a commitment to follow Jesus. Jesus called them, and they immediately left their nets and followed him. We might ask, "Why?"

The first time I heard this story, I got the impression that it happened just like that. It sounds like Jesus suddenly appears, wags his finger at four complete strangers, and they immediately start following him as if they are in some kind of a trance. But when we look more closely at it, we see that there is more to it than that. What we have here is a condensation of what happened. Mark doesn't give us all the details, only a bare outline. It is likely that Andrew and Simon, James and John already knew Jesus.

We know that Andrew was a follower of John the Baptist, and several of John's followers went on to become disciples of Jesus. Mark tells us that before this incident, Jesus spent some time in Galilee preaching. New Testament scholar William Barclay suggests that all four of these men probably had heard Jesus speak. Perhaps they had even talked with Jesus in small groups or one-on-one. And so it is likely that Andrew and Simon already knew Jesus, and it is possible that James and John did also.

But we can push the question deeper. Even if they already knew Jesus, why would they drop everything to become his disciples? What was in it for them? What prompted them to make that kind of radical commitment?

To be honest about it, we cannot say for sure. No one can know another person's mind and heart. But we can make an educated guess. We can guess what their motivation was because these four men were not the only ones attracted to Jesus. There were many more than just the twelve disciples who were committed to Jesus. For example, a number of women followed Jesus. Mary and her sister Martha, Mary Magdalene, another Mary, the wife of Zebedee, Joanna, Salome, and many other unnamed women followed Jesus. They were not merely curious onlookers. These women were deeply committed to Jesus. Many of these women followed Jesus all the way from Galilee to Jerusalem, ministering to him. Some of these women were there when Jesus died. And so we are talking about a deep and sincere commitment, not only for Andrew and Simon, James and John, but for many others.

What was it that led so many people to leave what they were doing and follow Jesus? Was it his teaching? No doubt that was part of it. In contrast to the religious leaders, the experts, the intelligentsia, Jesus taught with authority. He spoke of love and self-sacrifice and service to others. He spoke of God in a way that many of them had never heard. Forgiveness, compassion, mercy for sinners—this was all new and wonderful stuff.

Was it his healings, the miracles, the mighty signs? No doubt that played a part too. Was it the force of his personality? Yes, to be sure. Jesus had a way of looking at people with so much warmth, so much understanding, so much authenticity that people were naturally attracted to him. His teaching, his mighty acts, his personality were all factors. But behind all that was something more basic. Somehow, even though they didn't fully understand it, there was a feeling of "deep calling to deep." This was not just another man. Somehow when Jesus called them to follow him, it was a call from God himself.

Jesus still calls people to follow him. He still asks people to make a commitment to him. In fact, Jesus asks every one of us to do that. It doesn't matter how busy you are. It doesn't matter what other commitments you have. Some things are simply more important. I'm sure that Andrew and Simon, James and John had to reorder their priorities to follow Jesus. They had to rearrange their schedules; they had to give up some responsibilities; they had to make some changes in their lives. Mark is telling us something when he says that *immediately* they left their nets and followed Jesus. This was too important to put off. Jesus didn't wait until they had some free time. He didn't wait until their schedules became less complicated, or the workload let up, or the kids left home, or it was time to retire. Jesus went to men who were already hard at work in the prime of their lives, and he called them to something even more urgent.

What we're saying here is that our commitment to Christ must take precedence. Of course work is important; family is even more important. But God must be ultimate. To paraphrase Jesus, "Seek first the will of God, and everything else will fall into its proper place."

What, then, does it mean for us to follow Jesus, to make a commitment to him? Our commitment to Christ can be expressed in many ways. Perhaps the most basic Christian commitment is to accept Jesus Christ as the savior and Lord of our lives and to be baptized. If you have never made that kind of public commitment to Christ, I invite you to think about doing that, even this morning. Another level of Christian commitment is joining the church. I try not to make that ultimate—you are certainly welcome to be a part of our church family, to attend, to participate, without being a member. But church membership is one aspect of making a Christian commitment. Or if you have been baptized as a believer, if you are a church member, your Christian commitment can be expressed in other ways. Maybe you need to become more deeply involved in the life of the church. Maybe you need to become more regular in worship attendance. Maybe you need to take more seriously your spiritual formation and start coming to Sunday school. Maybe you need to take a look at the level of your giving. Or maybe your commitment to Christ will find expression outside the walls of the church. Maybe Jesus is calling to you to become a fisher of people, to help draw people to him.

I cannot specify exactly where Jesus might be leading you, but this I do know: Jesus calls every one of us to follow him in some way. It doesn't matter how busy we are. If we ignore the call of God in our lives, we cannot become all that God intends for us to be. In a real sense the quality of our lives depends on the level of our commitment to Jesus Christ.

I don't think my friend Slade MacTaggart will mind my telling this story. When the MacTaggart family first moved into their house, there was some confusion about the property lines which divided their yard from the neighbors' yards. Initially, no one had fences up, so everyone had to guess where their property ended and the other neighbors' began. Then, when some of them did put up fences, they discovered they had been miscalculating the perimeters of their respective backyards.

Slade had been mowing a corner of one neighbor's yard, and another neighbor had been mowing a corner of his. In fact, Slade had planted a tree in what he thought was his own backyard, but what turned out to be the backyard of the house behind theirs. After they put up fences, it became clear whose yard was whose. Slade decided to move his tree from the neighbor's yard into his own. He dug a huge hole, larger than the circumference of the branches, so that the tree could be lifted out with a great ball of dirt around the roots. With the help of several neighbors, he lifted the tree over the fence and placed it down in the hole in his own yard. That was several weeks ago, but sad to say, the tree is not doing well. Apparently, even with his careful calculations, he accidentally cut the tap root to the tree, and now there is some question whether the tree will even survive.

So it is with us. In a real sense, the tap root to our lives is our commitment to Jesus Christ. The deeper our commitment to Christ, the more God can fill our lives with purpose and power. But when our commitment is shallow or superficial, when we are not deeply rooted in the Bible, in the church, in Christian service, our lives will suffer. It may not be apparent at first, but sooner or later, our lives will show the effects. The tap root to life, and life eternal, is Jesus Christ.

What if Andrew and Simon, James and John had said to Jesus, "No thanks"? What if they had said, "We're busy, Jesus; we've got other responsibilities; we've got more than we can manage right now. We are not ready to make a commitment to you"? What if they had refused? They would have missed the power and the peace, the purpose and the glory of a personal relationship with Jesus Christ.

What about you? What kind of Christian commitment would you make? Have you publicly accepted Jesus Christ as your savior and Lord and followed him as a believer in baptism? Have you joined the church? Have you made Christian living a priority? Have you shared your faith with others? Have you served others in Jesus's name? Have you become a fisher of people?

What about it? Too busy, too many commitments, too many other things to do? How will you answer when Jesus calls you?

May 15, 1988

Chapter 7

2000-2002

Everything changed on the morning of Saturday, January 8, 2000. The Village Baptist Church building was destroyed by fire. Linda and I stood in the parking lot and helplessly watched as firefighters put out the blaze. One of the firefighters asked me if there was anything in the building I wanted him to try to retrieve. I told him there was a brass altar cross on the Communion table. If he could save that, we would be grateful. A few minutes later he emerged from the smoldering ruins with the altar cross in his hands. News photographers took pictures of him carrying the cross out through the smoke and rubble. By now the parking lot was filled with stunned church members. We spent most of the day consoling each other and trying to figure out what to do next. The fire chief offered us use of the community room at the Pointer Ridge fire station for worship the next day. It was the beginning of a plan. We would meet in the parking lot for prayer at 8:30 a.m. and again at 11:00 a.m. on Sunday morning. Then we would drive over to the fire station for the two worship services. We needed to gather in front of the destroyed building to begin to come to grips with our loss and to support one another. Plus, it was impossible to get the word out to the entire congregation about what had happened. No doubt some people would show up for worship unaware. We needed to be there to meet them and to collectively share our grief.

I was on my way to the fire station to set up for the early service when I decided to stop by the church. I pulled my car into the parking lot and surveyed the destruction. For the first time since the fire, I allowed myself to cry. Then I went to the fire station to set up and returned to the church to wait for the early-service crowd. After we had assembled in front of the burned building, I began by quoting the psalmist: "This is the day the LORD has made; let us rejoice and be glad in it" (Ps 118:24). To be honest about it, I didn't feel like rejoicing. None of us did. But we needed to place our tragedy in the larger context of God's loving care. The words of the psalmist would become the every-Sunday call to worship for the rest of my ministry at Village.

Once at the fire station, it became apparent that this was only a temporary solution. There was no space for childcare or Sunday school classes. The restroom facilities were limited. We had a portable keyboard for music accompaniment, but not much else. I placed the altar cross that the fireman had rescued on a table at the front of the room. The atmosphere for both services was surprisingly upbeat. We weren't exactly joyful, but we weren't morose either. I preached a sermon that I had written the night before, in place of the sermon I had written during the week. A news reporter was there, as well as some visitors who had heard about the fire and wanted to come and show their support.

We worshiped at the fire hall one more Sunday, and then the Bowie Alliance Church invited us to share their building on Sunday mornings. Several churches had offered us space on Sunday afternoons, but I knew our only chance of keeping the congregation together was finding a place to meet on Sunday mornings. We had visited a school, a hotel, a community center, even an empty retail space as possible options, until the invitation from Bowie Alliance Church came along. Their congregation was small, with a part-time interim pastor, and they were willing to adjust their schedule to accommodate ours. Plus, since we would pay them rent, the extra income would allow them to hire a full-time minister.

So beginning two weeks after the fire, we met at Bowie Alliance Church for what would be thirty-four months. Our adult choir met at the United Parish Church for weekly rehearsals, and counselor Rose Schrott set up her office at United Parish too. For a couple of months, the basement in our house functioned as the church office. An office equipment company donated a used copier, and the church phone number was transferred to our home phone line. Then a local family practice physician, Dr. Surendra Kumar, rented us office space.

We learned how to be a church without a building. We held baptisms at Cresthill Baptist Church, and Belair Baptist Church, and the swimming pool in the backyard of Leslie and Pete Parreco. The Christmas carol sing was held at the Collington Lifecare Community, with some Collington residents joining us. Benefit concerts for our building fund were held at Cresthill Baptist Church, Temple Solel Synagogue, the Bowie Church of Latter-day Saints, as well as a multichurch effort called ChurchAid at the Allen Pond amphitheater. There was also a benefit golf tournament organized by one of our members, Mike Sowers, that netted over $10,000 for the building fund. We were greatly encouraged when Dr. Daniel Vestal, coordinator of the Cooperative Baptist Fellowship, preached on a Sunday morning during our displacement. After the services at Bowie Alliance, Daniel went with me over to our under-construction new building for a tour.

Because no church rebuilds as it was before, we built for the future. Our insurance would only replace what had been destroyed, so we had to raise funds and borrow for building improvements. The new structure included a fellowship hall and commercial kitchen, as well as more restrooms and storage space. We used the existing slab for the sanctuary and educational wing, but we made the ceilings higher in the foyer and worship space. We added a choir room and a parlor and an expanded coat closet. My office and the secretary's office remained in basically the same locations as before.

Investigators determined that the fire that destroyed the church building had started in my office. Apparently it was caused by an electrical short in the wiring. All my books were fuel for the fire. I lost my entire professional library, except for one Bible that I had taken home the night before. The week after the fire I conducted a funeral. I discovered I could plan and lead the funeral with nothing other than my Bible and my experience of having officiated at many previous funerals. For the first few months after the fire, I wrote my sermons with few resources other than the Bible. Eventually, word got out about a pastor who had lost his entire library. Friends (and even ministers I did not know) started sending me books. One seminary classmate who was no longer in the ministry sent me his entire library. After meticulously documenting the books that had burned, I submitted a claim to the insurance company. From that settlement I was able to purchase commentary sets and other reference books.

The first year after the fire, the congregation held together. I decided to "get back to basics" by preaching from the Gospels of Mark, Luke, and John. I preached through Mark from the middle of January until the end of April. I preached through Luke from May until the end of the summer. I preached from John from September until the second Sunday of Advent. I concluded the year with the nativity stories from Matthew and Luke. My thought was that focusing on the life of Jesus would help us to be a church without a building.

During the second and third years of our displacement, we began losing people, especially families with children and youth. By the time we entered our rebuilt church, we had lost about a third of the congregation.

Many people had drifted away or moved away or joined other churches. Our intake of new members was less because we were meeting in another church's building and our visibility in the community was greatly reduced. Some Sundays during our displacement, I went home after services and just held my head in my hands. It was the most discouraging phase of my ministry. My wife and those who stuck with us kept me going, along with the hope of a brighter day. I knew that God was with us and that God would see us through.

The Sunday we occupied the new building was a joyous day. We met for one combined service at the Bowie Alliance Church to say goodbye. Then we processed on foot up Mitchellville Road, passing St. Edward the Confessor Catholic Church along the way. The priest at St. Edward's recessed mass so that their congregation could come out on the church lawn and cheer us as we passed by. Les Owen, a member of our congregation and a member of the U.S. Army band, led the procession, playing "When the Saints Go Marching In" on his saxophone. The co-chair of the building committee, Gracen Joiner, and his wife, Dottie, carried the altar cross. We entered our rebuilt church and went straight into the sanctuary to continue our worship.

At the dedication service on a Sunday afternoon a few weeks later, the same firefighter who had rescued the altar cross brought it back into the sanctuary. Area clergy took part in the dedication service. The mayor of Bowie was there. It was a celebration. Then the reality hit me. We had rebuilt the building; now we had the challenge of rebuilding the congregation.

Captures the devastation, and the hope, after the fire that destroyed Village Baptist Church on January 8, 2000." © Tom Carter. Used by permission.

The Beginning of the Good News
Mark 1:1-8 (NRSV)

The beginning of the good news of Jesus Christ, the Son of God. As it is written in the prophet Isaiah,
"See, I am sending my messenger ahead of you,
who will prepare your way;
the voice of one crying out in the wilderness:
'Prepare the way of the Lord,
make his paths straight,'"
John the baptizer appeared in the wilderness, proclaiming a baptism of repentance for the forgiveness of sins. And people from the whole Judean countryside and all the people of Jerusalem were going out to him, and were baptized by him in the river Jordan, confessing their sins. Now John was clothed with camel's hair, with a leather belt around his waist, and he ate locusts and wild honey. He proclaimed, "The one who is more powerful than I is coming after me; I am not worthy to stoop down and untie the thong of his sandals. I have baptized you with water; but he will baptize you with the Holy Spirit."

When the telephone rings at 7:00 a.m., it is seldom good news. Two weeks ago, our phone rang at 7:00 a.m. It was Linda's brother Skip telling us that his wife Ruthie was in the hospital and was not expected to live through the day. That's not the kind of thing you want to hear the first thing in the morning. We knew that Ruthie was sick, but we didn't know how sick she was. It was a sad day. After a hurried trip to Louisville for Ruthie's funeral, we were back home last weekend when the phone again rang at 7:00 a.m. on Saturday morning. It was Steve Harris telling us the church was on fire. Not good news at all. Linda and I threw on some clothes and rushed to the scene. We spent the rest of the day watching the building being destroyed by smoke and water and fire. It was another sad day we will never forget.

But today is a new day, and I have good news. The good news comes from our Scripture passage for this morning, found in Mark's Gospel, chapter 1, verse 1. For the next three months I plan to base all my sermons on the Gospel According to Mark. You might know that most scholars believe that Mark was the first Gospel, the first written account of the life and death and resurrection of Jesus. They think Mark was the first because the Gospels of Matthew and Luke incorporate most of Mark into their own stories about Jesus. So we begin our year-long study of the life of Jesus with Mark, the shortest and probably the first written record of Jesus.

Who was Mark, and where did he get his information? Traditionally, he has been identified as John Mark, not one of the original twelve disciples, but an early Christian mentioned numerous times in the book of Acts and the letters of Paul and Peter. We know that Mark was a close associate of Paul, and later tradition says that he had a special relationship with Peter. In fact, an early church historian named Papias said that Mark used Peter as the source for much of his material, perhaps even serving as a kind of scribe who wrote down what Peter told him. Another early church father, Jerome, went so far as to claim that "Peter spoke, and Mark wrote it down." So much of Mark's Gospel may include the personal reminiscences of Peter.

Mark was very careful about the way he began his Gospel. He let us know from the very beginning what it was all about. First, Mark told us that his writing was "good news." The Greek word for *good news* is the same word for *gospel*. So the word *gospel* means "good news." Mark had a story to tell that would make a difference for the people who read his Gospel in the first century, and a difference for us who read his Gospel in the twenty-first century. The question is, why is this story such good news? The story is good news because of who the story is about, namely Jesus Christ, the Son of God. From the outset Mark wants us to understand that God sent his son Jesus into the world to be the Christ, the Messiah, and that this coming of the Son of God is good news for everyone who believes in him.

I know that sometimes religion gets a bad rap. To some outside the church, Christianity seems rigid and confining and restrictive. But the heart of the gospel message is good news, not bad news. God sent his son Jesus into the world to make our lives better. Perhaps we have a hard time convincing the world that Christianity really is good news because there is some bad news contained within the Christian message. The bad news is that all of us are sinners, in need of repentance. That was the message of John the Baptist, who came before Jesus to prepare the way for his message. John preached a message of repentance for the forgiveness of sins, and he invited people to be baptized as a sign of their repentance. That's the bad news of the Christian message—all of us are sinners, and the only way we can get right with God is to repent.

But it is only after we hear the bad news that we can receive the good news. The good news is that our sin is not the final word. The good news is that God sent his son to save us from our sin and to make us right with God.

It seems like there has been a lot of bad news lately with regard to our church. Our building was destroyed by fire. We have no place for worship (other than the generous offer of the fire hall). We have no space for a nursery, or classrooms, or offices. We're probably going to have to go deeper in debt after this is all over. That's the bad news. But there is a lot of good news. And that's what I want to share with you for the rest of this sermon. I want to tell you about the good news.

The first good news is that we have a place to meet. Even before the fire was completely out, representatives from the Bowie volunteer fire department invited us to meet here for as long as we need to. And that was only the beginning of a tremendous outpouring of support from the community.

The second good news is the media. They covered the fire and its aftermath with sensitivity, compassion, and genuine concern. Some of you got on television or were quoted in the newspaper as a result of the fire. We're going to compile a scrapbook of all the newspaper articles and a videotape of all the television news reports. The media coverage has been good news because it has raised awareness of our church. In a way the media coverage has allowed us to give a greater witness to our faith.

More good news is the support we have received from other pastors and churches. This past week I have personally spoken with over two dozen pastors who called to express their concern. Another dozen or so pastors called and left messages, but I haven't had the chance to talk with them yet. We've received many letters and notes of condolence. Some of the other churches are helping in practical ways. The United Parish Church has invited our adult choir to hold their weekly rehearsals in their building. Another church has offered us hymnals. The Maryland Bible Society has offered us Bibles. There are many other Christians who are praying for us.

Some more good news. We've received offers of several pieces of office equipment for free, from people or businesses not even connected with our church. Mr. Larry Grier from IKON business systems donated a copier and fax machine. A lady in the community donated a printer. Chandra Knabel's employer, Choice Hotels, donated two computers. When we do get temporary office space, we will have the equipment we need to get back to business.

More good news. We've received monetary donations from various individuals and organizations. I did a live interview on WAVA radio last Tuesday night, and several listeners sent donations to the church. I'm not going to tell you about all the donors, but I want to mention two. My brother-in-law Skip, who lost his wife Ruthie just two weeks ago, used to work for a company owned by Lee and Carolyn Grossman. The Grossmans are Jewish, active in their synagogue in Louisville. But when they heard that our church had burned down, they sent a contribution to our building fund, in memory of Ruthie. Another donation came from Tom Yoder's Masonic Lodge—for $1,000. Normally, we don't identify donors or the size of their gifts, but these were remarkable and deeply appreciated.

More good news. The Bowie Alliance Church has invited us to share their building while we rebuild. They're not saying, "You can come in on Sunday afternoons and use our building." Several churches would be willing for us to do that. The Bowie Alliance Church has invited us to come in on Sunday mornings! They have offered to adjust their schedule so we can share the space together. That is extraordinary!

More good news. People in our church are pulling together, and working together, and putting aside personal preferences for the good of the entire church. Now, I have no illusions that the next year of rebuilding is going to be easy. We're going to have to make some sacrifices and make some tough decisions to get through the next year. But this crisis can pull us all closer together. It can give us a common purpose and a common bond. I firmly believe that our church can grow during this time of rebuilding. We can grow in our faith in God and in our love for one another. And we can grow numerically. This is an exciting time to be a part of Village Baptist Church! The future is bright with hope. We have good news to share—good news of forgiveness, good news of salvation, good news of Jesus Christ, who came to bring us closer to God and closer to one another too.

One of our younger members, Jean Joiner, sent me her take on the fire that destroyed our church building. Jean titled it "Ten Things the Fire Didn't Destroy":

   10. Our appetites. Ever been to a Village potluck dinner?
   9. Our voices. We can still sing praises to our Lord.
   8. Our laughter. We love to laugh. We always will.
   7. Our friendship. We will always be there for each other.
   6. Our hope. It's frail, but hard to kill.

5. Our faith. When you believe, miracles can occur.
4. Our family. We come together as one.
3. Our prayers. God is always listening.
2. Our spirit. This lives inside all of us.
1. Our future. This is not the end of Village Baptist!

Thank you, Jean. You said it exactly right! This is not the end of Village Baptist Church! This is only the beginning, the beginning of the good news of Jesus Christ; the beginning of the good news of Village Baptist Church too.

January 16, 2000

Jesus Was Baptized
Mark 1:9-15 (NRSV)

In those days Jesus came from Nazareth of Galilee and was baptized by John in the Jordan. And just as he was coming up out of the water, he saw the heavens torn apart and the Spirit descending like a dove on him. And a voice came from heaven, "You are my Son, the Beloved; with you I am well pleased." And the Spirit immediately drove him out into the wilderness. He was in the wilderness forty days, tempted by Satan; and he was with the wild beasts; and the angels waited on him.

Now after John was arrested, Jesus came to Galilee, proclaiming the good news of God, and saying, "The time is fulfilled, and the kingdom of God has come near; repent, and believe in the good news."

One of the most difficult phone calls I had to make after our church building burned three Saturdays ago was to my parents in Texas. As you know, my mother was diagnosed with ovarian cancer last October, and after surgery she began a series of chemotherapy treatments that will continue for several more months. I didn't want to call and add to their worries, but I had to tell them about the church. So I was somewhat relieved when my father answered the phone. After asking him how Mom was, I got right to the point. "I have some bad news," I said. "The church burned down today." Of course it was a shock to him, but I didn't see any merit in beating around the bush. I had something important to tell him, so I might as well say it at the outset.

Unlike my phone call to my parents, Mark began his message with good news, not bad news. But like my phone call, he had something important to say, and he said it at the outset. He didn't beat around the bush. He said his good news was about Jesus Christ, the Son of God. But as he began his story about Jesus, the first thing he told us was not what we would expect. When you are telling the story of someone's life, you usually begin at the beginning. But Mark didn't do that. Mark didn't tell us anything about how Jesus was born, or who his parents were, or what his ancestry was. Mark didn't even go back as far as Jesus's childhood. Rather, Mark began his story almost in mid-sentence, with Jesus as a grown man. As Hershel Hobbs said in his Exposition of the Gospel of Mark, "Jesus springs full-grown into the arena of history." And the first thing that Mark told us about Jesus is that Jesus was baptized.

You may recall from last week that Mark began his Gospel by introducing John the Baptist, or John the baptizer as he is called in the New Revised Standard Version. John was like a prophet preaching in the wilderness, "proclaiming a baptism for the repentance of sins." Dressed in a camel skin with a leather belt around his waist, subsisting on a diet of locusts and wild honey, John was not exactly the poster boy for the local chamber of commerce. He was a radical, a wild-eyed fanatic, who attracted the curious and the truly repentant to his baptismal rituals in the Jordan River. This was highly unorthodox. Baptism was not unknown in the Jewish religion. Gentile proselytes might be baptized upon their conversion to the Jewish faith. But the idea of baptism as a sign of repentance for Jews was new. For orthodox Judaism the way to express repentance was to go to the temple and offer a sacrifice under the auspices of the priests. John had no official credentials. It was under his own auspices that John set up shop in the wilderness and baptized in the Jordan. It's no wonder that John got into trouble with the authorities. He was meddling in their business and jeopardizing their livelihoods as well. If all people had to do to repent was to take a dip in the river, the income from temple sacrifices would go way down.

Incredibly, Jesus began his public ministry by being baptized by John. It doesn't seem like a very prudent thing to do. You would think Jesus would want to get started in the best possible light. It's like the presidential campaigns in Iowa and New Hampshire. All the candidates are looking for endorsements from the political establishment. The last thing they want is to be identified with some wacko, fringe group. But Jesus didn't go after the endorsement of the political and religious establishment. Jesus identified himself with a rogue preacher who had absolutely no political connections. And to make matters even more confusing, Jesus was baptized by John, just like everyone else.

To be honest about it, the baptism of Jesus is confusing. What sense did it make for Jesus to be baptized? He was without sin. He had no need to repent. Why, then, did Jesus begin his public ministry by being baptized by John? And why did Mark tell us about the baptism of Jesus as the very first thing he told us that Jesus did?

Many of you know that I am originally from Texas. Growing up in Fort Worth, I was a Dallas Cowboys fan. I hated the Washington Redskins. But then we moved to this area, and I was surrounded by Redskins fans. For a couple of years, I held out, secretly rooting for the Cowboys. Then, when George Allen was no longer the Redskins' coach, I had a change of heart. I figured that as long as I was living around Washington, I ought to do the things that Washingtonians do, which was root for the Redskins. Shortly after that, Joe Gibbs became the Redskins' coach, and you know the rest of the story. I've been a Redskins fan ever since.

One of the reasons I became a Redskins fan was to better identify with the people I was ministering to as a pastor. That may be part of the reason that Jesus was baptized by John. It was a means of identifying with the message that John was preaching. It was a way of Jesus saying, "What John is about and what I am about are the same thing. We are both calling people back to God."

Baptism is still a powerful way of calling people back to God. Jesus did not sin, so Jesus did not need to repent. But Jesus was baptized as a sign of his identifying with God. This is still the mission of the church—calling people back to God.

After the fire I was deluged with calls from people offering help. I soon discovered that some people were offering help out of the goodness of their hearts, and others were offering help with a profit motive in mind. There were people who wanted to intercede for us with the insurance company so they could get a cut of the settlement. There were people who had fundraising plans they wanted to present to the church. There were building contractors and demolition contractors who hoped to make a profit from our misfortune. It took a bit of discernment to sort through dozens and dozens of offers of help to determine which were really offering to help and which were out to get money.

Thankfully, it is not my job to discern people's hearts. I cannot say who is close to God and who is self-centered and self-serving. Our mission is to do what Jesus did—to serve others for God and to call them back into relationship with God.

Jesus' baptism was a way of saying he was not going to live a life that was self-centered and self-serving. Rather, his baptism was a way of saying that he was going to live a life dedicated to God. That's why Jesus saw the heavens open and the Spirit descend like a dove. That's why he heard the voice from heaven saying, "You are my Beloved Son, and I am well pleased with you." God was pleased with Jesus because Jesus had given his life to his Father in heaven. God is pleased with us when we give our lives to the Father too.

Notice one more thing, however. The baptism of Jesus did not put him on easy street. It didn't take away all his problems. It didn't mean he would live happily ever after. Immediately after he was baptized, Jesus was tested. He was tempted to compromise his trust in God and to weaken his dedication to God.

Like that temptation in the wilderness following his baptism, times of testing come to every Christian. The Christian life is not without obstacles, problems, hardships, and temptations. Looking back, we may very well see the destruction of our building as a time of testing for our church. It may be a time of testing our dedication to God. But as the angels of God ministered to Jesus in the wilderness, we can be sure that God will minister to us during this wilderness experience. Indeed, the fact that we are here this morning in this church building is a sign that God already is providing for our needs.

So Jesus was baptized as a sign of his dedication to God. It may be that some of you here today would be baptized as a sign of your faith in Jesus Christ. We don't have a baptistry in this church, but I have made arrangements with another church for a baptismal service on a Sunday afternoon in the near future. Many of you have been baptized, but maybe you would rededicate your life to God. I can think of no better time to do that, as we begin to rebuild our church building.

Jesus was baptized as a sign of his commitment to God. That's the first thing that Mark told us about Jesus. Maybe that's the first thing that we need to think about too.

January 23, 2000

The Source of My Strength
Mark 1:32-39 (NRSV)

That evening, at sunset, they brought to him all who were sick or possessed with demons. And the whole city was gathered around the door. And he cured many who were sick with various diseases, and cast out many demons; and he would not permit the demons to speak, because they knew him. In the morning, while it was still very dark, he got up and went out to a deserted place, and there he prayed. And Simon and his companions hunted for him. When they found him, they said to him, "Everyone is searching for you." He answered, "Let us go on to the neighboring towns, so that I may proclaim the message there also; for that is what I came out to do." And he went throughout Galilee, proclaiming the message in their synagogues and casting out demons.

Richard Foster was fresh out of seminary and ready to conquer the world for God. He was appointed to a small church in a thriving region of Southern California. He could hardly wait to get started. Foster was only momentarily sobered when the former pastor of the church, upon learning of his appointment, put his arm on his shoulder and said, "Well, Foster, now it's your turn to be in the desert!"

"No way," Foster thought to himself. "This church will become a shining light set on a hill. The people will literally flood in." After three months, the young pastor was almost ready to quit. He had given that tiny congregation everything he knew and then some, and it had done them no good. So much for a "shining light on a hill." He was spiritually bankrupt, and he knew it. His problem was more than having something to say from Sunday to Sunday. His problem was that what he did say had no power to help people. His messages had no substance, no depth. The people were starving for a word from God, and he had nothing to give.

It was out of this situation of desperation that Richard Foster discovered a source of strength that would change his ministry and change his life. It began with an influx of genuinely needy people into the small congregation. Normally you would think that a pastor would be happy to have anybody new join his church. But these were high-maintenance people. These were people with difficult personalities and deep-seated problems. These were people who needed substantive pastoral care. Sensing his lack of spiritual depth, Forster began to read the writings of the spiritual giants of the

Christian faith—people like Augustine, and Francis of Assisi, and Julian of Norwich, and many others. Foster sensed that these ancient Christian writers had a substance to their faith that he longed for. As he read these classics of Christian devotional literature, he discovered that these "saints" knew God in a way that he did not. As Foster put it, "They experienced Jesus as the defining reality of their lives. They possessed a flaming vision of God that blinded them to all competing loyalties. They experienced life built on the Rock" (*Celebration of Discipline*, p. xiv).

As Foster continued to read and to soak in the stories of these men and women who were on fire for God, he began to desire this kind of life for himself. And that desire led to seeking, and that seeking led to finding. What Foster discovered is that a deeper life with God doesn't just happen by accident. He discovered that the common denominator of all those great Christians of the past was that they devoted themselves to certain spiritual disciplines, like meditation and prayer and fasting and Bible study. Foster called these the "inward spiritual disciplines." Foster discovered that through these disciplines of the spiritual life, the great Christians of all ages have been able to move beneath the surface level of daily life into the depths of the life of the spirit. Foster is not talking about some otherworldly mysticism here. He's not talking about the super-saints and spiritual giants who spend all their days in meditation and prayer. Foster discovered that the source of spiritual strength is the same for everybody, including average men and women who have jobs, and care for children, and mow lawns, and wash dishes. The primary requirement for a deeper Christian life, Foster says, is simply a longing after God.

Through the centuries Christians have discovered that certain spiritual disciplines can open the door for a deeper and more fulfilling relationship with God. It's not that meditation and prayer and fasting and Bible study guarantee intimacy with God or guarantee spiritual growth, but they open the door for God's spirit to come in. The disciplines of the spiritual life allow us to place ourselves before God in such a way that God's grace can come into our lives.

In his book *Celebration of Discipline*, Foster uses the analogy of a television set. Broadcast signals are filling the airwaves all the time, but unless the television set is equipped with an antenna to receive them, and unless the television set is plugged in and turned on and tuned in to the proper channel, the set will never receive the signals.

A few years ago Linda gave me a satellite dish for Christmas. Television reception through an antenna is notoriously bad for most of the homes around here. Some days the Baltimore stations would come in better, and some days the Washington stations would come in better, and some days none of them would come in well. We tried cable for a while, but the cost kept going up, and the quality kept going down. So a few years ago Linda gave me a satellite dish, and it's been great. As long as the receiver is turned on and the channel is tuned in, the reception is excellent. There are hundreds of stations available through the satellite dish, if you're willing to pay for them. Those hundreds of stations are beaming satellite signals twenty-four hours a day. But to receive the signals, you've got to have the right equipment, and pay the subscription fee, and point your antenna in the right direction. The spiritual disciplines of meditation and prayer and fasting and Bible study help us to receive the signals that God has been sending all along.

So where did Christians get the idea they needed to engage in spiritual disciplines? They got it from the Bible and from the example of great men and women of faith that have gone before. Preeminently, we see the example of living a spiritually disciplined life in Jesus. Even though he was the Son of God, Jesus regularly meditated and prayed and fasted and read God's word. Our scripture for today provides a window into the spiritual life of Jesus, which was a part of his everyday life.

It was near the beginning of his public ministry, and Jesus already was making quite a name for himself. Jesus had healed a man of an unclean spirit, and his fame had begun to spread throughout the region. He was staying at Simon Peter's house in Capernaum, and by the end of the day, the whole city had gathered at the door. Jesus cured many who were sick, and he cast out many demons. Only with the falling darkness of night did the people go home. Early in the morning, while it was still dark, Jesus got up and went out to a deserted place to pray. Sometime after that, Simon Peter and the other disciples came looking for him. When they found him, they said, "Everyone is searching for you." The implication was that they wanted Jesus to go back into town and continue healing people and casting out demons and doing other miracles. Perhaps a crowd had already gathered once again at Peter's house. But Jesus didn't seize the moment as they had expected. Jesus didn't go back into the city to take advantage of his rising popularity. Instead, he said, "Let us go on to the neighboring towns, so that I may proclaim the message there also; for this is what I came to do."

Jesus got up early in the morning to go off by himself to pray. That was the source of his strength—Jesus maintained a vital relationship with God. I'm not a morning person myself. Because I have a lot of nighttime meetings, I have to program my body so that I am awake and alert at night. Then I go home, and it takes me an hour or so to unwind. So some nights I don't go to bed until 11:30 p.m. or so. Thus, early mornings are not a good time for me. Some of you, on the other hand, go to bed early and get up early. Like Jesus, some of you get up well before sunrise. Apparently Jesus was a morning person. He got up before dawn to spend some time with God in prayer.

The point is not so much *when* we pray, but *that* we pray. Prayer is our vital link with God. We can pray almost anywhere and anytime. The point is that we set aside some time to pray. Each of us needs to find our own time and place. Find a place that is quiet and free from interruptions. If possible, turn off the cell phone. It's worth being "out of touch" for a few minutes to allow yourself to be "in touch" with God.

In his study of the great Christians of the past, Richard Foster discovered that prayer was not some habit tacked on to the periphery of their lives; prayer was at the center of their lives. Adoniram Judson, one of the first American Baptist missionaries, spent most of his adult life on the mission field in Burma. Seven times a day Judson would stop whatever he was doing and spend a few moments in prayer. He began at dawn, then stopped to pray at nine, noon, three, six, nine, and right before he went to sleep. Maybe that sounds extreme, but for Judson his prayer life was the source of his strength. So it has been for all the great men and women of God.

An example like Judson may be more likely to discourage us than encourage us. "I could never discipline myself to pray that often," we say to ourselves. But God doesn't expect us to become spiritual giants overnight. God meets us where we are right now and moves us into a deeper life with him. Someone who jogs a few miles every now and then is not ready to run a marathon. But over time the occasional jogger can become more disciplined in his or her training. The same is true of prayer. Maybe a more realistic goal for you would be to begin by setting aside a minute—one minute—to pray every day. Then, over time, maybe you could increase the duration or the frequency of your prayer time.

Prayer is talking to God, but prayer is also listening, not with our ears, but with our hearts. I think that's what Jesus was doing early that morning when he went off by himself to pray. As a result of listening, Jesus received God's directions for his ministry and his life. Circumstances might have suggested that Jesus go back into Capernaum and continue the work from the day before. A crowd was already beginning to assemble—he had a ready-made audience! But Jesus didn't listen to circumstance—Jesus listened to God in prayer. And God was telling him to go on to other towns and villages and take the message there.

Imagine this—God cares about the direction of our lives too! But God will not force us to go anywhere we do not choose to go. God loves us too much to control us against our will. Rather, God wants to lead and guide us, but only if we allow him to lead and guide us.

Maybe God is leading you this morning to give your life to Jesus Christ, to accept him as your savior and Lord, to follow him as a believer in baptism. Maybe God is leading you to join this church. Maybe God is leading you to deepen your spiritual life, to commit yourself to spend time every day in prayer. In just a moment I'm going to invite you to pray. Will you listen to what God has to say?

January 27, 2002

Another Step in the Journey
Joshua 4:1-7 (NRSV)

When the entire nation had finished crossing over the Jordan, the LORD said to Joshua: "Select twelve men from the people, one from each tribe, and command them, 'Take twelve stones from here out of the middle of the Jordan, from the place where the priests' feet stood, carry them over with you, and lay them down in the place where you camp tonight.'" Then Joshua summoned the twelve men from the Israelites, whom he had appointed, one from each tribe. Joshua said to them, "Pass on before the ark of the LORD your God into the middle of the Jordan, and each of you take up a stone on his shoulder, one for each of the tribes of the Israelites, so that this may be a sign among you. When your children ask in time to come, 'What do those stones mean to you?' then you shall tell them that the waters of the Jordan were cut off in front of the ark of the covenant of the LORD. When it crossed over the Jordan, the waters of the Jordan were cut off. So these stones shall be to the Israelites a memorial forever."

It had been forty years of waiting, forty years of wandering in the wilderness, forty years of looking longingly toward the promised land. Finally, after forty years, Joshua led the people of Israel across the Jordan River to the land of Canaan. Joshua, sensing the momentous nature of the occasion, organized a special service of commemoration as they reached the other side. He instructed the people to select from among them twelve men, one from each tribe, to be their representatives. Each of these twelve was to pick up a stone from the middle of the Jordan River and carry that stone into the promised land. Like the crossing of their ancestors from captivity in Egypt, the waters of the Jordan were miraculously held back as the people crossed over. The twelve men picked up their twelve stones, and when they had reached the camp, they stacked the stones into some kind of an altar, a place of worship, that would be a memorial forever for what the Lord had done. In future generations when their children and their children's children would ask "What do these stones mean?" they would tell the story. The stones would remind them how the Lord had rescued them from bondage in Egypt, and how the Lord had led them safely through the wilderness, and finally how the Lord had delivered them into the promised land.

We have not been wandering in the wilderness for forty years, but at times we wondered if we would ever see the promised land. Thirty-four months ago our church building was destroyed by a devastating fire. Some of you were here that Saturday, January 8, 2000, when the building burned. You stood with me in the parking lot and watched in shock and horror and disbelief and grief as the firefighters fought to contain the blaze. After the fire was put out, a fire department spokesman estimated that the building had suffered $350,000 in damage. Oh, that his estimate had been accurate! In reality, it was three times that much, and the building was destroyed. Some of the walls were left standing, some of the contents were saved, but the building was a total loss. When it came time to rebuild, about all that could be reused were the concrete slab and the exterior brick walls along the backside of the east wing and the sanctuary. Virtually everything else had to be replaced or rebuilt. Some of the bricks from the original building are cemented in place in this new structure. Some of you helped to clean the bricks that were recovered from the rubble, and those bricks were added to the sanctuary walls to accommodate a higher roofline. So everything was not lost, but most of the building was. Except for the original concrete slab and a few exterior brick walls, this is a new building, incorporating the old, but mostly new.

The Sunday after the fire we worshiped in the Pointer Ridge fire hall. We gathered first on the parking lot in front of our burned building to pray.

Then we went over to the fire hall to continue our worship there. The media were here in full force. I got to be on television more than enough for the rest of my life. For a few weeks after the fire, just about everywhere I went, someone recognized me as the pastor whose church had burned. I've had my "fifteen minutes of fame," thank you very much! We deeply appreciate all the publicity we received and the hundreds of expressions of sympathy.

While the church was still burning, I started to try to find a place for us to meet on Sunday (the next day). I had Linda on her cell phone calling United Parish and Temple Solel to see if there was any chance we could meet in either of their buildings. United Parish would have been happy for us to use their building Sunday afternoon, but Sunday morning was not available. Temple Solel was using their building on Sunday morning as well. Then one of the firefighters said we could use the fire hall. It was the first of many gracious offers of hospitality. The week after the fire we started looking for a place to meet. We checked out schools and hotels and community centers and empty storefronts. Nothing looked promising. Then I got a handwritten note in the mail from Bowie Alliance Church. It was like dozens of other notes of sympathy that were pouring in, except this note made an offer I could hardly believe. They were inviting us to use their building on Sunday mornings, and they would even alter their schedule to accommodate us. It was like a gift from heaven. No, it *was* a gift from heaven.

Now, thirty-four months later, we are finally back home. What have we learned from our wilderness wandering, and what do we discern to be our calling as we occupy the place that God has provided for us? Let me share a few observations.

First, we have learned that God is faithful. On the day of the fire, a verse of Scripture was planted in my mind, and it became the theme verse for our displacement, Romans 8:28: "We know that all things work together for good for those who love God, who are called according to his purposes." At the time it was hard to see what good God would bring out of that tragedy. But now looking back, we can see many evidences of how God has been at work to bring good out of bad. This beautiful new structure is one evidence of God's hand at work. All of you here are another evidence of God's hand at work. Yes, the first thing we have learned, maybe the most important thing we have learned, is that God is faithful.

A second lesson we have learned is that people can be incredibly generous. When our building burned, we had about $3,000 in our building fund.

Immediately, donations began to pour in. The first donation came from Rev. Charles Galbreath, whose church, Bowie New Life Assembly, was meeting in the Pointer Ridge Elementary School at the time. They didn't have a building of their own, but they sent a donation to our building fund as an expression of support. We received donations from former members, from friends and family of church members, and from people in the community who had no connection to our church. Three benefit concerts were organized for the building fund—Cresthill Baptist Church had a praise band concert; Trinity Community Church organized a ChurchAid concert at the amphitheater at Allen Pond and recruited six other churches to participate; and the Tackett sisters, Ginny and Beth, along with Les Owen, presented a Christmas concert at the Latter-day Saints church on Route 3. Temple Solel's seventh-grade class organized a spaghetti dinner; Edna Jamison's granddaughter organized a basket bingo fundraiser in honor of her grandmother to benefit our building fund. A Jewish resident at Collington donated a host of original paintings she had done for auction and sale. And there are many other stories of generosity.

I haven't yet mentioned your generosity. You gave sacrificial, over-and-above gifts to the building fund. You supported yard sales and estate sales and bake sales and eBay auctions and craft fairs and bazaars and many other fundraising projects. You bought keys for a new piano. You donated to showers for the kitchen and the nursery. You gave and gave and gave, and then you gave some more. But it wasn't just the money that got us here. It was the prayers and the encouragement and the support from so many generous, compassionate people.

A third lesson that we have learned is that God has a purpose and a mission for our church. Shortly after the fire, Ron Knode asked the startling question, "Why should Village Baptist Church continue to exist?" Why go through all the trouble of rebuilding? Why not cut our losses and grab whatever insurance money we could and disband? Why endure almost three years of displacement and frustration? The answer is very simple: We are convinced that God has a purpose and a mission for this church. We are convinced that God wants us here, in this building, on this property, in this community, because Village Baptist Church has something to offer in the name of our Lord Jesus Christ.

God has given our church a mission and a purpose because God can use a church like ours. We aren't the biggest church around; we aren't the richest; we aren't the most talented; we aren't the most sophisticated; we aren't a lot of things, but God can use us nonetheless. Here is some of what we are that God can use. We are a church that is centered around Jesus Christ. We proclaim Jesus Christ, crucified for our sins, raised for our salvation, and coming again for our ultimate redemption. Next Sunday we are going to have a believer's baptisms in both services. I wanted to have the baptisms this Sunday, but there wasn't enough time to get everything ready. But next Sunday, our first full Sunday back in our new building, we're going to celebrate the baptism of believers because we are a church centered around Jesus Christ.

We are also an inclusive church. We reserve the right to accept everybody. That doesn't mean we have no moral standards, but it does mean we don't judge people; we leave judgments to God. If you come in sincerity to worship God with us, then you are welcome here. You don't have to fit into some narrow, preconceived mold. You are welcome here, flawed as you are, because all of us are flawed, yet God loves us anyway. We are all sinners saved by God's grace.

We are also a serving church. We are active in worldwide missions and in community ministries. We have partnered with missionaries to reach out to the Gypsy peoples around the world. In less than a month, two of the original missionaries to the Gypsies, T and Kathie Thomas, are coming to be with us. We also have a growing relationship with Christian sisters and brothers in Zimbabwe, Africa. On the local front we support various ministries, such as Martha's Table, Habitat for Humanity, the Bowie Food Pantry, and many more. Our building is in use seven days a week to serve this community. We host an Alcoholics Anonymous group, two Chemically Dependent Anonymous groups, four Girl Scout and Brownie groups, mental health counselor Rose Schrott, and most recently the Mitchellville Community School of the Arts. This is a serving church, and we continually look for more opportunities to serve others in Christ's name.

This is also a learning church. We read and study the Bible often. We have an active Sunday school program with Bible study classes for all age groups. We encourage each other to approach the Bible with open minds and open hearts.

This is also a church characterized by fellowship and friendships and love. We see ourselves as an extended church family. Everyone is important; everyone is valued. We have a deacon family ministry plan that links every active participant in our church with a deacon. One of the biggest improvements in our new building is a fellowship hall and commercial-style kitchen.

We want to start having dinners and other social events as soon as possible so we can strengthen our fellowship with one another and reach out to newcomers who come to see this new place.

The fire destroyed a building, but it did not destroy our church. The essential qualities remain. The day after the fire a reporter interviewed Maury Sweetin. Maury told the reporter that it was just "another step in the journey." Then Maury went on to predict that our church would survive the fire and go on to even more meaningful ministry and service in the future. That is what lies before us, now that we are finally back in our building—more meaningful ministry and service.

When Joshua instructed the people of Israel to collect twelve stones as a memorial, he wanted some tangible way to remind the people of their past and also to call them into the future. One day shortly after the fire, Jo Reiter snuck up to the ruins and dug a brick out of the rubble to take home as a remembrance. That brick served as a reminder of what had been, but also as a sign of hope for what is to come. Seizing Jo's idea, I gathered some bricks from the old building and stacked them on the old Communion table at the back of this sanctuary. There are thirty-four bricks back on the table, one for each month of our displacement. They are both reminders of what was and signs of hope for what will be. This morning I invite anyone who wants one to take a brick from the old building. If you take all the old bricks off the table, there are more brick pieces in boxes in my office. Let the old bricks be a reminder to you of what this church stands for and what God calls this church to be. Then, when your children or your children's children ask you, "What does this brick mean?" you can tell them the story. It's a story that is not over yet—not by a long shot.

Today is a great day, but it's not the end. It's just another step in the journey. We're home, but we're not really home yet, if you know what I mean. The journey continues. "I am bound for the promised land, I am bound for the promised land. Oh, who will come and go with me, I am bound for the promised land." ("On Jordan's Stormy Banks," *Celebrating Grace*, p. 556).

November 10, 2002

Chapter 8

2003-2010

The rebuilt structure changed the look of the church building, and the years that followed changed the look of the congregation. Returning to our "church home" on Mitchellville Road was both exhilarating and sobering. It was exhilarating to occupy a new church building; it was sobering to return with fewer congregants than we had before the fire. As I said in the last chapter, we had rebuilt the building; now we had to rebuild the congregation.

The family that had worshiped with us for the first time in the fire house on that first Sunday after the fire were the Larsons, Don and Thelma and their adult daughter, Heather. They came that first Sunday after the fire, and they kept coming as we worshiped in the Bowie Alliance Church building. Sadly, Don died the following year, in 2001. But Thelma and Heather kept coming. In fact, Heather was baptized during the first baptism in the rebuilt church.

I don't remember exactly when it started, but Thelma appointed herself as greeter in the new building. She would stand inside the front entrance and greet people with a hearty "hello," and a big smile, and an even bigger hug. She would hug everybody, members and visitors alike, unless they preferred a handshake or a wave. That set the tone for the welcoming spirit that infused the loyalists who remained. We had lost about a third of our congregation during the almost three years of displacement, but the two-thirds who were still with us were really with us. Thelma's hugs were symbolic of how all of us felt. We were going to "hug" anybody who came our way.

Visitors did come, and they were welcomed, and many of them joined. Reflecting the increasing diversity of the community, the congregation became much more diverse. When Linda and I came to Village in 1985, we had two African-American members, both married to white spouses. Their biracial children were the only other "minorities" at Village. By the time of the fire in 2000, a handful of African-American families had joined, but it was still a predominantly white church.

My how that changed after we occupied the rebuilt church! By the time I retired at the end of 2017, the congregation on Sunday morning was roughly

50/50, black and white, with Latinos and Asians too. Immigrants from Kenya, Uganda, Nigeria, Cameroon, Bahamas, Jamaica, Canada, Chile, Guyana, Philippines, India, and other countries enriched our fellowship. I wish I could take credit for the transformation, but I had no secret formula or brilliant strategy. We just tried to welcome everybody.

Beginning in 2003 we began to host a series of emissaries from the Baptist Convention of Zimbabwe, under the auspices of the Alliance of Baptists. First, Rev. Champion Chasara and Mrs. Joice Ngozo; then, Rev. Dennis Dhula and Mr. Elias Maponga; later, Rev. John Mazvigadza; later, Rev. Champion Chasara again with his new wife, Isabel. We also welcomed Rev. Kingsley Perrera of the Sri Lankan Baptist Sangamaya and Mr. Paul Montacute and Dr. Denton Lotz and Dr. Neville Callam of the Baptist World Alliance. CBF field personnel visited and spoke at Village almost every year: Frank and Cindy Dawson, T and Kathie Thomas, Ralph and Tammy Stocks, Eddie and Macarena Aldape, Darrell and Kathy Smith, Karen Morrow, Earl and Jane Martin, two couples serving in high security-risk areas, as well as Bonnie Dixon from Journey Partners, and Katherine and Rolf Buehler from Wycliffe Bible Translators.

Villagers began making mission trips: to Appalachian Outreach in Tennessee; to Detroit, Michigan; to Baton Rouge, Louisiana, for the Baptist Build Blitz; to Samaritan Ministry in Knoxville, Tennessee; to Kenya and China with Buckner International. In 2005 Linda and I went with Mark and Michele Miles to the Baptist World Congress in Birmingham, England.

In 2009 Village raised funds for a church building in Bamunkumbit, Cameroon. The pastor, Rev. Chenyi Marcel, then asked if Village would provide him with a scholarship to attend the Cameroon Baptist Theological Seminary in Ndu. It was the beginning of a seven-year partnership that would support him and eventually his wife and two children.

In 2010 Linda and I attended the Baptist World Congress in Honolulu, Hawaii. While there, we met two leaders from the Cameroon Baptist Convention, Mrs. Elizabeth Samandi, president of Cameroon Baptist Women; and the general secretary, Rev. Donald Ndichafah. We told them about our seminary student in Cameroon, and both agreed to meet with him upon their return. Later, Mrs. Samandi and Rev. Ndichafah spoke at Village during trips to the United States.

Other guest preachers during those early years in the new building included Dr. Morris Vickers, a former director of missions and member of our congregation; Dr. Stan Hastey from the Alliance of Baptists; Dr. Tom Rogerson from Centerpointe Counseling; Dr. Jere Allen and Dr. Jeffrey Haggray and Dr. James Langley from the D.C. Baptist Convention; Rev. Brent Walker and Mrs. Holly Hollman from the Baptist Joint Committee for Religious Liberty; Rev. Jerry Bucker, retired Baptist campus minister at the University of Maryland; Rev. Elizabeth Evans Hagan; Dr. C. J. Malloy Jr.; Dr. Daniel Vestal of the Cooperative Baptist Fellowship; Rev. Gary Javens; and former Village pastor Dr. Dan Ivins.

All this is to say that the preaching at Village was enriched by many guest preachers, representing many of our mission partners. As a "solo practitioner," I still did the lion's share of the preaching. But my efforts were tremendously augmented by an array of outstanding proclaimers, and our fellowship was richer for it.

One in Christ Jesus
Galatians 3:27-29 (NRSV)

As many of you as were baptized into Christ have clothed yourselves with Christ. There is no longer Jew or Greek, there is no longer slave or free, there is no longer male and female; for all of you are one in Christ Jesus. And if you belong to Christ, then you are Abraham's offspring, heirs according to the promise.

I was born in 1951. Go ahead—do the math! I will turn sixty-five this year. To some of you, that makes me an old soul. To others of you, that makes me your contemporary. To a few of you, that makes me a young whippersnapper. Well, maybe not so young. Anyway, the point is that I am old enough to remember Rev. Dr. Martin Luther King Jr. I never met him or saw him in person, but I remember him. He was one of the major figures of my youth. I remember some of the significant events of his life, because they were important for our time.

When I was growing up in Texas in the 1950s and 60s, our society was even more racially divided than it is today. I never had an African-American classmate in school until my junior year in high school. I had Latino classmates, and Asian-American classmates, and Jewish classmates, but no African-American classmates. There were no African Americans in my Boy Scout troop. There were no African Americans on my Little League baseball team. There were no African Americans in our youth group at church. There were no African Americans in my neighborhood. Our society was far more segregated than it is today. I remember two water fountains in the grocery store, one labeled "White" and the other labeled "Colored." I don't remember many people of color shopping at that store, but there was a water fountain for them in case they did. One day when no one was looking, I took a drink out of the "Colored" fountain.

The only African American I knew personally when I was growing up was the lady who cleaned our house one day a week and my grandmother's house another day a week. She was the only African American who was invited to my sister's wedding in 1966. Only after I started working at Snow White Laundry while in high school did I meet other African Americans and get to know them on a personal level. I remember Freddie, who swept the floors, and a lady named Theodoris, who ironed shirts and pants. But I really didn't have any African-American friends until I got to college.

That's the way our society was in the 1950s and 60s—it was racially divided. I remember hearing about the March on Washington in 1963 and the "I Have a Dream" speech. I certainly remember when Dr. King was assassinated and the riots that followed. I talked with Freddie, the African-American man who cleaned the building at Snow White laundry. He was as perplexed about the rioting as I was. Sure, there was anger after Dr. King was killed. But what good did the rioting do, we both wondered. I admit, I was reacting as someone who had enjoyed "white privilege" his entire life. The problem was, I didn't realize I was privileged. I did not understand what it was like to be discriminated against.

I began to understand a little bit the summer after my freshman year in college. A friend and I spent the summer doing mission work in a small Baptist church in Cheney, Washington, near Spokane. There was an interracial couple in the church who invited us for dinner in their home on several occasions. The husband was black, and his wife was white. He was originally from Mississippi. The couple was living in Cheney, Washington, because he was on the faculty at Eastern Washington State University. They told us that when they traveled back to Mississippi to visit his family, they had to be very careful and keep a low profile. This was in 1970, and interracial couples were not welcome in many places in the South.

The summer after my sophomore year in college, I was youth director in a church in a transitional neighborhood in Memphis, Tennessee. The church was trying to reach the kids in its community, but integrated church youth groups were not common in 1971. The summer after my junior year in college, I was youth minister at a church in Waco, Texas. There were African-American kids living in the community not too far from the church, but it was hard to attract those kids to a predominantly white church. The summer after I graduated from college, before I went to seminary, I was still youth minister at the church in Waco. My roommate for that summer was an African-American friend I had met at the church. I never told my parents I had a black roommate that summer, because I wasn't sure how they would have reacted in 1973.

After college I went to seminary in Louisville, Kentucky. One summer I did youth work at an inner-city Baptist church. That summer I coached a baseball team of youth from the neighborhood. We played other youth teams from churches in the local association. Ours was the only team that had all black players and a white coach. There were a few African-American students at the seminary, but not many. I did become friends with several seminary students from Africa. It was only after I moved to Maryland in 1977 to serve a church in Silver Spring that I was part of church that was significantly integrated.

I share this personal history because, like many of you, I have lived through major changes in race relations in our country. We have come a long way, but we have a long way yet to go. The sin of racism is still a blight upon our culture. Racial inequality is still pervasive in many areas. The election of a black president did not automatically change race relations for the better. In some respects it seems like racial divisions have gotten worse.

That's why what we are doing in this church is so important. We are creating a new paradigm of race relations. When I came to Village as pastor thirty-one years ago, this community and this church were predominantly white, although we did have a couple of African-American members and their children. But as our community has become more diverse, our congregation has become more diverse. That's a credit to the people who began this church and to the pastors who came before me. Former pastor Dan Ivins, who grew up in segregated Tennessee, remembered seeing signs in businesses which said, "We reserve the right to refuse service to anyone." Dan turned that around and coined the slogan "We reserve the right to accept everyone."

I think Paul would have agreed with that slogan. Paul wrote in his letter to the Galatians, "There is no longer Jew or Greek, there is no longer slave or free, there is no longer male and female," for we are all one in Christ Jesus.

I think Dr. King would be pleased to see a church that reserves the right to accept everyone. That's what Jesus did. He accepted all kinds of people, even those people the religious leaders of his day would not accept. Jesus came for all people, and he died for all people, to show every one of us how much God loves us. And Jesus came to show us that God wants us to love each other too.

So happy birthday to Dr. King, our Baptist brother! We are trying to continue what he gave his life for—to see people not by the color of their skin, but by the content of their character. We are all one in Christ Jesus. Can anybody say "Amen"?

January 17, 2016

Freedom in Christ
Galatians 3:23-29 (NRSV)

Now before faith came, we were imprisoned and guarded under the law until faith would be revealed. Therefore the law was our disciplinarian until Christ came, so that we might be justified by faith. But now that faith has come, we are no longer subject to a disciplinarian, for in Christ Jesus you are all children of God through faith. As many of you as were baptized into Christ have clothed yourselves with Christ. There is no longer Jew or Greek, there is no longer slave or free, there is no longer male and female; for all of you are one in Christ Jesus. And if you belong to Christ, then you are Abraham's offspring, heirs according to the promise.

My friend Gary Javens is a graduate of Eastern Baptist College, just outside of Philadelphia. It's now called Eastern University. He is also a graduate of Eastern Baptist Theological Seminary, also outside of Philadelphia. It's now called Palmer Theological Seminary. Both schools are affiliated with the American Baptist Churches, USA. But over the years both schools dropped "Baptist" from their names. The college became Eastern University to appeal to a broader constituency. It still maintains a Christian identity, but it strives to attract students from a variety of backgrounds, not just Baptists. The seminary changed its name in 2005 in honor of a large bequest. The seminary still has a Baptist identity, but it too wants to attract students from a larger pool of churches.

Some Baptist churches have dropped the word "Baptist" from their names. Among older churches in the D.C. Baptist Convention, First Baptist Church, Bethesda, is now simply Church in Bethesda. Riverside Baptist Church in the

District is now simply Riverside Church. First Baptist Church of Wheaton is now Streams of Hope Church. Many newer churches within the D.C. Baptist Convention have never had "Baptist" in their names. For example, there are Salem Gospel Ministries, 3 Strands Community Church, Balm in Gilead Ministry, Beloved Community Church, Christ Our Shepherd House of Worship Ministries, The Church of the Restoration, Evangelical Missionary Church, Liberation Temple, Lighthouse Christian Church, Olive Branch Community Church, Redeemed Christian Worship Center, Word for Life Church Ministries, International Christian Church, New Life Congregation, Dayspring Community Church, Johenning Temple of Praise, Metropolitan Outreach Ministries, and Rivers of Joy Bible Fellowship Church. Whew! These are all Baptist churches, but none of them have "Baptist" in their name. What's going on here? Are they ashamed to be identified as Baptist? Perhaps!

Of course, one motivation for removing a denominational label is to appeal to a wider audience. After our building burned in 2000, we shared worship space with the Bowie Alliance Church. Their building is still there down the street, but you could drive up and down Mitchellville Road all day and not find Bowie Alliance Church. A few years ago they changed their name to Christ Community Church. They are still affiliated with the Christian and Missionary Alliance denomination, but you would never know it from their name. Some Baptist churches think the word "Baptist" does more harm than good. The name "Baptist" conjures up negative stereotypes in some people's minds. And for good reason! Those fanatics from Kansas who protest at military funerals call themselves Baptists. We certainly don't want to be associated with them. My friend Jerry Buckner said that when he was the Baptist campus minister at the University of Maryland, he found that the name "Baptist" closed more doors than it opened. Some university administrators associated Baptists with religious zealots and proselytizers.

The truth is that some of the negative images that Baptists have been given are well-deserved. Baptists don't have a reputation of being the most tolerant or easygoing or fun-loving people. I graduated from Baylor University, the largest and one of the oldest Baptist colleges in the world (which, by the way, never did have "Baptist" in its name). When I enrolled at Baylor, there were a lot of activities that were prohibited. Alcohol was not allowed on campus, of course, but neither was dancing. Girls were not allowed to wear shorts on campus, except in gym class. There were no coeducational dormitories, nor were male and female students allowed to visit one another's dorm rooms. Female students had a strict curfew in their dorms. Male students didn't have a curfew, but without the girls there wasn't much point in staying out late. Sororities and fraternities were not allowed to have their own houses, and wild parties were out of the question. It was a rather restrictive atmosphere for a college campus in the 1970s, but that's the way Baptists were back then. There was almost a puritanical quality to it.

That's understandable, because the Baptists and the Puritans grew out of the same movement. In fact, most of the early Baptists came out of the Puritan church. And the Puritans were not exactly the "life of the party." Remember, it was the Puritans who banned the celebration of Christmas in Boston in the seventeenth century. It was the Puritans who hauled you before the magistrate for missing Sunday church services. It was the Puritans who passed laws banning secular entertainments, such as games of chance and, heaven forbid, maypoles. There was a restrictive atmosphere in Puritan ethics that some of the Baptists inherited.

The Puritans didn't call themselves "Puritans." They called themselves "the godly." It's not surprising that those who called themselves "the godly" would want to force their morality on everyone else. It is somewhat ironic that the Puritans who came to the New World seeking religious freedom were unwilling to grant it to others. But some Puritans recognized the incongruity of wanting religious freedom for themselves and denying it to everyone else. Thomas Helwys in England and Roger Williams in America left the Puritan church because they believed that governments had no business telling people what to believe or how to worship. Helwys and Williams were so radical in their commitment to religious liberty that they rejected infant baptism because an infant could not make a voluntary faith commitment. For their trouble, Helwys was thrown into Newgate Prison, where he would perish, and Roger Williams was banned from Boston and expelled from Massachusetts. Roger Williams eventually founded the colony of Rhode Island and the first Baptist church in America in a place he called Providence.

So although Baptists inherited some of the Puritan ethical DNA, they became a distinct movement based on the radical idea of complete religious liberty. That radical idea had two logical corollaries: the voluntary baptism of believers only (not babies) and the separation of church and state. From the outset, Baptists wanted to do more than "purify" the Church of England. Baptists, above all, wanted to follow Christ according to the dictates of their own consciences. They wanted to be guided by the Bible and by the Holy

Spirit, not human authorities. They were deeply suspicious of church officials who sought to tell them what to do or, even worse, what to believe. So Baptists rejected manmade creeds and hierarchical church organizations and anything that would limit the freedom of the individual soul. At its essence the Baptist faith was a freedom movement, founded in absolute commitment to Jesus Christ and Christ alone. As our friend James Dunn says, "Ain't nobody but Jesus gonna tell me what to believe."

One of the most important recent books about the Baptist faith is a slender volume by Walter Shurden titled *The Baptist Identity: Four Fragile Freedoms*. In the book Shurden asks the question, "What makes a Baptist a Baptist?" Shurden acknowledges that there are all kinds of Baptists and all kinds of Baptist churches. But what are the distinctive beliefs, the ideals, the principles that make a Baptist a Baptist? According to Buddy Shurden, it's all about freedom. He identifies four freedoms that are the hallmarks of the Baptist faith: Bible freedom, soul freedom, church freedom, and religious freedom. Shurden arrived at those four freedoms by studying and analyzing sermons and addresses given by Baptists from around the world at meetings of the Baptist World Alliance since its founding in 1905. Shurden also notes that "the Baptist passion for freedom is a major reason why there is so much diversity in Baptist life." (p. 2). Let me briefly describe what those four fragile freedoms mean.

First, there is Bible freedom. That means that the Bible is central to the life of the individual Christian and central to the life of the church. Under the Lordship of Christ and guided by the Holy Spirit, we are free and obligated to read and study and interpret and follow the scriptures for ourselves. Another Baptist church historian, Penrose St. Amant, described the process as "an open Bible and an open mind." (*Whitsett Journal*, January 1995).

Second, there is soul freedom. That means each individual is free to deal with God directly, as Shurden puts it, without "the imposition of creed, the interference of clergy, or the intervention of civil government." The only intermediary between the individual and God is Jesus.

Three, there is church freedom. That means that each local church is autonomous under the Lordship of Christ. The local Baptist church determines its own membership, elects its own leadership, develops its own style of worship and ministry, and cooperates with other churches and organizations according to the freedom of its own decisions.

Fourth, there is religious freedom. That means that, again quoting James Dunn, "the best thing that government can do for religion is to leave it alone." As the First Amendment to the Constitution says, it is not the business of the government either to establish religion or to prohibit the free exercise of religion.

So the Baptist identity is wrapped up in those four fragile freedoms: Bible freedom, soul freedom, church freedom, and religious freedom. That is what made those early Baptists leave the Puritan church. The Puritans wanted to be free from the Church of England, but they didn't understand the radical freedom that is ours in Christ. Baptists have no pope, no creed, no church hierarchy, because Jesus Christ is Lord and no one else.

I have a pastor friend whose grown children have left the Baptist church for other nondenominational churches. They no longer want to be identified as Baptists. Maybe that's because some churches and pastors and denominations have given Baptists a bad name. Ironically, some of those nondenominational churches are neither free nor democratic. Some are run by the pastor or a small group of elders, handpicked by the pastor. Some have a narrow set of beliefs that everyone in the church must agree to. Some have a coercive atmosphere or peer pressure to conform. In leaving the Baptist church, some of my pastor friend's kids have given up some of their freedom.

In his letter to the Galatians Paul wrote, "For freedom Christ has set us free. Stand firm, therefore, and do not submit again to a yoke of slavery" (Gal 5:1 NRSV). The "yoke of slavery" that Paul was referring to was a narrow, restrictive, legalistic, authoritarian religion. Such legalism might make people aware of their sin, but it will not save them. The only true forgiveness, the only true salvation, the only true freedom comes through faith in Jesus Christ.

A few weeks ago Mary Ann Brannan asked me if it would be okay for her to sing "Ave Maria" in church today. Mary Ann asked because she knew "Ave Maria" as a Roman Catholic song, and she would be singing it in Latin. Would that be okay in a Baptist church? Of course it would be okay here at Village! We are free to sing whatever songs we want to sing. After all, "Ave Maria" is based on Scripture, on the annunciation of the angel Gabriel to Mary in the Gospel According to Luke. It's okay to sing in Latin in a Baptist church! "For freedom Christ has set us free." We are guided by the Bible, and by the Holy Spirit, and by the love that binds us together. Thank you, Mary Ann, for singing "Ave Maria" and for reminding us that we are a part of a family of faith much larger than ourselves. And thank you, Holly Hollman, for standing up for religious freedom, for Baptists, and for all people through the Baptist Joint Committee for Religious Liberty.

Some folks have given Baptists a bad name. Maybe it's time for some folks to give Baptists a good name, a name that stands for freedom in Christ. Can I get an "Amen" to that?

August 21, 2011

Liberty and Equality
Galatians 3:27-28; 5:1 (NRSV)

As many of you as were baptized into Christ have clothed yourselves with Christ. There is no longer Jew or Greek, there is no longer slave or free, there is no longer male and female; for all of you are one in Christ Jesus....

For freedom Christ has set us free. Stand firm, therefore, and do not submit again to a yoke of slavery.

July 4, 1776—the American colonies had been at war with Great Britain for over a year. Still, even with the fighting, some colonies were reluctant to declare independence. Maryland was a holdout; so was New York. Some hoped for reconciliation with King George III. Others prayed that the British would tire of the bloodshed and just go home. For many, the only resolution was separation from Britain, even if it meant an armed revolution. Benjamin Franklin of Pennsylvania had been pushing for a formal declaration of independence for a long time; so had John Adams of Massachusetts and Thomas Jefferson of Virginia. But unless they could persuade all the delegates to the Second Continental Congress to vote for independence, freedom would be a long way off.

Although there was resistance to declaring independence, Congress had appointed a committee to draft such a document. The principal writer was Thomas Jefferson, although Franklin and Adams and two others had input. The "rough Draught" was first read to Congress on June 28 and debated from July 1–4. About one-fourth of Jefferson's original text was deleted, including a condemnation of the slave trade. The delegates reasoned that the revolution would succeed only if it had the support of all the colonies, and condemning slavery would alienate those in the South.

Even without any mention of slavery, there was still a fundamental contradiction. Jefferson wrote, "We hold these truths to be self-evident, that all men are created equal, that they are endowed by their Creator with certain unalienable Rights, that among these are Life, Liberty, and the pursuit of Happiness." A nation dedicated to the cause of liberty that continued to practice slavery was "defective from the start," as the late Supreme Court justice Thurgood Marshall put it. "All men are created equal" did not include women, Native Americans, and African slaves. And those unalienable rights of life, liberty, and the pursuit of happiness were not universal either.

That may be why after the Revolutionary War was over, the Declaration of Independence was largely ignored. Having served its original purpose in declaring independence, the truths of the Declaration were "inconvenient" (even if self-evident). The ideals of liberty and equality for all were pushed aside, but they were never forgotten.

At the time of America's founding, there were about half a million slaves of African descent living in the United States, mostly in the five southern states, where they comprised forty percent of the population. Many of the founding fathers were slave owners, including George Washington and Thomas Jefferson. Jefferson in particular had a conflicting attitude toward slavery. During his first term in the House of Burgesses, he proposed legislation to emancipate slaves in Virginia, but his motion was soundly defeated. He included that paragraph in the original draft of the Declaration of Independence, condemning the slave trade, while he himself owned about 200 slaves that he had inherited. Yet even without an overt reference, "all men are created equal" was a rebuke of slavery.

Some patriots noted the paradox between demanding liberty and accepting slavery. Both John Adams and Benjamin Franklin were strong advocates for the abolition of slavery. John Adams called slavery "a foul contagion in the human character" and "an evil of colossal magnitude." Benjamin Franklin said that slavery was "an atrocious debasement of human nature" and "a source of serious evils." In 1774 Franklin co-founded the Pennsylvania Society for Promoting the Abolition of Slavery. Even George Washington was against slavery. In 1786 he wrote, "There is not a man living who wishes more sincerely than I do to see a plan adopted for the abolition of it." At the end of his presidency, Washington quietly freed some of his household slaves, and in his will he decreed that all his slaves would become free upon the death of his wife.

Thomas Jefferson may have hoped that slavery would die out on its own. In 1776 Adam Smith had argued in his book *The Wealth of Nations* that slavery was uneconomical because slaves cost more to maintain than free laborers and because the plantation system was a wasteful use of land. But after Eli Whitney invented the cotton gin in 1793, the dramatic growth of the cotton industry led to an increased demand for slave labor.

In 1819, during the debate over the admission of Missouri as a slave state, John Adams worried that the struggle over slavery might tear the country apart. He appealed to Jefferson for guidance. Jefferson wrote in 1820 that the Missouri crisis was a "fire bell in the night." He continued, "We have the wolf by the ears and we can neither hold him nor safely let him go. Justice in one scale, and self-preservation in the other." Sadly, Jefferson would not publicly support emancipation or even free his own slaves. He wrote, "This enterprise [namely, the struggle against slavery] is for the young."

But others took up the cause when Jefferson would not. A young journalist named William Lloyd Garrison became one of the leading abolitionists of the nineteenth century. Garrison made his first public speech against slavery at the Park Street Church in Boston in 1829 when he was only twenty-four years old. He moved to Baltimore and became co-editor of an antislavery newspaper. One of his regular features was a column that reported on "the barbarities of slavery." Sued for libel in a state then known for its proslavery courts, Garrison was convicted and sentenced to six months in jail, serving seven weeks before an antislavery philanthropist paid his fine. After leaving Baltimore, Garrison returned to New England, where he founded the antislavery newspaper *The Liberator*.

William Lloyd Garrison was in constant danger. After his imprisonment in Baltimore, the state of Georgia offered a $5,000 reward for his arrest. He received frequent death threats. But Garrison would not be deterred. He said the "twin rocks" of his convictions were the Bible and the Declaration of Independence. Garrison wrote, "As long as there remains a single copy of the Declaration of Independence, or of the Bible, in our land, we will not despair." Later, after slavery was abolished, Garrison became a leading voice for women's suffrage, again basing his convictions on the Declaration of Independence and the Bible.

William Lloyd Garrison was deeply influenced by the writings of an Ohio pastor, Rev. John Rankin, one of the early "conductors" of the Underground Railroad. From Reverend Rankin, Garrison came to see the Bible as the foundation of the antislavery movement. Garrison had titled his newspaper *The Liberator*, but Jesus was the ultimate liberator. As Paul wrote in

Galatians 5:1, "For freedom Christ has set us free. Stand firm, therefore, and do not submit again to a yoke of slavery." Garrison was also influenced by the Bible in his approach to emancipation, stressing nonviolence and passive resistance.

Abraham Lincoln also was a student of the Bible and an admirer of the Declaration of Independence. In his famous debates in 1858, Lincoln argued with Stephen Douglas about the meaning of the phrase "All men are created equal." Douglas said that the Declaration referred only to white men and did not proclaim the equality of any "inferior race." Lincoln said that the language of the Declaration was deliberately universal and that it set a high moral standard toward which the American republic should strive. After he became president, Lincoln said in the opening sentence of his Gettysburg Address, "Four score and seven years ago [i.e., in 1776], our fathers brought forth on this continent a new nation, conceived in Liberty, and dedicated to the proposition that all men are created equal." From where did Lincoln derive such ideas? From the Declaration of Independence and from the Bible. As Paul wrote in Galatians 3:28, "There is no longer Jew or Greek, there is no longer slave or free, there is no longer male or female, for all of you are one in Christ Jesus."

Liberty and equality were at the heart of Paul's letter to the Galatians. Liberty and equality were at the heart of the Declaration of Independence too. Yet in Paul's time, just as in Thomas Jefferson's time, liberty and equality were more ideals than reality. In a sense, liberty and equality remain a high moral standard toward which we continue to strive as a nation and as a community of faith.

On this Fourth of July we celebrate the ideals of liberty and equality upon which our country was founded. But more than that, on this Communion Sunday, we celebrate the liberty and equality that is ours in Christ. Because Jesus died for us, we are free from the power of sin and free to live faithful lives for God. Because Jesus died for all, we are equal recipients of God's forgiveness and love and grace. Distinctions of race or social class or gender don't matter anymore, for we are all one in Christ Jesus.

Just as the flag is a symbol of our freedom as Americans, the bread and the cup are symbols of our freedom as Christians. Christ died to make us free.

July 4, 2010

Chapter 9

2011–2017

David Potter wanted to be ordained. A military veteran, David had heard the call to ministry while he was driving semis across the country for a long-distance trucking company. At first he tried to ignore it, but over time he became convinced that God wanted him to do more than drive trucks. He enrolled in college online, and he was almost finished with his bachelor's degree when he showed up at our church. His plan was to complete seminary online too and then become ordained for hospital chaplaincy. He had moved to Bowie to live with his parents and to work for his brother, who owned a pest control company. His wife would join him later after she had taken care of some family responsibilities on the West Coast.

At first I just listened to his story. Then I asked a few probing questions to better understand his motivation. I didn't try to talk him out of becoming a minister, but I wanted to understand what he understood about it. As my friend Don Harris once said, "Don't go into the ministry—unless you have to!" Over the next two years David demonstrated his commitment. He was working on his master of divinity when he applied for a chaplaincy internship at a regional hospital. The CPE supervisor was willing to admit him into the program if he were ordained to the gospel ministry.

We had ordained deacons almost every year, but ordaining someone to the gospel ministry was new territory for me. I called the D.C. Baptist Convention and spoke with the staff person responsible for the advisory committee on ordination. Her name was Rev. Starlette McNeill (now Rev. Starlette Thomas), a graduate of Colgate Rochester Crozier Theological Seminary. We had not yet met face to face, but our phone conversation led me to invite her to preach at Village on a Sunday I would be gone in 2011. In 2012 I invited her to come to Village again to give the charge during David Potter's ordination service. Rev. McNeill came again early in 2013 on a Sunday I would be away. Sometime during this period, I began to get a "crazy" idea. Maybe Rev. McNeill would be open to coming to Village as our associate pastor.

It was a "crazy" idea because Rev. McNeill already had a job with the D.C. Baptist Convention and because Village did not have a budget line item or position description or even an awareness that we needed an associate pastor. But I knew I was going to retire one day, and I knew that churches often struggle after a long-haul pastor leaves. My thought was that if Rev. McNeill were to become our associate pastor, she could get to know the congregation, and they could get to know her, and maybe she would help the church to carry on after I was gone.

I invited Rev. McNeill to lunch at Olive Garden in the spring of 2013. I asked her if she felt any calling to local church ministry. She said, in fact, she did. Then I told her about my "crazy" idea. She said she would pray about it. I told her it was far from certain, because I still had to sell the idea to the church and come up with the money to make it happen. So I would pray about it too.

The annual gathering of the Baptist World Alliance was in Ocho Rios, Jamaica, in the summer of 2013. Linda and I were there, and it was a rich experience of meeting Baptist leaders from around the world. One afternoon the group was transported by buses away from the conference site to a dinner meeting with leaders from the Jamaican Baptist Union. On our way back to the conference center, I noticed Dr. Daniel Vestal sitting on the bus. I sat down by Daniel and explained to him my idea of calling Rev. McNeill as our associate pastor. I wanted his input and feedback. Daniel listened carefully and asked a few pertinent questions. Then he told me he thought it was a worthy idea, and he encouraged me to pursue it further after I got back to Maryland. Daniel's affirmation was just the encouragement I needed.

Over the next few weeks I began to share the "crazy" idea with key church leaders. Some were skeptical, but they were willing to think about it. One advantage of being at the same church a long time is the trust factor. A bank account of credibility had grown over the years that I drew upon. Some longtime members didn't even want to think about the day I might retire. Others wondered if the church were ready for a female, African-American associate pastor. Some suggested we should establish a search committee and advertise for an associate pastor. I told them I believed God had led me to Rev. McNeill and no one else. If she were not willing to come or if the church were not willing to call her, I didn't want to create the position and search for another candidate. It was one of the few times as a pastor that I orchestrated instead of collaborated.

Rev. McNeill did accept the call to become our part-time associate pastor in the fall of 2013. She would continue to work part-time for the D.C.

Baptist Convention, but she would be with us every Sunday and a couple of other days during the week. Rev. David Potter was accepted into the intern program as a hospital chaplain, and Rev. Starlette McNeill joined the staff of Village Baptist Church. I gave Pastor Star as many opportunities to preach as I could. It averaged out about once a month. I still preached most Sunday mornings, but Pastor Star preached the Sundays I was away and for special occasions such as New Year's Eve and Maundy Thursday and Thanksgiving Day and for the early service on choir cantata Sundays. We learned she was an excellent writer and an eloquent preacher. It was still a long shot that my retirement strategy would ever come to fruition, but we were going to give it a chance.

As Pastor Star approached her fourth anniversary of coming to Village, I told her I was thinking about retiring at the end of 2017. I said there was no guarantee that the church would ask her to become the interim pastor but that I would recommend it to the personnel committee. A pastor search committee would be elected according to the church bylaws. But I thought there was a good possibility Pastor Star would be asked to become interim pastor, if she were willing to serve in that capacity. She was willing, and the personnel committee did ask, upon my strong recommendation. Once again, I drew on the credibility accrued from thirty-three years as pastor.

I announced my retirement in a letter mailed to everyone on the mailing list. The letter went out the day before Thanksgiving so that most people would have received it before they came to church on the Sunday after Thanksgiving. The church bylaws specified that the pastor should give the church one month's notice before leaving, and this was my one month's notice. I had alerted the personnel committee previously so they could begin making plans for a smooth transition.

At first I had not been sure it was wise to retire at the end of December. The Christmas season is the busiest time of the church year, and we had family coming in for the holidays. But the funeral for my friend Rev. Gary Javens convinced me the time was right. At the funeral I learned that Gary had retired as pastor of Clifton Park Baptist Church on the last Sunday of December after a thirty-one-year pastorate. If Gary could do it, I could too.

I Thank God for You
Philippians 1:2-6 (NRSV)

Grace to you and peace from God our Father and the Lord Jesus Christ.

I thank my God every time I remember you, constantly praying with joy in every one of my prayers for all of you, because of your sharing in the gospel from the first day until now. I am confident of this, that the one who began a good work among you will bring it to completion by the day of Jesus Christ.

I thank God for you! Today I am announcing my upcoming retirement as pastor of Village Baptist Church. December 31, 2017, will be my last Sunday. It will mark the end of thirty-three years of service as your pastor. It has been a privilege, and a blessing, and a joy—to serve you, and to know you, and to love you. As Paul said to the church in Philippi, "I thank my God every time I remember you, constantly praying with joy in every one of my prayers for all of you, because of your sharing in the gospel from the first day until now" (Phil 1:3–5).

Why am I retiring, and why now? I am retiring because I am sixty-six years old, and I have served this church half my life. I am retiring now because Village is in good hands, and I can leave knowing that the work of God will continue among you. For the time being, Linda and I will continue to live in Bowie. But after December 31 we will no longer come to Village. We will worship elsewhere to allow the interim pastor and eventually the new pastor to serve without interference. Undoubtedly, we will see some of you in the grocery store, or in a local restaurant, or elsewhere. We are not ending our friendships with any of you! But we will not attend Village after December 31 to give the interim pastor and the new pastor some breathing room to begin a new ministry among you.

Our plans are somewhat indefinite. In January we will go to Texas to visit my mother. She will be ninety-four in February. Although she is doing incredibly well, there may come a time when we will need to move closer to her. All that is to be determined. In February we are going to Florida to visit our friends Don and Norma Harris. We hope to see Belinda Franklyn while we are there and also to see Angela Sweetin. Kathleen Rowe will travel with us, as she has done for many years. We are grateful to Dr. Kumar for allowing us to stay in his timeshare condo in Orlando. That will help us adjust to living on a retirement income. At some point we may sell our home, both to downsize and to reduce our cost of living. We love living in Bowie, but we may need to relocate, both to help my mother and to live more economically.

The decision to retire has been several years in the making. Back in 2012 I started looking for a younger associate pastor. The idea was for the associate to come alongside me, to get to know the congregation, and perhaps to lead the church when I did retire. God led me to Pastor Star, and she became our associate pastor in 2013. She is ready, willing, and able to serve as interim pastor. I felt the need to find someone to help the church carry on after I retired, because I knew that many churches struggle after a longtime pastor leaves. I wanted to do everything I could to minimize the impact of my retirement. I believe God led us to Pastor Star and that God led Pastor Star to us. She knows and loves this congregation, and the congregation knows and loves her. She has recently completed extensive interim pastor training. She is well-prepared and well-equipped to be an excellent interim pastor.

The church bylaws describe the process for calling a new pastor. During the interim period a pastor search committee will evaluate possible candidates for the new pastor. The pastor search committee will recommend one person for the church to consider. In the meantime Pastor Star will serve as the interim pastor until a candidate for pastor has been recommended and voted on by the church. This is the process the church followed when it called Dr. Kenneth Bradshaw as the first pastor in 1969, and Rev. John Woodall as the second pastor in 1971, and Rev. Dan Ivins as the third pastor in 1974, and me as the fourth pastor in 1984. The pastor search committee will recommend the best candidate as the fifth pastor. The church will vote on the candidate they recommend.

Since this is the Sunday after Thanksgiving, let me devote the rest of this sermon to expressing thanks for the last thirty-three years. First, I thank God for calling me to this church. It was the Lord's doing, and not my own. I knew very little about Village and even less about Bowie. In 1984 Linda and I were living in Silver Spring with our two children, Amy and Marc. I was serving as associate pastor of Montgomery Hills Baptist Church. It was my first full-time ministry position after seminary. I had graduated from seminary in December of 1976. The pastor at Montgomery Hills, Rev. Don Harris, came to the campus of The Southern Baptist Theological Seminary in Louisville, Kentucky, early in 1977 to interview recent seminary graduates. I was among those he interviewed. Linda and I were not yet married. For some reason Linda wanted me to have a job before she would marry me. So my being called to Montgomery Hills was an answer to two prayers. It meant I would get a job in a church, and it meant I would get a wife (and a daughter too, since Linda had a four-year-old child, Amy). Life was good!

Life continued to be good. Our son, Marc, was born in 1980. We enjoyed serving the Montgomery Hills church. Don and Norma Harris were more than pastor and first lady. They became close friends. That's why we have continued to visit them every winter in Florida since they retired. We were happy at Montgomery Hills and not looking to move. But in 1984 a woman named Leslie Parreco cold-called our house in Silver Spring. Leslie identified herself as a member of the pulpit committee at Village Baptist Church in Bowie. She said that she had been given my name by Dr. James Langley, the executive director of the D.C. Baptist Convention. Leslie asked if I would be willing to meet with the search committee. For some reason I said yes. The committee was chaired by Maury Sweetin. Besides Leslie and Maury, other members included Jo Reiter, Mark Miles's mother (Janis Miles), Ron Knode, Walt Townshend, and Pete Parreco's sister (Julie Terrell). The Village Baptist Church secretary, Gloria Newton, served as an ex-officio, non-voting member of the search committee. Some members of the committee came to Montgomery Hills and heard me preach. Then I came to Village one Sunday morning in the fall of 1984 and preached a trial sermon. The church voted after the worship service that Sunday morning. The vote to call me to Village was 64–1. I am thankful to the sixty-four members who voted for me. I am even thankful for the one member who voted against me. I have done my best over the past thirty-three years to win over that one negative voter to my side.

I am thankful for so many other members of Village. I am thankful for Carlynn and Dave Thompson. Carlynn has been leading the early service music for twenty-five years! Dave has done almost everything in the church (except sing in the choir!).

I am thankful for Loretta and Marion Shipman. They have served as deacons, commission chairpersons, and many other roles over the past twenty years. I am thankful for Joel and Linda Smith, who have been at Village almost as long as we have. Linda has served as our pianist since 1992. She and Joel have been deacons, commission chairs, choir members, and more.

I am thankful for our choir director/organist, Jeanine Warden-Jarrett. Jeanine started playing the organ at Village when she was a lowly medical student back in 2004. Now, Dr. Jarrett is a primary care physician here in

Bowie and serves as our choir director as well as our organist. I am thankful for our former music leaders and accompanists—Dianne Webster, Ruth Dugan, Jo Reiter, Betty Swaffield, Jennifer Claybrook Helwig, Kevin Bennear, Ron Knode, Doug Quinzi, Phil Wyrick, Angela Corbett, as well as our substitute organist, Jeannine Case. I am thankful for soloists like Kasey Malatesta and Ron Hawkins and Ken Fisher and Denise Fenrick.

I am thankful for Judy Woodall, the editor of *The Village Voice*, our monthly church newsletter, and now a member of our choir. I am thankful for Karen Woodson, deacon, committee chairperson, former Vacation Bible School director, member of the personnel committee. I am thankful for Ray Chatary, our moderator and seafood feast organizer. I am thankful for Rhonda Hamby, our church clerk and Sunday school director, who has served as a deacon and commission chair and nursery coordinator. I am thankful for Frankye Taylor and the Jacknewitzes and all the members of my Sunday school class—you know who you are! I am thankful for our deacon chair, Jimmie Winston, and his wife, Martha. I am thankful for Judy and Ed Dellinger, who have been deacons, and encouragers, and friends. I am thankful to Thelma and Heather Larson—to Thelma for her hugs and to Heather for her sweet spirit. I am thankful to the Parrecos, the Duelleys, the Miles, the Kirks, the Grahams, the Dearrings, the Porters, the Browns, the Boggs, the Moultries, the Sassers, and so many more. If I haven't mentioned your name, it's only because there is not enough time. I thank my God for all of you!

One more story. Allison Miller was twenty-three years old, living in Brooklyn. A guy she was dating invited her to go up to the Catskills, two hours north of the city, for the weekend. The proprietor of the inn where they would be staying was a friend of the guy she was dating. The friend comped them accommodations in the Victorian bed and breakfast. That weekend Allison hiked, sat around a campfire, and fell in love—not with the guy she had come with, but with his friend, the young innkeeper! Two years later Allison walked down a grassy aisle in the backyard of the inn to become the innkeeper's wife.

Now, eight years later Allison and the innkeeper greet guests together, along with their three-year-old daughter. The inn dates to 1893 when a twenty-eight-year old doctor returned to the Catskills after finishing medical school in New York City. He had the house built, and he lived there with his family until 1945. For the next forty years it belonged to another family who ran the supermarket down the street. After that, a woman lovingly restored the house and turned it into a bed and breakfast. Now the inn belongs to Allison and her family. She said their tenure is merely a chapter, just like those who came before them. She said, "We're stewards of a place that many have called home."

That's how Linda and I feel about Village. We have been stewards of a place that many have called home. After another month we will turn over the keys to those who will come after us.

We have a month to say goodbye to one another. I can't promise I won't get choked up. But I can promise we will remember with gratitude, and we will look to the future with hope. I'm not worried about Village. You're in good hands. You're in God's hands.

Paul wrote, "I am confident of this, that the one who began a good work among you will bring it to completion by the day of Jesus Christ" (Phil 1:6 NRSV).

November 26, 2017

The Story of Village
Philippians 1:1-6 (NRSV)

Paul and Timothy, servants of Christ Jesus, To all the saints in Christ Jesus who are in Philippi, with the bishops and deacons: Grace to you and peace from God our Father and the Lord Jesus Christ.

I thank my God every time I remember you, constantly praying with joy in every one of my prayers for all of you, because of your sharing in the gospel from the first day until now. I am confident of this, that the one who began a good work among you will bring it to completion by the day of Jesus Christ.

The year was 1968. Some of you were not born yet, while others may remember it well. Here are some highlights (and lowlights) of what happened in 1968 (cds.library.brown.edu/projects/1968/reference/timeline.html).

January 23
North Korean patrol boats capture the U.S.S. Pueblo, a U.S. Navy vessel, and its eighty-three-man crew on charges of violating the country's twelve-mile territorial limit. This crisis would dog U.S. foreign policy for eleven months, with the crew finally freed December 22.

January 31
North Vietnamese launch the Tet offensive. Nearly 70,000 North Vietnamese troops will take part in the action, taking the battle from the jungles to the cities. The offensive will carry on for weeks and is a major turning point for American attitudes toward the war.

February 1
During police actions following the first day of the Tet offensive, a South Vietnamese security official is captured on film executing a Viet Cong prisoner. The Pulitzer Prize-winning photograph becomes yet another rallying point for antiwar protestors.

February 18
The U.S. State Department announces the highest U.S. casualty toll of the Vietnam War. The previous week saw 543 Americans killed in action and 2,547 wounded.

March 16
Senator Robert Kennedy, former attorney general and brother of former president John F. Kennedy, announces he will enter the 1968 presidential race.

March 16 (same day)
Although it will not become public knowledge for more than a year, U.S. ground troops from Charlie Company rampage through the hamlet of My Lai, killing more than 500 Vietnamese civilians, from infants to the elderly.

April 4
Martin Luther King Jr. spends the day at the Lorraine Motel in Memphis working with local leaders on plans for his Poor People's March on Washington to take place later in the month. At 6:00 p.m., as he greets friends in the courtyard, King is shot with one round from a 30.06 rifle. After an international manhunt James Earl Ray will be arrested on June 27 in England and convicted of the murder. The King assassination sparks rioting in Baltimore, Boston, Chicago, Detroit, Kansas City, Newark, Washington, D.C., and other cities. Across the country forty-six deaths will be blamed on the riots.

June 4/5
Robert Kennedy addresses a crowd of supporters at the Ambassador Hotel in San Francisco. After he leaves the stage, Kennedy is shot by Sirhan Sirhan, a twenty-four-year-old Jordanian living in Los Angeles. The forty-two-year-old Kennedy dies in the early morning of June 6.

August 8
At their convention in Miami Beach, the Republicans nominate Richard Milhous Nixon to be their presidential candidate. The next day Nixon will appoint Spiro Agnew of Maryland as his running mate.

August 20
The Soviet Union invades Czechoslovakia with over 200,000 Warsaw pact troops, putting an end to the "Prague Spring" and beginning a period of oppressive "normalization."

August 26
Mayor Richard Daley opens the Democratic National Convention in Chicago. While the convention moves toward nominating Hubert Humphrey for president, the city's police attempt to enforce an 11:00 p.m. curfew. The next two days bring increasing violence. Police beat some marchers unconscious and send 100 to emergency rooms while arresting 175.

October 3
George Wallace, running an independent campaign for president, names retired Air Force chief of staff Curtis E. LeMay to be his running mate. At the press conference the general is asked about his position on the use of nuclear weapons and responds: "I think most military men think it's just another weapon in the arsenal.... I think there are many times when it would be most efficient to use nuclear weapons.... I don't believe the world would end if we exploded a nuclear weapon."

October 11
Apollo 7 is launched for an eleven-day journey, which will orbit the Earth 163 times.

October 12
The Summer Olympic Games open in Mexico City. The games have been boycotted by thirty-two African nations in protest of South Africa's participation. On the 18th Tommie Smith and John Carlos, U.S. medalists in the 200-meter dash, further disrupt the games by performing the black power salute during the "Star-Spangled Banner" at their medal ceremony.

November 5
Election Day. The results of the popular vote are 31,770,000 for Nixon, 43.4 percent of the total; 31,270,000, or 42.7 percent, for Humphrey; 9,906,000, or 13.5 percent, for Wallace; and 0.4 percent for other candidates.

November 17
A worship service is conducted in a house at 15725 Pointer Ridge Drive in Bowie, Maryland. The service is led by Rev. Richard Brackin, pastor of Belair Baptist Church in Bowie. The house would serve as home for the congregation until January 6, 1980.

In 1968 I was a senior in high school. I remember just about everything in the timeline, except for the last item, namely, the first worship service of a little mission church that met in a house on Pointer Ridge Drive in Bowie, Maryland.

[The year] 1968 was a tumultuous time for our country. The Vietnam War was raging. Thousands upon thousands of American soldiers were dying in southeast Asia. Antiwar protests here at home were growing by the day. Race relations were at a fever pitch in 1968. My high school in Fort Worth, Texas, had integrated two years before, but most neighborhoods and churches and organizations were still racially segregated. I worked after school and on Saturdays at a laundry and dry-cleaning business. I remember talking with an African-American co-worker about the assassination of Martin Luther King Jr. and the riots that followed. He was as bewildered as I was. We didn't know what was going to happen next. It seemed our country was falling apart. After Robert Kennedy was assassinated, we felt more insecure. There were a few bright spots, like the Apollo space program, but mainly I remember how messed up our world was in 1968.

It was during this tumultuous time that a group of visionary souls had the dream of starting a Baptist church in south Bowie. They didn't just dream about it—they did it. They converted a Levitt rancher on Pointer Ridge Drive into a church house and began meeting there on Sunday mornings. The first service was held November 17, 1968, shortly after Richard Nixon was elected president the first time. Most of the worshipers came from Belair Baptist Church on the more established north side of town. Shortly after that refugees from another Baptist church in Bowie started worshiping with the pioneers from Belair and residents of the community. A year after the first worship service, in November of 1969, Dr. Kenneth Bradshaw came as the first pastor. He wasn't pastor for very long. Nine months later Dr. Bradshaw resigned for a teaching position at the University of Corpus Christi. But the story of Village did not end.

Maury Sweetin chaired the pulpit committee that would recommend a second pastor, Rev. John Woodall. He helped the congregation adopt a constitution and bylaws and covenant and to become an autonomous church. There were seventy-two charter members, but that included the four Bradshaws who had since moved to Texas. Maury was elected a deacon, along with Gracen Joiner and Hugh Lytton. Martha Potter helped start a choir, and then George Robinson (Jeanette's husband) became the director in November 1971. That was also the year of the first Thanksgiving celebration. The next year, 1972, Joan King started a mother's day out program, and Doug Miles (Mark's father) was elected a deacon. The choir presented a Christmas cantata that year.

In 1973, after the church purchased an annex, Rev. Woodall resigned for another church. But the Village story continued. A new pastor, Rev. Dan Ivins, came to Village in 1974. Dick Price (Michele Miles's and Lauren Kirk's dad) was elected a deacon that year. In 1975 Village purchased four acres here on Mitchellville Road. Also in 1975, an AA group began to meet in the annex, the first issue of the *Village Voice* newsletter was published, and Ruth Dugan began as church organist. The next year, 1976, the choir presented an Easter cantata. In 1977 Gloria Newton became the church secretary. Also that year, 1977, Carlynn and Dave Thompson sponsored a yard sale for the building fund. In 1978 Jo Reiter became church pianist, and Jo was elected as the first female deacon at Village. In 1979 counselor Rose Schrott started the Family Enrichment Center at Village.

The last worship service in the church house was on January 6, 1980. For three months the congregation worshiped at the South Bowie Community Center, then moved into the new building. Village joined the D.C. Baptist Convention that year. Angela Sweetin hosted the first women's retreat in 1981, and Pete Parreco was elected a deacon in 1982. Maxine Brown (Ray's mother) started telling the children's story every Sunday in 1983. In 1984 Dr. Dan Ivins resigned as pastor, and Dr. James Dunn came as interim pastor.

Linda and I came to Village the first Sunday of 1985. Betty Swaffield became the church organist later that year. In 1986 we bought a new organ and approved plans to expand the building. In 1987 we completed the west wing addition, and we collected hunger banks for the first time. In 1988 we began taking sandwiches to Martha's Table in the District. In 1989 we installed lights in the parking lot. In 1990 we helped pay for a roof for a church in Burkina Faso. In 1991 a Chemically Dependent Anonymous group began meeting in our building. In 1992 we started an early service with contemporary music. In 1993 we installed eight new pews in the back of the sanctuary. In 1994 we installed a new church sign out by the road.

[The year] 1995 was the year we began to donate to the Cooperative Baptist Fellowship Global Mission Offering. In 1996 Dave Thompson posted our first home page on the internet, then known as the world wide web. In 1997 we voted to purchase choir robes (believe it or not, that was a controversial subject back then—not everybody was in favor of it!). The altar cross on the Communion table was purchased in 1998 from the Memorial Fund. In 1999 we formed a long-range planning committee. Then Saturday, January 8, 2000, the church building burned. For the next thirty-four months we worshiped on Sundays at the Bowie Alliance Church, and we rented office space from Dr. Kumar.

It took all of 2001 and most of 2002 to construct this edifice on the foundation of the original building. The first service in the rebuilt church was held on November 10, 2002. In 2003 we had rebuilt a new church building, but we needed to rebuild the congregation. We had lost almost a third of our people during the long thirty-four months of our displacement. This is where many of you have come in. Just for fun, let's see who has come to Village since 2002. Would you stand so that we might recognize you? In many ways the story of Village Baptist Church is still being written, by you and by all of us. Rather than continuing my historical timeline, I'd like to make some observations about what Village has been and what Village has become.

First, Village has been, and continues to be, a place of refuge. Some of our most active charter members were refugees from another church that didn't welcome them anymore. Later, a number of divorced people affiliated with Village because their former churches didn't welcome them. Over the years a number of interracial families have affiliated with our church because they felt welcome here. More recently, many immigrant families have joined our church after coming to this area from other countries of origin. Village began as a predominantly white church because this community was predominantly white in 1968. But from the beginning, Village has had members from racial minorities. Shortly after Linda and I came to Village in 1985, the south Bowie community was becoming more racially diverse, and our church has increasingly reflected that diversity. Even before Linda and I arrived at Village, former pastor Dan Ivins created the slogan "We reserve the right to accept everybody." Dan and many members were committed to making Village an inclusive church, a place of welcome for any who would come.

A second characteristic is that Village has been, and continues to be, a house of prayer. We take time every Sunday morning to share our joys and our concerns and to pray for one another. Prayer is at the heart of our fellowship. In 2015, under the leadership of Pastor Star, we have begun a monthly first Wednesday night service of prayer, in addition to our prayer time on Sunday mornings. Our church covenant says, "Believing in Jesus Christ as our Lord and Savior, and on the profession of our faith, having been baptized in the name of the Father, Son, and Holy Spirit," we will "watch over one another in prayer, and aid one another in times of distress and illness." We may not agree on everything, but we agree to pray.

Third, Village has been, and continues to be, a family of faith. A strong sense of family was present from the very beginning. Those who were around in the house-church days remember how the congregation was like an extended church family. Even after the congregation outgrew the church house and moved into the original building on this site, that sense of family persisted.

Our guest preacher last Sunday, Rev. Dr. Pam Durso, told me that she has never received as many hugs while visiting a church as she received here at Village. Of course, not everybody likes to be hugged by strangers, but if we have anything to do about it, newcomers will not feel like strangers for long. Thelma Larson is going to hug you, and Pastor Star is going to hug you, and

I'm going to hug you if you give me the chance. That's because we're family here, and you are family here, if you want to be.

The church at Philippi was like family to Paul. It was the first church that Paul established on the European continent. It's not that the church was without problems. Paul experienced opposition, as he did in most places. But Paul felt a close bond with the members of the church in Philippi. The Greek word that Paul uses is *koinonia*. It could be translated *sharing* (as it is here in the New Revised Standard Version), or *partnership* (as it is in the New International Version), or *fellowship* (as it is in the King James Version).

The point is, it was this spirit of *koinonia*, of fellowship, of partnership, of sharing that characterized the church in Philippi. And it is that spirit of *koinonia* that has also characterized Village over the years.

Back when Dianne Webster was our choir director, the adult choir would sometimes sing a song as a call to worship on Homecoming Sunday. I'm not going to sing it, but I will quote the opening verse:

> All are welcome here in this fellowship we share
> A fellowship of Christian love and faith
> Where we reach to one another in friendship and in prayer
> Thankful for the blessings of God's grace.
>
> Welcome friends, we're glad you came our way.
> Welcome friends, now rest awhile and stay.

October 11, 2015

The Fellowship of Kindred Minds
Philippians 1:1-11 (NRSV)

Paul and Timothy, servants of Christ Jesus, To all the saints in Christ Jesus who are in Philippi, with the bishops and deacons: Grace to you and peace from God our Father and the Lord Jesus Christ.

I thank my God every time I remember you, constantly praying with joy in every one of my prayers for all of you, because of your sharing in the gospel from the first day until now. I am confident of this, that the one who began a good work among you will bring it to completion by the day of Jesus Christ.

It is right for me to think this way about all of you, because you hold me in your heart, for all of you share in God's grace with me, both in my imprisonment and in the defense and confirmation of the gospel. For God is my witness, how I long for all of you with the compassion of Christ Jesus.

And this is my prayer, that your love may overflow more and more with knowledge and full insight to help you to determine what is best, so that in the day of Christ you may be pure and blameless, having produced the harvest of righteousness that comes through Jesus Christ for the glory and praise of God.

In 1989 a group of world Baptist leaders met in Zagreb, Yugoslavia (now Croatia), under the auspices of the Baptist World Alliance. The purpose of their meeting was to draft a statement of distinctive Baptist beliefs and practices. The group was called the Baptist Heritage Commission, and the statement they drafted was titled "Toward a Baptist Identity." We've included a brief summary of that statement in the bulletin. The report of the Baptist Heritage Commission states that Baptists:

> stress the experience of personal salvation through faith in Jesus,
> symbolized in baptism and the Lord's Supper;
> under the Lordship of Jesus Christ, bond together in free local congregations;
> follow the authority of Scriptures in all matters;
> claim religious liberty for all people;
> believe the Great Commission to take the Gospel to the world
> is the responsibility of the whole membership.

The statement is descriptive, not coercive. It states what is typical or common or characteristic in most Baptist churches around the world.

The New Testament pictures the church in two ways. First, there is the broad concept of the church, namely, the church universal, made up of everyone who believes in Jesus Christ and who has been baptized into his body, regardless of denominational label. Second, the New Testament speaks of the church in a more narrow way, namely, the local congregation of believers that gathers in specific times and places to worship and study the scriptures and share the Lord's Supper and fellowship together and serve others in Christ's name. As Christians we are members of both the church universal and the church local.

As Baptists we have a distinct understanding of the nature of the local church: "Under the Lordship of Jesus Christ, we bond together in free local congregations." The tie that binds us together is our love for Jesus Christ and our desire to live according to his will.

Because of our love for Jesus Christ, we have a love for each other too. We are not just a group of strangers who come to listen to the music or to hear a sermon, like a disconnected audience. We bond together through personal relationships. One of the advantages of a church our size is the opportunity to get to know each other and feel connected to one another.

Our church covenant states that we will "watch over one another in prayer" and "aid one another in times of distress and illness." That's why our worship services on Sunday mornings always include a time of sharing concerns and intercessory prayer. When I tell someone, "We'll be praying for you," that's not just a cliché. We really do pray for people in need. Every Sunday morning we "watch over one another in prayer."

Last month some cherished members of our church, the Cutcliffe family, moved to Georgia. Linda Cutcliffe wrote me an email about their beginning to search for a new church home. Linda said that they visited one church not too far from their new home because it didn't seem to be quite as big as some of the other Baptist churches in the area. But even that "medium size" church has about a thousand members. Linda said it was a little overwhelming to be in a congregation that large.

Now, I'm not knocking big churches. I grew up in a big church in Texas. Big churches have a lot to offer. But it's easy to get lost in the crowd in a big church. It's easy to feel like a spectator rather than feeling like a vital part of the fellowship. Village can't compete with megachurches when it comes to programs and church staff and professional-quality worship services. The church that the Cutcliffes visited has a budget almost ten times our church budget. But we can focus on personal relationships, and caring, and being bonded together through our love for Christ.

Apparently the church in Philippi had that kind of fellowship and personal relationships among the congregation. Some biblical commentators believe that the church at Philippi was Paul's favorite congregation. It's obvious that Paul had a warm, personal relationship with the people in the church at Philippi. Normally, Paul would refuse financial support from any of the local congregations because he didn't want to be indebted to anyone, and he didn't want any of the churches to think he was an apostle for the money. Typically, Paul supported himself by his tent-making occupation. But Paul made an exception with the church at Philippi. There was such a level of mutual trust between them that Paul could accept their gracious offer of financial support. That special bond that Paul felt comes through in his letter to the Philippian church.

In the Baptist way we bond together in free local congregations. That means each church is autonomous, or self-governing. But it also means we value the relationships we have with one another. When members of our church are hurting, other members feel their pain. When anyone in the church is in trouble, others will try to help. At least that is the goal. We want to do whatever we can to insure we aid one another in times of illness and distress.

Three hundred forty years ago, a man named John Fawcett was ordained for Christian ministry and accepted the call to become pastor of a small church in Wainsgate, Yorkshire, England. It wasn't a "choice" position—Fawcett described Wainsgate as "less than a village," and the people in the church he described as "uneducated, pagan, and hot-tempered." (www.cyberhymnal.org). Nonetheless, Fawcett began to serve faithfully in that little congregation, and the church began to grow. Eventually, a balcony had to be added to the sanctuary; then more land was acquired, and another building was erected.

For nine years Fawcett and the people served together and bonded together. Then he received a call to become pastor of the Carter Lane Baptist Church in London, a much more prestigious position. Because of his small salary at Wainsgate and because the needs of his family of four children were growing, he accepted the call to London. He preached his farewell sermon, and the next morning he and his family prepared to leave. The wagons were loaded with furniture and books, and the family was ready to depart when parishioners began to gather at the parsonage with tears in their eyes. They begged him not to go. Fawcett began to rethink his decision. His wife said to him, "Oh, John, I cannot bear this." "Neither can I," the pastor replied. "We will not go."

Fawcett told the men of the church to unload the belongings while he sent word to the church in London that he would not be coming. John Fawcett stayed at Wainsgate for another forty-five years, founding a training school for pastors, writing books and hymns. Near the end of his ministry, King George III offered him anything he desired because the king had been so impressed by one of Fawcett's essays. Pastor Fawcett declined, saying, "Thank you, but I live among a people who love me. The Lord has blessed my labors among these people, and I need nothing that a king can supply."

One more thing you might know about John Fawcett—in honor of the congregation that wooed him back with their love, he wrote the hymn "Blest Be the Tie That Binds," saying, "We just cannot break the ties of affection that bind us to you dear friends."

> Blest be the tie that binds our hearts in Christian love;
> The fellowship of kindred minds is like to that above.

What a challenge—to make the fellowship we have with one another in the church like the fellowship of heaven. No congregation has the power to do that in its own strength, but under the Lordship of Jesus Christ, we can pray for one another and support one another and welcome one another and love one another. May our love overflow more and more until this fellowship of kindred minds is like that above.

July 27, 2003

Chapter 10

2017–

By far the hardest part of being a long-term pastor is saying goodbye to people you love. I'm talking about more than announcing my retirement. I'm talking about saying goodbye over the course of thirty-three years to people I loved. Of course every pastor must deal with losses. But because relationships deepen over time, the loss seems greater when those deepened relationships end.

In 2007 we dedicated a memorial garden behind the church building, between the sanctuary and the fellowship hall. We installed engraved bricks in the memorial garden for members and friends who had passed away. Each year we added new engraved bricks, and we held a dedication service after worship on the Sunday before Memorial Day. The printed program for each dedication service included the names of all those who were remembered with bricks in the garden, as well as the names of those on the new bricks to be dedicated. The week before the dedication service, I would spend some time in the garden, making sure we hadn't inadvertently left any names out of the printed program. As I reviewed the names, I reflected upon those who were no longer with us.

There were bricks for a father and his ten-year-old daughter who were killed in an auto accident. Linda and I were in Houston for the annual gathering of the Cooperative Baptist Fellowship when we got word about the tragedy. We changed our plane tickets and rushed back to Maryland the following day so we could be with the young widow who had lost her husband and her only child.

There was a brick for a man who died in the prime of life, leaving behind a wife and their five-year-old daughter.

There were bricks for six members of the same family. Over the years I had conducted six funerals for those people I loved.

There were bricks for people who had died far too soon and bricks for people who had died after a ripe old age of a good life. Thank God we have the promise of heaven, but the pain of loss is nonetheless real.

Conducting funerals was one of my most important ministries. It is a ministry that will continue after retirement. As I am able, I will officiate the funeral for any family that asks. My goal in each eulogy is to remember the person with honesty and love and to lift up our Christian hope.

By far the most fulfilling part of being a longtime pastor is making a difference in people's lives. After announcing my retirement, I began to receive messages of thanks from many who were touched by my ministry. Some reminded me of something they had heard in a sermon years ago. Others recalled a particularly tough time in their lives when I was there for them. I am certainly no hero. Sometimes I didn't know what to say to make things better. But God can use the "ministry of presence" to make a difference.

The final sermon I preached at Village on December 31, 2017, was "God's Love Made Visible."

God's Love Made Visible
John 1:14-18 (NRSV)

And the Word became flesh and lived among us, and we have seen his glory, the glory as of a father's only son, full of grace and truth.

(John testified to him and cried out, "This was he of whom I said, 'He who comes after me ranks ahead of me because he was before me.'") From his fullness we have all received, grace upon grace. The law indeed was given through Moses; grace and truth came through Jesus Christ. No one has ever seen God. It is God the only Son, who is close to the Father's heart, who has made him known.

My brother, John Salmon, is a pianist. He doesn't just play the piano—it's his life's work. John is a piano professor in the music school at the University of North Carolina, Greensboro. He's also a concert pianist. Linda and I attended a concert he played last year in North Carolina with the Piedmont Wind Symphony. The bio in the program for the concert reads, "Pianist John Salmon has distinguished himself on four continents, as both a classical and jazz artist." John has given piano recitals and played in concerts in many places—Chicago, New York City, Mexico City, Spain, Hungary, China. He even gave a recital in Washington, D.C., for the Music Teachers National Association annual meeting.

John started taking piano lessons when he was five years old. When in high school, he wrote a fan letter to the jazz pianist Dave Brubeck. For some reason Dave Brubeck wrote him back. They became almost like pen pals. Eventually they met. Years later they collaborated on arrangements for some of Dave Brubeck's compositions. John recorded three compact discs of Dave Brubeck's piano music. In that Washington, D.C., performance John played an all-Brubeck program with Dave Brubeck in attendance. Linda and I were blessed to be in attendance that night when John and Dave Brubeck jammed together on "dueling pianos" before an audience of appreciative piano teachers from all over the country. In another concert with the Wilmington Symphony, John played in a trio with two of Dave Brubeck's sons, bassist Chris and drummer Dan. After Dave Brubeck died in 2012, John played a tribute in one of the memorial services.

It might surprise you to know that jazz composer Dave Brubeck has a piece in our hymnal. It was written in 1975 in collaboration with his wife, Iola. She wrote the words, and Dave wrote the music. The hymn is titled "God's Love Made Visible." (*Celebrating Grace*, p. 142). When I asked John about the hymn, of course he was familiar with it. John described it as "an attractive but not easy piece (it's in 5/4 meter!)." I was attracted to the hymn, not by the 5/4 meter of the music, but by the words that Iola wrote.

> God's love made visible! Incomprehensible!
> Christ is invincible! His love shall reign!
> From love so bountiful, blessings uncountable
> Make death surmountable! His love shall reign!
>
> Open all doors this day of His birth,
> All of goodwill inherit the earth.
> His star will always be guiding humanity
> Throughout eternity! His love shall reign!

Admittedly, the song is hard to sing, thanks to the 5/4 meter, but the message is what Christmas is all about. God's love was made visible when Jesus came to dwell among us. The Gospel writer John said as much in our scripture for this morning. John wrote, "And the Word became flesh and lived among us, and we have seen his glory, the glory of a father's only son, full of grace and truth" (John 1:14). John concluded the prologue to his Gospel with this declaration: "No one has ever seen God. It is God the only

Son, who is close to the Father's heart, who has made him known" (John 1:18). In other words God's love was made visible in his Son!

Iola first met Dave Brubeck when he was an aspiring musician in the 1940s. After they were married, Iola helped manage Dave's career as a jazz composer and performer. By the 1950s the Brubecks were playing on college campuses and other venues. I read this description in an online account: "As champions of racial justice, they refused to play at colleges where black musicians were treated differently. In 1958, the State Department sent them on a people-to-people cultural exchange tour of Eastern Europe. [It was] the first time jazz musicians were used as emissaries of the U.S. behind the Iron Curtain. Four years later, Dave and Iola Brubeck co-wrote a musical, *The Real Ambassadors* starring Louis Armstrong, [as] a reaction to racial segregation in the U.S. It premiered at the Monterrey Jazz Festival in 1962 to critical acclaim." (www.pbs.org/wnet/religionandethics/2009/07/10/july-10-2009-dave-brubeck/3488/).

Iola collaborated with Dave on several oratorios and cantatas, including *La Fiesta de la Posada* (The Festival of the Inn) in 1975. Included within that Christmas choral pageant is "God's Love Made Visible." In a PBS interview Dave said, "My wife was driving, and I said, 'I've finished this (*La Posada*).' And she said, 'No, you haven't finished it.' And I said, 'Well, what did I leave out?' And she said, 'God's love made visible. He is invincible.'" Her lyrics resonate, from the title of the piece to the emphasized phrase "His love shall reign." Though it could be sung any day of the year, it's a Christmas song, as it declares, "Open all doors this day of His birth."

Today I give my last sermon as your pastor. I've been thinking and praying about what to say in this final sermon. What could I possibly say that you have not heard before? Well, what I want to say in this final sermon is what Iola Brubeck wrote in the hymn and what John wrote in the prologue to his Gospel: In Jesus, God's love is made visible! That's what Christmas is all about. That's what our Christian faith is all about. That's what I want you to remember from all the words I have ever spoken in this place. In Jesus, God's love is made visible! That's the most important thing I want to say in this last sermon.

The second most important thing I want to say is simply, "Thank you." Thank you for allowing me to be your pastor. It has been a privilege, and a blessing, and a joy. You've allowed me to walk alongside you in some of the most personal moments of your lives. I dedicated some of you as infants. I baptized a good number of you upon your profession of faith in Christ. I officiated at your wedding for some of you. For many of you, I prayed beside your bed when you were sick or in the hospital. For many of you, I officiated the funeral for a loved one. I don't take those personal moments alongside you for granted. Being able to be with you in those most personal times has been one of the most meaningful parts of my ministry.

I thank you for your support all these years, and I thank my wife, Linda, for her support. Village got a great deal when you called me as pastor because you got Linda too. She has contributed so much to this church, not because she had to, but because she wanted to. She has been a banner maker. She has been a Sunday school teacher. She co-chaired the missions commission. She helped coordinate the warm nights ministry. She helped coordinate the silent auction for summer mission projects. She has served as a deacon. She has led a women's evening Bible study. She helped lead the craft team for Vacation Bible School. She prepared meals for Lenten Bible studies. She represented our church at meetings of the Cooperative Baptist Fellowship and the Baptist World Alliance. In the early years she volunteered in the nursery. She has been a friend and confidant to many. So thank you, Linda, for all you have done!

For the time being, Linda and I will continue to live in Bowie. But we won't be coming here to church. We will continue to be friends with you. We will socialize outside the church. But for the sake of the next pastor, it's important that we remove ourselves.

Now, Village will go on without Linda and me. But I want to say this loud and clear—VILLAGE WILL GO ON. By God's grace, Village will go on. Village flourished before we came, and I am confident Village will continue to flourish after we are gone. You have a very capable interim minister in Pastor Star. She knows the congregation. She brings many gifts to ministry. She is well-prepared to help Village carry on. I'm not worried about the future of Village. Village is in good hands. We are all in God's hands.

So this is not our final goodbye. This is "'til we meet again." And we will meet again, if not on this earth, then in the great reunion in heaven. Until then, let us remember: "No one has ever seen God. It is God the only Son, who is close to the Father's heart, who has made him known" (John 1:18). "God's love made visible—his love shall reign!"

December 31, 2017

Contradiction from the Start
John 1:9-14 (NRSV)

The true light, which enlightens everyone, was coming into the world. He was in the world, and the world came into being through him; yet the world did not know him. He came to what was his own, and his own people did not accept him. But to all who received him, who believed in his name, he gave power to become children of God, who were born, not of blood or of the will of the flesh or of the will of man, but of God. And the Word became flesh and lived among us, and we have seen his glory, the glory as of a father's only son, full of grace and truth.

This past week I took my car in for an oil change. While I was waiting in the customer lounge, I overheard an interesting conversation between two men. There was a talk show on the television about single men who adopt children. These two men in the waiting room were debating the wisdom of single fathers adopting young children. One man pointed out that a child needs two parents; or if a child can have only one parent, a mother is better equipped to be a single parent than a man is. He was especially wary of a single man adopting a little girl. He wondered how the single father could be an adequate role model when it came to raising a young daughter.

The other man in the customer lounge disagreed. Although he conceded that having two parents was the ideal, he thought these men on the TV talk show could give their adopted children a good home. He based his belief on the fact that these particular men were highly motivated to be fathers. He pointed out that these men were fathers by choice. They did not have to adopt their children. Rather, theirs was a conscious decision to become fathers by adoption. He argued that because of their love for their children, these single fathers would be able to give their adopted children what they really needed.

It was not the kind of conversation you would expect to hear in an auto service waiting room, particularly among two men. But it got me to thinking about our Scripture text for this morning. As it happened, I was working on this Scripture passage at the very time the talk show was on the television and the two men were having their debate. I had my Bible open on my lap to these verses in the first chapter of John as I listened to the discussion about single fathers and adopted children. Then I began to see some connection between what they were saying and what John is talking about here in the prologue to his Gospel. John is saying that God is like a Father who, out of love, wants to make us his children. God sent his son, Jesus, into the world so that we might believe in him and become part of God's family.

The problem, the contradiction, is that not everybody wants to be God's children. Not everybody wants to be born again into God's family. Not everyone accepted God's son when he was sent into the world. Indeed, many of his own people rejected him. Jesus came as the very embodiment of the grace and truth of God, but many of those to whom he came wanted nothing to do with him. How do you explain that?

Tonight at 7:00 p.m. we begin a three-month Bible study of the life of Jesus. During the next twelve weeks we will be working our way through the accounts of Jesus's life that we find in the Gospels of Matthew, Mark, Luke, and John. It's interesting that the Bible doesn't give us just one long narrative about Jesus, but rather four different narratives from four different points of view. Matthew, Mark, Luke, and John each have their own perspective on the life of Christ. Each of them sees Jesus in a slightly different way. At many points their stories about Jesus correspond, but they also differ at key points. The Gospel of John is the most different of all the Gospels. Matthew and Luke begin their Gospels by talking about Jesus's lineage, his parents and his ancestors. Mark begins his Gospel by talking about the forerunner to Jesus, John the Baptist. But John goes all the way back to the beginning, even before the world was created, when Jesus was with God. Theologians call John's point of view a "high Christology," or a "Christology from above." John begins with the divinity of Jesus, and then he describes how the divine Word became a human being.

In John's Gospel there is contradiction from the start. Jesus, who is one with the Father in heaven, surrenders his divine status to take on human flesh. He comes to the world which was created through him, and the world rejects him. Jesus comes to the chosen people, and his own people turn against him. What a contradiction!

According to the Old Testament, God had a plan. God chose a particular people to be the means through which he would draw all people back to himself. For centuries God revealed himself to the Jews, to prepare them for his ultimate self-disclosure, through the gift of his Son. This was God's plan, but the chosen people did not cooperate. Those with whom God had been working for centuries to prepare for his coming, the Jews who should have been most ready to receive him, were the very ones who by and large rejected Christ when he did come. How do you explain something like that?

During our study of the life of Christ, we are going to consider yet another perspective on Jesus. Not only will we turn to Matthew, Mark, Luke, and John; we'll also hear from a modern-day disciple of Jesus, a songwriter named Michael Card. We have printed the words to one of his songs about Jesus on the back of the bulletin. Like Matthew, Mark, Luke, and John, Michael Card has tried to tell us who Jesus was, not through the words of Holy Scripture, but through his music. The song is called "The Nazarene":

> The Nazarene had come to live the life of every man.
> And He felt the fascination of the stars.
> And as He wandered through this weary world,
> He wondered and He wept,
> For there were so few who'd listen to His call.
> He came. He saw. He surrendered all,
> So that we might be born again.
> And the fact of His humanity was there for all to see.
> For He was unlike any other man
> And yet so much like me.

If you ever studied any Latin, you might remember that famous phrase *veni, vidi, vici*, which means, "I came; I saw; I conquered." It was a quote attributed to Julius Caesar after his victory in Zela in 47 B.C. "I came; I saw; I conquered" became the motto for Julius Caesar's life. By the time of his assassination in 44 B.C., Julius Caesar had conquered much of the Mediterranean world into the mighty Roman Empire.

Only a few decades after Julius Caesar, another conqueror was born. Eventually, he too would establish a kingdom, a kingdom far greater than the Roman Empire. This one born only forty years after the death of Julius Caesar would prove to be a conqueror of a very different sort. He would conquer not by a force of arms but by the power of love. His victory would be won not with violence but with self-sacrifice.

While Julius Caesar lived by the motto "I came; I saw; I conquered," Jesus lived by the motto "I came; I saw; I surrendered." No wonder Jesus was rejected by his own people. They were looking for a savior like Julius Caesar, a mighty warrior, a victorious general, a conquering hero. In the words of George Macdonald ("That Holy Thing"),

> They all were looking for a king to slay their foes and lift them high;
> [He came], a little baby thing, that made a woman cry.

Because Jesus was not the kind of king they were looking for, many of the people rejected him. But not all. Some people would grasp the contradiction of a king born in a stable and laid to rest in a manger. Some people would see beyond the humble exterior of this Nazarene carpenter. Some people would even recognize the glory of his cross.

An ancient creed said: "He became like us, so that we might become like Him." That's what our Christian faith is all about—becoming like Jesus. And to become like Jesus means that we will find victory by surrendering ourselves to him. To become like Jesus means that our motto will be not power and might, but service and love. To become like Jesus means that through our own acts of self-sacrifice, we will find a glory that can only come from God. The gospel of Jesus Christ is shot through with contradiction. As Michael Card wrote (www.songlyrics.com/michael-card/the-nazarene-lyrics/),

> He came. He saw. He surrendered all,
> So that we might be born again.
> And the fact of His humanity was there for all to see.
> For He was unlike any other man
> And yet so much like me.

January 9, 1994

All I Want for Christmas: Love
John 1:1-5, 14, 16-18; 3:16 (NRSV)

In the beginning was the Word, and the Word was with God, and the Word was God. He was in the beginning with God. All things came into being through him, and without him not one thing came into being. What has come into being in him was life, and the life was the light of all people. The light shines in the darkness, and the darkness did not overcome it....

And the Word became flesh and lived among us, and we have seen his glory, the glory as of a father's only son, full of grace and truth....

From his fullness we have all received, grace upon grace. The law indeed was given through Moses; grace and truth came through Jesus Christ. No one has ever seen God. It is God the only Son, who is close to the Father's heart, who has made him known....

"For God so loved the world that he gave his only Son, so that everyone who believes in him may not perish but may have eternal life.

Santa was having a bad day. Four of his elves got sick, and the replacement trainee elves didn't know what they were doing and totally messed up the toy order. Then Mrs. Claus told him that her mother was coming for a long visit. Then, when he went to harness the reindeer, he discovered that two of them had jumped the fence and were flying around who knows where. Then, while loading his sleigh, a large bag of toys fell off and scattered gifts everywhere. Totally frustrated, Santa went inside for a mug of cider with a shot of rum. He discovered the cider jug was empty and the elves had drunk all the rum. Then the doorbell rang. Santa yanked open the door, and there stood a little angel with a great big Christmas tree. "Merry Christmas, Santa," the angel said. "Isn't this a lovely day? I have this beautiful tree for you. Where do you want me to stick it?" And so began the tradition of a little angel on top of the Christmas tree.

Not everyone is happy this time of year. Christmas adds a level of stress that can put even Santa in a bad mood. And then there are those people who seems to be in a bad mood all the time. Did you see any episodes of the latest season of *Survivor*, the "reality" series on CBS? The show was set in Gabon, Africa, and one of the contestants was an especially bitter, middle-aged man named Randy. Throughout the series Randy was mean and insulting to just about everyone. When Randy finally got eliminated from the competition, you could see the glee on the faces of his fellow competitors. Surprisingly, Randy's profession is a wedding photographer. Considering his personality, it seems like an odd choice of a career. But Randy relishes his sour demeanor. Randy says he is a ruthless bully who enjoys picking on those who lack his strength and intellect. He describes himself as "angry, blunt, mean, sarcastic (yet charming)." I think his charm must be an acquired taste.

Randy readily admits that his personal life is a trainwreck. He says he has no living relatives, except for an older brother whom he hasn't heard from in years. He lives by himself on a lake in rural southwest Missouri. Randy says he has never met a person who didn't eventually disappoint him. His best friend, the only one he ever really loved, was his recently deceased black Labrador retriever mix, with whom he lived for thirteen years. Randy says he has no use for cell phones or overly religious people, and he won't allow either in his home or car. On the final show of the season, where the winner of *Survivor* was announced live, each contestant was allowed to bring six guests. Most of the other contestants brought family members or friends. Randy brought six people he had never met before. Apparently they were members of an unofficial Randy fan club.

During that final show the viewers learned more about Randy. We learned that he has an engineering degree from Vanderbilt University. We learned that he has a commercial pilot's license and has competed in many marathons and triathlons. We also learned that he has the second highest IQ of any of the contestants, bested only by a physician whose IQ is off the charts. With all that going for him, one wonders why Randy became such a bitter, isolated, disagreeable, angry person.

We've all known them—otherwise intelligent, competent, capable people who are nonetheless miserable in their lives and who find a way to make everyone around them miserable too. What gives a person such a negative outlook on life? I suppose there are many possible reasons. Some people seem to have just a naturally gloomy disposition. Others were raised in a negative environment. Some turn sour because of negative life events. But my guess is that at the bottom of every bitter person is a fundamental lack of love. If people do not feel loved, it is hard for them to be happy and to have a positive outlook on life.

There are a lot of unhappy investors after the most recent financial calamity on Wall Street. Bernard Madoff, one of the most experienced and respected brokers on Wall Street, apparently bilked investors out of fifty billion dollars. According to the Securities and Exchange Commission, he set up an elaborate Ponzi scheme where he used the money from new investors to pay attractive returns to older investors. A lot of very smart, very wealthy people got taken. Some people lost everything. I saw an interview with a man in Florida who lost his entire nest egg of eight million dollars. He said he should have known better than to put all his assets in one place. But Bernie Madoff had a sterling reputation, and the returns were phenomenal. The man in Florida said he made a nice return every year with Madoff managing his money. Even when the stock market was down, he made money.

The word got around that Madoff's clients were getting a healthy ten percent return (or more) on their investments every year. So wealthy clients were clamoring to get in on the action. Some investment advisors were skeptical. The returns seemed too good to be true. No one, they argued, could be that market savvy to make such money every year. Either Bernie Madoff was the smartest guy on Wall Street, or he must have been doing something illegal, like insider stock trading. It turned out he was doing something illegal—not insider trading, but a giant Ponzi scheme.

Madoff got away with it for years. Only when the stock market began to fall and clients began to ask Madoff to cash out their investments did the whole scheme come crashing down. It was when investors demanded withdrawals from their accounts of some seven billion dollars that Madoff finally had to admit he didn't have the money. He had used it to pay returns to other investors. Bernie Madoff had portrayed himself as a financial genius, making money even when the stock market was going down. In reality, he admitted, it was "all one big lie." As Warren Buffett observed, it is only when the tide goes out that it becomes clear who was swimming naked. Well, the financial crisis was the tide going out, and Bernie was swimming naked, exposing a lot of naked investors with him.

I can understand how so many people got taken in. Bernie Madoff was a former chairman of the Nasdaq stock exchange. He ran a legitimate trading business that at one point handled almost ten percent of all stock trades in America. But at the same time, he was running this fraudulent financial management service that fleeced a lot of trusting investors. One official with the SEC called it "a stunning fraud of epic proportions." I can understand how investors would want to get in on what seemed to be a sure thing. Who would not want a ten percent or more return year after year, even in bear markets?

What I don't understand is the motivation of Bernie Madoff to engage in such fraud. He had already made a name for himself as a legitimate stock trader for more than forty years. He had become a legendary player on Wall Street, both for his stock trading business and for his role in developing electronic trading networks. He and his wife owned three multimillion-dollar homes and were members of six prestigious golf and country clubs in New York and Florida and elsewhere. They moved in elite social circles. He had friendships with financiers, philanthropists, and politicians all over the world. He had developed such a reputation that hundreds of banks, hedge funds, and wealthy individuals entrusted him with billions of dollars. Why would he risk all that? He already had plenty of money. How many multimillion-dollar bonuses and country club memberships does anyone need?

On the surface it looked like Bernie Madoff had it all, but underneath he must have been lacking something. My guess is that he enjoyed being viewed as a financial genius. He craved the adulation that came from investors who thought he had a magic touch and could spin gold even in down markets. There must have been something lacking in Bernie Madoff that made him risk everything. Could it have been a lack of love?

To be sure, he had plenty of people around him who care about him. He has a wife, and a brother, and two sons, and other family members. The fact that his sons turned him in to the SEC doesn't mean they don't love him. Doing the right thing was the only way they could really help him. My guess is that a lot of people do love Bernie, but somehow he wasn't able to be satisfied with their love. Somehow he needed more to feel good about himself. Perhaps that's why he did it—in an effort to build himself up in the eyes of others and in his own eyes too.

We all need someone to love us. We all need someone to let us know that we matter, that our lives count for something. And that's what Christmas is all about. Christmas is about love, the love from God in his son, Jesus Christ. God sent Jesus to show us how much he loves us. Jesus, the Word of God, became flesh and lived among us. No one has ever seen God. But God's son, who is close to the Father's heart, has made him known.

"For God so loved the world that he gave his only Son, so that everyone who believes in him may not perish but may have eternal life" (John 3:16 NRSV). That's what Christmas is all about—God sent his son because he loves us. God sent Jesus because we matter; our lives count for something. In the end Christmas is all about love.

There are a lot of bitter people out there like Randy. There are a lot of people who are driven by ego needs to self-destructive behavior like Bernie Madoff. And those bitter, egocentric people can hurt a lot of other people in their wake. But Jesus came to change all that. Jesus came to change bitter, empty hearts and to fill them with his love. Maybe your heart, like mine, could use some changing too. O holy child of Bethlehem, be born in us today.

December 21, 2008

Light in the Darkness
John 1:1-5, 14 (NRSV)

In the beginning was the Word, and the Word was with God, and the Word was God. He was in the beginning with God. All things came into being through him, and without him not one thing came into being. What has come into being in him was life, and the life was the light of all people. The light shines in the darkness, and the darkness did not overcome it....

And the Word became flesh and lived among us, and we have seen his glory, the glory as of a father's only son, full of grace and truth.

The year was 1692. It was one of the darkest times in American history. Salem, Massachusetts, was a small community of about ninety families, with a total population of less than 600. Their days were filled with fear and drudgery and hard work and prayer. The Puritans were so "puritanical" in their religious extremism that they didn't even celebrate Christmas and Easter. Their daily monotony was punctuated by quarrels over property and firewood, terror of Indian raids, and Sunday church meetings filled with heavy obligations and very little joy.

In her book *The Witches: Salem, 1692*, Stacy Schiff describes what it was like to live in Massachusetts in the seventeenth century. She writes, "New Englanders lived very much in the dark." Their sky, she continues, was black, "crow black, pitch-black, Bible black, so black it could be difficult at night to keep to the path." It was in the midst of this perpetual darkness that a hysteria erupted about suspected witchcraft. Based largely on the emotional testimony of a few teenage girls and a South American slave, a paranoia spread that there were agents of the devil among them. Beginning in the cold winter of 1692 and continuing through the summer into the fall, accusations led to the arrest of somewhere between 144 and 185 suspected witches and wizards. Subsequent trials led to the conviction of nineteen men and women, who were hanged to death. Before their executions each victim denied being part of sorcery, but the reign of terror continued until it finally burned itself out.

Historians are still trying to figure out why it happened. Was it some kind of group mental disorder that led those girls to such theatrical outbursts and accusations? Did the young women get so caught up in the celebrity of being the center of attention that they leveled increasingly outlandish charges against their fellow citizens? Did the magistrates and judges and clergy see this as an opportunity to increase their power and to rid the community of misfits and undesirables? Or was it simply an expression of the dark underside of human nature, an evil mania that can infect a whole society and lead to witch hunts, even today?

There was darkness in Salem, Massachusetts, in 1692—physical darkness, spiritual darkness, and an evil darkness that led otherwise God-fearing people to accuse and kill their fellow citizens in the name of religion.

In our scripture for this morning, John wrote, "The light shines in the darkness, and the darkness did not overcome it." John was speaking metaphorically, of course. He was speaking about Jesus as the light of the world, and he was speaking about the spiritual darkness that exists in human hearts apart from God. Those metaphors of light and darkness have been rooted in the physical experience of most people throughout history. In ordinary contexts, light is good, and darkness is bad. That is, unless you are trying to get some sleep, and then darkness is good, and light is bad. Up until the discovery of electricity and the invention of illuminating devices, the vast majority of people throughout history have lived in darkness.

There was an article in last Sunday's *Washington Post* (November 8, 2015, A11), "Living in the Dark." Even today, some 1.3 billion people around the world live in the dark because they lack access to electricity. In Latin America, five percent of the population has no electricity. In the Middle East, it's eight percent of the population. In Asia, it's seventeen percent of the population. In Africa, fifty-seven percent of the people have no electricity, including seven out of ten in sub-Saharan Africa. In some countries, the percentages are even higher. In Haiti, for example, seventy-one percent of the people have no electricity. In North Korea, seventy-three percent of the people do not have electricity. In Ethiopia, it's seventy-six percent. In Somalia, it's eighty-seven percent. In Malawi, ninety-two percent of the population does not have electricity. These are people who literally live in the dark much of their lives.

There is a correlation between poverty and lack of electricity. If you want to see where people are impoverished and go hungry, look for places without electrical power. According to the World Food Programme, "Three-quarters of all hungry people live in rural areas, mainly in villages of Asia and Africa." These are also the areas with the lowest access to electricity. So darkness can be a metaphor for human need. But John wrote, "The light shines in the darkness, and the darkness did not overcome it."

For many years our church has received a Thanksgiving offering for world hunger. We receive the offering next week on the Sunday before Thanksgiving. What better way to express our thanks to God than to share with those in greater need? According to the United Nations Annual Hunger Report, over 795 million people globally suffer from malnutrition. According to the Bible, responding to the needs of the poor and the hungry is our Christian responsibility. William Epps, a Baptist pastor in Los Angeles and a former vice president of the Baptist World Alliance, says, "Poverty is mentioned in the Bible more than 2,000 times." As the book of James says, if someone lacks daily food and you do not supply their bodily needs, what is the good of that (Jas 2:15–16)? Jesus said what we do for "the least of these," we do for him (Matt 25). One way the light of God shines into the darkness of human need is through Christians who work together to feed the hungry.

Our Thanksgiving offering hunger gifts go to Baptist World Aid, the relief and development agency of the Baptist World Alliance. Baptist World Aid provides both emergency food assistance and long-term development aid in many countries around the world. Although the aid is not just for Baptists, or even just for Christians, Baptist and Christian partners make requests and distribute aid in the places where they already serve. Here are a few examples of how Baptist World Aid has used our donations this year:

- Shipped 1.5 million meals to Liberia, Sierra Leone, and Guinea during the peak of the Ebola disease outbreak;
- Provided food, clothing, and basic necessities to over 5,000 Syrian refugees and persecuted Iraqi Christian refugees and other ethnic minorities forcibly displaced by ISIS (Islamic State in Iraq and Syria) in Lebanon, Jordan, and Turkey;
- Provided food and tarpaulins for shelter to 600 households immediately after the devastating earthquake in Nepal;
- Provided food assistance to people affected by natural disasters like floods and cyclones in Malawi, the Democratic Republic of Congo, Burundi, India, and the Philippines;
- Supported small landholder farmers with seeds, tools, and training in sustainable agriculture in Sierra Leone, Bangladesh, Zimbabwe, Ethiopia, DR Congo, Rwanda, and Angola;
- Supported income-generating projects for people living in poverty in India, DR Congo, Zimbabwe, Cameroon, and Indonesia.

After the earthquake that struck Haiti in 2010, about ninety percent of the schools in and around Port-au-Prince were severely damaged or destroyed. The Haiti Baptist Convention appealed to Baptist World Aid for help. Baptist World Aid allocated money to build a new school and an orphanage on land owned by the Haiti Baptist Convention. The Virginia Baptist Mission Board contributed to the project, and Hungarian Baptist Aid supervised the construction. The total cost was about $1.5 million.

Today the school provides education for thirty-five orphans who live at the center and another 120 children from the surrounding community. In addition to primary education classes, there are computer classes, English classes, music classes, and soccer classes. In addition, twelve disabled children receive free daily therapy, and the center provides potable water to the community. "Most important," says the vice president of the Haiti Baptist Convention, "we preach the gospel." Would you like to guess the name of this school in Haiti funded by Baptist World Aid? It is called "Source of Light." Our gifts to Baptist World Aid shine the light of Christ into some of the darkest places of human need.

Of course, there is more than the darkness of poverty and hunger in the world. There is spiritual darkness—the darkness of those who don't know God or the darkness of those who forget about God. Even Christians can live in the dark if we try to go it alone. But Jesus came into the world so that we don't have to go it alone. Jesus came into the world to shine the light of God into the dark places of our lives.

Some of you may feel like you are in a dark place right now. Maybe you are sick or someone you care about is sick. Maybe you feel like the weight of the world is on your shoulders. Maybe you feel like a shadow is hanging over you and your life seems to be getting darker and darker. Maybe you feel all alone. This, then, is God's word for you: "The light shines in the darkness, and the darkness did not overcome it."

There are many places without power in the world, but we who believe in Jesus are never without power. We may be weak and heavy laden, but God is strong and mighty. The world may be a dark place, but we live in the light of Christ. We are never without hope.

Jesus said, "In this world you will have trouble. But take heart! I have overcome the world" (John 16:33 NIV). "The light shines in the darkness." What more do we need?

November 5, 2015

Epilogue

I never wanted to be a preacher. But I learned from many preachers along the way, and somehow I became a preacher myself. I was smart enough to ask questions and to listen to what those role models had to say. I once asked Dr. George Buttrick how many biblical commentaries I should consult in preparing to write a sermon. He replied, "Study the commentaries until you have enough." Dr. David Matthews once told me that he always had three or four books on his desk that he was reading to give him ideas for sermons. I tried to keep three or four books on my desk that I was reading to give me ideas for sermons. Dr. J. P. Allen once told me that people would come out of the church and say, "Pastor, that was one of the best sermons I have ever heard." He said, "Don't you believe them!" I didn't. I was never completely satisfied with any sermon I ever preached. I always aspired to do better. Dr. John Claypool was my primary role model. Dr. Wayne Oates described Claypool's preaching as a "disciplined confession." In Claypool's first book, *Tracks of a Fellow Struggler*, he opened up about his own life in order to be a help and encouragement to others. As he told me, the goal of his "confessional" preaching was not to come across as a hero, but to allow his own struggles to give others hope.

Some time ago, I was riding in a car with the pastor of a very prestigious church. I had heard him preach, and I was impressed. I asked him, matter-of-factly, "Do you consider yourself a naturally gifted preacher?" He thought a minute, and then he replied, without a trace of arrogance, "Yes, I guess I do." Some preachers are naturally gifted. I do not consider myself to be one of them. Yet for thirty-three years, Sunday after Sunday, I did the best I could.

Lee Trevino was a professional golfer, and a very successful one at that. He was inducted into the World Golf Hall of Fame after a career in which he won twenty-nine PGA Tour events, including six major championships. But Trevino came from an unlikely background for a professional golfer. He was born in Dallas, Texas, into a family of Mexican ancestry. Lee never knew his father. He dropped out of school at age fourteen and earned money as a caddie and shoe shiner at a local golf course. At age seventeen he joined the U.S. Marine Corps, where he continued to work on his golf game. After being discharged from the Marines, he got a job as an assistant professional at a golf club in El Paso, Texas. Not yet a member of the PGA Tour, he qualified for the U.S. Open in 1966 and again in 1967, finishing high enough to gain provisional tour status. He had an unorthodox self-made swing, but a gregarious personality that belied his humble beginnings. He played in an era that included such golf greats as Arnold Palmer, Jack Nicklaus, and Gary Player. An interviewer once asked Trevino what gave him the idea that he could compete against such legends of the game. Trevino replied, "I figured somebody's got to win this golf tournament. It might as well be me."

That became my attitude about preaching. I figured somebody's got to preach this sermon. It might as well be me.

Balcony People
Ephesians 4:29-30 (NRSV)

Let no evil talk come out of your mouths, but only what is useful for building up, as there is need, so that your words may give grace to those who hear. And do not grieve the Holy Spirit of God, with which you were marked with a seal for the day of redemption.

The author Keith Miller calls them "basement people." He's not talking about people who live on the bottom floor. He's talking about people in the subconscious of our minds. We all have them. These are people in our past or present who have helped shape how we feel about ourselves. These are people whose words stay with us and whose expectations continue to influence us. Basement people are anyone who has exerted a significant influence upon our lives—a parent or grandparent, a teacher, a coach, a boss, a pastor, perhaps even a spouse. Basement people are authority figures, persons we have sought to please, persons (living or dead) who exert control over the way we think and act and feel and live.

However well-intentioned, basement people tend to be critical individuals, persons with a negative point of view, persons who find fault or point out our shortcomings or tell us where we need to improve. In a way, that's good. In a way, offering constructive criticism is a parent's job, or a teacher's job, or a coach's job, or a boss's job, and even a pastor's job. We all need correcting now and then. We all need someone to nudge us when we have gotten on the wrong path and to get us going in the right direction. But the problem is, most of us don't take criticism very well. For most of us, it is difficult to hear a critical word and not take it personally. If a person we care about says something negative, we take it to heart. A critical word from someone important to us can be devastating to our self-esteem.

I've got some basement people in my life. A couple of my schoolteachers were basement people. If I did not do well, their disappointment was almost palpable. There was a baseball coach who criticized me whenever I made a mistake on the baseball diamond. As a consequence he had me terrified of striking out or making an error. Of course, I was so nervous, there was no way I could play well. There was a professor in college who was constantly pushing me to do better. He was a brilliant teacher of literature who specialized in the English Romantic movement. I admired him so much that I kept taking courses from him, even though I could never do enough to earn an "A" in his class. Two straight years he had me doing extra work over the Christmas holidays to earn extra credit so I could improve my grade. I look back now and wonder about his control over me. Why was I trying so hard to please that guy? Why did his critical comments have such a hold on me?

You've got basement people in your life too. On a conscious level you may not realize they are there, but they are. Whenever you begin to doubt yourself or to second-guess yourself or to berate yourself or to feel bad about yourself, somebody's negative comments are down there at the bottom of it. Some of us who are adults are still carrying around our parents in the basement of our subconscious. Some of us are still trying to please them, still trying to live up to their expectations, still trying to avoid their disapproval. In other cases we live our lives in rebellion against the expectations of our parents. Basement people can make our lives miserable if we allow ourselves to be tyrannized by their critical influence.

I see the same phenomenon taking place in some families today. I see parents who deeply love their children, but whose critical comments and rigid expectations have made their children almost gun-shy. We parents need to realize what awesome power our words can have over our children. We might think that our words are weak because our children don't always listen to us or don't always do what we tell them to do. But disobedience and inattentiveness can be defense mechanisms. Our children may seem to be ignoring us because they cannot bear the threat to their fragile egos when they take our negative judgments to heart. Basement people can dominate our lives if we give them the power to do so.

But life does not have to be lived from the basement. We can stop listening to basement people. Just as important, we do not have to be basement people in other persons' lives. There is an alternative—what pastor and author Carlyle Marney called "balcony people." Balcony people are encouragers. Balcony people build up rather than tear down. Balcony people are those persons (living or dead) who cheer us on. They are those who inspire us, those who affirm us, those who help us to believe in ourselves. And the same categories I listed for basement people can also be balcony people. Balcony people can be parents or grandparents, teachers or coaches, bosses or pastors, or even spouses. Again, these are people of authority, people we care about, people whose words have helped to shape who we are. But instead of depositing negative images into the basement of our psyches, they have left powerful positive images in the balconies of our minds. Their words have lifted us up instead of putting us down. Their encouragement has helped us to become more of the persons God wants us to be.

Thank God I've had some balcony people in my life. My grandmother was a balcony person. She got a twinkle in her eye whenever I came around. She made me feel that I was special, loved, cherished. There was a youth leader at my church who was a balcony person for me when I was a teenager. He selected me to be "pastor" during youth week at our church. That experience gave me the self-confidence to begin to consider the possibility that God was calling me into the ministry. There was a minister at my church in college who was a balcony person. During my senior year we went to lunch a number of times together, and occasionally he took me to play racquetball with him. He never came right out and said it, but his attitude toward me was, "I see something in you; I believe in you. You are a person of value and worth. You can believe in yourself too."

In our Scripture reading, Paul wrote about the difference between "basement people" and "balcony people." Paul recognized the powerful impact our words can have on other people. What we say, the kind of language we use, our tone of voice, our choice of words, our basic attitude can be crucial in another person's life. In effect, Paul told the Christians in Ephesus, "Don't be basement people, speaking critical words, tearing others down. Instead, be balcony people, speaking helpful words, building others up. Don't say anything that would hurt another person. Instead, say only what helps. At work, at school, at church, in the home (especially in the home), don't be a discourager. Instead, be an encourager."

There was a Western song we learned as children called "Home on the Range" ("My Western Home," Brewster Higley, 1872). I don't remember all the lyrics, but the refrain went something like this:

> Home, home on the range,
> Where the deer and the antelope play,
> Where seldom is heard
> A discouraging word,
> And the skies are not cloudy all day.

God wants our homes to be like that—not populated with deer and antelope, but places where seldom is heard a discouraging word. God wants our homes, our work, our church to be places where encouragement is far more common than criticism.

I once heard author and pastor Bruce Larson say that it takes ten "attah boys" to offset the effect of one "you jerk." In other words, it takes ten positive comments to counter the impact of one negative comment. There are more than enough negative people in the world. God calls us to be people of encouragement. You think I'm overstating the case? Let me read our scripture for you again: "Let no evil talk come out of your mouths, but only what is useful for building up, as there is need, so that your words may give grace to those who hear. And do not grieve the Holy Spirit of God, with which you were marked with a seal for the day of redemption."

Did you notice the second part of the passage? Paul said, "Do not grieve the Holy Spirit." Our critical comments, our negativity, our putdowns not only hurt other people; they grieve the Holy Spirit. God himself is wounded by our destructive words. This is important business—watching what we say, carefully choosing the words we speak. This has consequences not only for our relationships with others, but also for our relationship with God. When we speak hurtful words and tear people down, we grieve the Holy Spirit. But when we speak helpful words and build people up, we please the spirit of God.

When the musical *Les Misérables* opened at the Barbican Theatre in London in 1985, the critics panned it. The respectable newspapers in London didn't like it because they said the musical trivialized a classic of Western literature, the novel by Victor Hugo. The tabloids trashed it because they said the production was long and dreary, and musicals are supposed to be light and frothy. The critics hated it; the audiences loved it. The critics were basement people. The audiences were balcony people. Thankfully, the producers ignored the basement people and listened to the balcony people. *Les Misérables* went on to win eight Tony Awards and five Drama Desk Awards. Its message of hope and encouragement is still lifting up audiences around the world.

Jesus was a balcony person. He was always on the lookout for people who were down so he could lift them up. Jesus was always ready to speak a word of grace to a person who needed it. And the good news of the gospel is that Jesus wants to be a balcony person for you. Jesus sees something in you. Jesus believes in you. Jesus says you are a person of worth and value. He's up there in the balcony of heaven right now cheering you on. Even more, if you invite him into your heart, he's right there inside you, ready to help you become a balcony person too.

September 24, 1995

Justice and Kindness
Micah 6:8 (NRSV)

He has told you, O mortal, what is good; and what does the LORD require of you but to do justice, and to love kindness, and to walk humbly with your God?

This sermon has been percolating in my mind for about four months now. It started on a Saturday back in March, the day of Julia Bruce's wedding. I was invited to officiate the ceremony in the base chapel at the Patuxent Naval Air Station. Because it's a long drive down there, Julia's parents, Neal and Jeramie, graciously offered to put us up in a hotel so we wouldn't have to make the roundtrip twice. So Linda and I drove down on Friday afternoon for the rehearsal, and we spent the night at a hotel near the base. Because the wedding was Saturday afternoon, we had time on Saturday morning to do some sightseeing. On our way to Point Lookout State Park, we passed an enclosed memorial of some kind, with a tall granite tower in the middle of it. We noted a sign identifying it as the Point Lookout Confederate Cemetery. Not knowing the history, we were a little mystified to come across a Confederate cemetery in Maryland. We learned that Point Lookout had been the location of a prisoner of war camp during the Civil War.

It was during the Battle of Gettysburg in July of 1863 that Union forces captured thousands of Confederate soldiers. Unprepared to deal with so many POWs, the Union army hastily established many makeshift military facilities to accommodate the captives. A forty-acre prison compound was established at Point Lookout, Maryland, just north of an existing military hospital. A fifteen-foot-tall wooden fence was erected around the complex, and by the end of August, the stockade held more than 1,700 Confederate troops. By the end of the war, more than 20,000 Confederate prisoners were being held at the camp. As the prison population grew, conditions worsened. There were no barracks or permanent housing. Instead, the detainees lived in tents. Poor sanitation, contaminated water, inadequate rations, malaria and typhoid fever, and exposure to the elements took a terrible toll. It is estimated of the 50,000 total prisoners held at the Point Lookout camp, almost 4,000 died while incarcerated. Two cemeteries were established for the Confederate dead. A third cemetery contained the bodies of Union soldiers who had died while being treated at the nearby military hospital.

After General Lee's surrender at Appomattox, the U.S. quartermaster general's office discussed establishing a national cemetery at Point Lookout. Eventually, the remains of Union soldiers were transferred to Arlington National Cemetery. The two Confederate cemeteries remained until 1870 when the state of Maryland consolidated the two sites into one location. Because it was not possible to identify individuals, more than 3,000 Confederate remains were buried in a mass grave. In 1910 the state transferred the cemetery to the federal government. The United States erected an eighty-foot-tall granite obelisk the following year, affixed with bronze tablets carrying the names of 3,382 Confederate soldiers and sailors presumed to be buried there. For years the site was marked by both the American flag and the Confederate flag.

In 1998 the Confederate flag was removed by order of the U.S. Department of Veterans Affairs. Thereafter, only the American flag was flown over the cemetery. Some members of the Point Lookout Prisoners of War Descendants Organization objected to the removal of the Confederate flag. Eventually, the private organization bought the land right next to the federally owned Point Lookout Confederate Cemetery. On that adjacent property they built the privately owned Confederate Memorial Park in Point Lookout. The two sites, the cemetery and the memorial park, are basically right next to each other, separated only by a small grove of trees.

Linda and I knew nothing of this history when we came upon the Confederate Cemetery and then the Confederate Memorial Park. In fact, we visited the memorial park first. But almost from the outset, something seemed odd about it. We had no idea it was a private memorial. In fact, there is a sign that had been erected by the state of Maryland commemorating the location as the site of the Point Lookout POW camp. The state-erected sign led us to assume that the memorial park was government-owned, just like the cemetery. Linda was first to sense something was wrong when she noticed that the circle of flags around the pavilion of the memorial park contained the state flag of Kentucky. Being a Kentucky native, Linda knew that Kentucky never joined the Confederacy, even though it was a slave state. Then I noticed that the historical markers at the memorial park were surprisingly sympathetic toward the Confederacy. It was only later we learned the memorial park is a private enterprise, not government property.

When I went online to check out the memorial park, our suspicions were confirmed. The memorial park was established to present a more sympathetic view of the Confederacy. One of the founders of the memorial park said, "Now we'll have a place where we can say what we want to say and fly the [Confederate] flag 24/7" (confmemparkinc.plpow.com/CMP_CountyTimes_Article.htm). Among the guest speakers at the dedication of the memorial park in 2008 were two clergymen, one a Baptist pastor from Georgia and the other a retired Army chaplain. Both offered strong defenses of the Confederate cause. The Baptist pastor said, "When we think of our Confederate soldiers, we must remember that they were indeed right! They were not fighting for what they believed was right; they were fighting for what was right." The retired Army chaplain said, "Now we are free at last to tell the true story and history of the Confederate soldiers and civilians who suffered here so horribly at the hands of the federal government…and thank God for all our prisoner descendants' love of God, their love of the Southern Confederacy and her just and righteous cause." (www.plpow.com/Speech,%20for%20POWS/Speeches_JWeaver.htm).

As I said, this sermon has been percolating in my mind since that Saturday in March. It finally started to brew a couple of weeks ago when Dr. James Langley sent me his poem titled "Raid at Harpers Ferry." Perhaps you remember the story. John Brown, a radical abolitionist, led a raid on the federal armory at Harpers Ferry on the night of October 16, 1859. His goal was to seize the weapons from the armory in order that he might arm slaves to start an insurrection. Although he failed to start a rebellion, many historians believe that the raid on Harpers Ferry was the tipping point that led to the Civil War.

While Brown was successful in seizing the armory, his plot soon fizzled. After two days John Brown and his co-conspirators were defeated by military forces, led by an army officer named Robert E. Lee. Many of Brown's men were killed, including two of his sons. Brown was captured and quickly put on trial.

John Brown was a man motivated by deep religious convictions. In court he argued that his actions were just and right in the sight of God. He said, "Now, if it be deemed necessary that I should forfeit my life for the furtherance of the ends of justice, and mingle my blood with the blood of my children, and with the blood of millions in this slave country whose rights are disregarded by wicked, cruel, and unjust enactments, I submit; so let it be done." John Brown was convicted of treason and sentenced to be hanged to death. On his way to the gallows, he declared, "I, John Brown, am now quite certain that the crimes of this guilty land will never be purged away but with blood." (https://en.wikipedia.org/wiki/John_Brown_%28abolitionist%29).

There were strong reactions to John Brown's hanging. Many Southerners applauded his death. Among those present to witness his execution were the future Confederate general Stonewall Jackson and the future presidential assassin John Wilkes Booth. But many Northerners viewed John Brown as a hero and a martyr. Frederick Douglass later wrote, "His zeal in the cause of my race was greater than mine. I could live for the slave, but he could die for him" (www.wvculture.org/history/jbexhibit/bbspr05-0032.html). A song was written about John Brown's body "a-mouldering in the grave," but "his soul goes marching on" (Pete Seeger). The song became a kind of unofficial anthem of the Union army. Julia Ward Howe based her "Battle Hymn of the Republic" on the song.

I tell you these two stories, about the Confederate Memorial Park at Point Lookout and about John Brown's raid on Harpers Ferry, because both were purported to be in the cause of justice. The POW descendants organization that built the memorial park claims that the Confederate cause was right and just. John Brown believed that his cause to abolish slavery was right and just. Jim Langley helped me put these two stories together when he sent me his poem. Jim noted that most Christians rightly praise the German pastor Dietrich Bonhoeffer who was involved in a plot to assassinate Adolf Hitler and who died a martyr's death in a Nazi concentration camp. We view

Bonhoeffer's cause as just and right because he sought to end a great evil, even if it meant killing Hitler. Jim notes that like Bonhoeffer, John Brown plotted and engaged in violence, hoping to achieve a worthy goal and abolish a great wrong. And of course both John Brown and Dietrich Bonhoeffer were executed by hanging. But in the process of thinking about the violent abolitionist John Brown, Jim also remembers another Christian martyr, Martin Luther King Jr., who rejected bloodshed, working for justice through nonviolent protest, even at the cost of his own life.

So we finally return to our scripture for this morning, that famous verse from the Old Testament prophet Micah. This one verse sums up what the Lord requires of us, namely, to do justice, and to love kindness, and to walk humbly with our God. As people of God, and more as followers of Jesus Christ, we are called to do justice, and to love kindness, and to walk humbly with our God.

The question is: How do we do it? How do we do justice, and love kindness, and walk humbly with our God? Slavery was abolished 150 years ago, but our country is still marred by the legacy of that "peculiar institution." And you don't have to venture to the Deep South to see vestiges of it. Just drive an hour and a half to southern Maryland and see the Confederate battle flag flying proudly over the Confederate Memorial Park.

Although the Confederate flag no longer flies within the adjacent Confederate cemetery owned by the federal government, some Confederate sympathizers erected a flagpole just beyond the fence of the cemetery. It is so visually deceptive that I had to walk to the back of the cemetery to verify the battle flag wasn't indeed flying within those hallowed grounds. From the parking lot it is difficult to tell whether that Confederate flag is in the cemetery or not. No doubt Confederate sympathizers would argue that removing the battle flag was nothing but political correctness. But for the sake of justice, who would fly a flag that represents centuries of the systematic enslavement and violent oppression of millions of people? Coincidentally, it was only three weeks ago Washington and Lee University finally removed Confederate flags from the college's Lee Chapel.

I want to thank Dr. Langley for using his poem to raise important questions about justice and mercy. As followers of Jesus Christ, we are called to do justice, but we are also called to love kindness in our deeply troubled world. And those questions of justice and mercy keep coming at us. The influx of unaccompanied children from Central America is a challenge to our calling to do justice and to love kindness. It is estimated that 90,000 such children will cross our national borders this year, compared with 24,000 last year. Some of those children are being sent here to Maryland. What do we do with them? How do we treat them? What is just and right in the sight of God? With the continuing violence between Israelis and Palestinians in the Gaza strip, the tension between justice and kindness demands the best of our moral reasoning.

The poet T. S. Eliot wrote in his play, "Murder in the Cathedral," "The last temptation is the greatest treason: to do the right deed for the wrong reason." We might add that it is also the greatest treason to do the wrong deed for the right reason. A just cause does not mean that any action is just. Justice and kindness must go hand in hand. That's the only way we can walk humbly with our God.

Jesus is our exemplar of justice and kindness. He managed to maintain that balance between standing up for what is right and acting with mercy and kindness and love. And we who would follow Jesus, we who would walk humbly with our God, must do justice and love kindness too.

July 27, 2014

Raid at Harpers Ferry

By James A. Langley

John Brown was a man of outsize passion,
On fire with a burning zeal and compassion
To end vile bondage and set slaves free,
Reason futile, he would force the issue for history.

Where light a torch to start a firestorm
When passions were feverish and past reform?
At the confluence of the Potomac and Shenandoah,
A blow of no-return was struck forevermore.

The scheme was to seize a cache of arms,
For armed insurrection against the gravest harms;
The military resisted, not without reason,
Brown's rebellion was widely held to be treason.

A town with the ferry-founder's name Harper,
Would signal the world of divisions sharper
Than generally perceived and the prelude to war civil,
To save the union, and end a monstrous evil.

Ill-fated it was, and unwise it may have been,
The 'peculiar institution' would not yield an easy win;
The rebellion was put down by one Robert E. Lee,
But it foreshadowed emancipation by war and decree.

Attacked from all sides—slave advocates construed
Him a prime danger, as terrorists would later be viewed,
Proponents of compromise feared his fanaticism,
Some abolitionists worried their cause was doomed by cataclysm.

Militant abolitionist, Brown aided blacks, slave and free,
His anti-slavery bloodshed led to the uprising plot fatefully;
A hanging high, the tragic end of his descendance,
And a mournful ballad became his chief remembrance.

A dark cloud of rage and fear descended
Upon slave-holders for what the act portended;
The raid and its threat fed a frenzy for secession,
Wielders of chairs and the lash would soon opt for insurrection.

Contempt and outrage have been visited upon Brown,
Whereas violence in other plots have brought renown;
Apart from a firebrand, might the scourge have endured
Another century before freedom from bondage was secured?

The raid is commonly seen and reproached as John Brown's folly,
Ill-conceived, Brown's plan deserves its melancholy;
We may leave John Brown's actions to a Judge omniscient,
Yet praise and honor his obsession magnificent.

Note: Jim personally sent this poem to me. He read it during worship on the Sunday the accompanying sermon was presented.

Bibliography

Achtemeier, Paul J., General Editor. *HarperCollins Bible Dictionary.* New York, NY: HarperCollins Publishers, 1996.

Barclay, William. *Discovering Jesus.* Louisville, KY: Westminster John Knox Press, 2000.

Card, Michael. *Immanuel: Reflections on the Life of Christ.* Nashville, TN: Thomas Nelson Publishers, 1990.

Claypool, John R. *Tracks of a Fellow Struggler: How to Handle Grief.* Waco, TX: Word Books, 1974.

Comfort, Philip W. and Jason Driesbach. *The Many Gospels of Jesus: Sorting Out the Story of the Life of Jesus.* Carol Stream, IL: Tyndale House Publishers, 2008.

Culpepper, R. Alan. *John: The Son of Zebedee, The Life of a Legend.* Minneapolis, MN: Fortress Press, 2000.

Dant, James C. *1 & 2 Samuel: Surviving the Tensions of Life.* Macon, GA: Smyth & Helwys Publishing, 2002.

Dilley, Andrea Palpant. *Faith and Other Flat Tires: Searching for God on the Rough Road of Doubt.* Grand Rapids, MI: Zondervan, 2012.

Drane, John. *Introducing the New Testament.* New York, NY: HarperCollins Publishers, 1987.

Evans, Craig A. and N. T. Wright. *Jesus, The Final Days: What Really Happened.* Louisville, KY: Westminster John Knox Press, 2009.

Foster, Richard J. *Celebration of Discipline: The Path to Spiritual Growth.* New York, NY: HarperCollins Publishers, 1998.

Goldingay, John. *Exodus & Leviticus for Everyone.* Louisville, KY: Westminster John Knox Press, 2010.

Hobbs, Hershel H. *Exposition of the Gospel of Mark*. Grand Rapids, MI: Baker Book House, 1970.

Köstenberger, Andreas J. *John. Baker Exegetical Commentary on the New Testament*. Grand Rapids, MI: Baker Academic, 2004.

Lane, Tony. *Timeless Witness: Classic Christian Literature Through the Ages*. Peabody, MA: Hendrickson Publishers, 2004.

McAfee, J. Thomas, Project Chair, and John E. Simmons, Coordinating Editor. *Celebrating Grace Hymnal*. Macon, GA: Celebrating Grace, Inc., 2010.

McLaren, Brian D. *A Generous Orthodoxy*. Grand Rapids, MI: Zondervan, 2004.

Miller, Stephen M. *The Jesus of the Bible: An Illustrated Guide to His Life, World, Teachings*. Uhrichsville, OH: Barbour Books, 2009.

Olson, Mark J. *Romans: The Letter that Changed Christian History*. Macon, GA: Smyth & Helwys Publishing, 2003.

Salmon, Bruce C. *Storytelling in Preaching: A Guide to the Theory and Practice*. Nashville, TN: Broadman Press, 1988.

Sayles, Guy. *Matthew: Living as Disciples of Jesus*. Macon, GA: Smyth & Helwys Publishing, 2006.

Schiff, Stacy. *The Witches: Salem, 1692*. Boston, MA: Little, Brown and Company, 2015.

Shurden, Walter B. *The Baptist Identity: Four Fragile Freedoms*. Macon, GA: Smyth & Helwys Publishing, 1993.

Story, Laura. *When God Doesn't Fix It: Lessons You Never Wanted to Learn, Truths You Can't Live Without*. Nashville, TN: Thomas Nelson Publishers, 2014.

Wilkins, Michael J. *Matthew: From Biblical Text to Contemporary Life (NIV Application Commentary Series)*. Grand Rapids, MI: Zondervan Academic, 2009.

Appendix A

Guest Preachers at Village Baptist Church (1985-2017)

Eddie and Macarena Aldape, CBF field personnel—2006

Rev. James Allcock, music director, Baptist Convention of Maryland/Delaware—1986

Rev. Dr. Jere Allen, executive director/minister (emeritus), D. C. Baptist Convention—1996, 2000 (2), 2004

Milton Allred, SBC missionary to Mexico—1993

Rev. Dr. Raymond Bailey, professor of homiletics, The Southern Baptist Theological Seminary—1986*

Rev. Charles Barnes, executive director (1993–2000), Baptist Convention of Maryland/Delaware; interim pastor (1973), Village Baptist Church—1986

Rev. Jerry Buckner, campus minister, University of Maryland—2005 (2), 2008 (3)

Katherine and Rolf Buehler, Wycliffe Bible translators missionaries—2007, 2011

Rev. Dr. Otniel Bunaciu, founder, Ruth School, Bucharest, Romania; pastor, Providence Baptist Church, Bucharest; former president, European Baptist Federation—2016

Rev. Dr. Neville Callam, general secretary, Baptist World Alliance—2010

Rev. Reynold Carr, director of missions, Prince George's Baptist Association—2002

Rev. Champion Chasara, president, Baptist Convention of Zimbabwe—2002, 2003, 2011*

Rev. Tony Cupit, director, Division of Evangelism and Education and Study and Research, Baptist World Alliance—1995

Cindy and Frank Dawson, CBF field personnel—2000, 2007 (Cindy Dawson)

Rev. Dennis Dhula, president, Baptist Convention of Zimbabwe—2004, 2006

Rev. Bonnie Dixon, founder and executive director, Journey Partners—2008

Rev. Dr. James Dunn, executive director, Baptist Joint Committee for Religious Liberty; interim pastor (1984), Village Baptist Church—1985 (2), 1986, 1989, 1990, 1998, 2003

Rev. Dr. Pam Durso, executive director, Baptist Women in Ministry—2015

Rev. Dr. Ron Elville, executive director, Prince George's Baptist Pastoral Counseling Center—1995

Rev. Temukum Fidelis, visiting pastor, Cameroon Baptist Convention—2013

**CBF field personnel—2003

Rev. Carol Franklin, ABC National Ministries' Office of Governmental Relations, Washington, D.C.—1985

Rev. Dr. Bruce Gourley, executive director, Baptist History and Heritage Society—2016

Rev. Elizabeth Evans Hagan, candidate for pastor, Washington Plaza Baptist Church, Reston, Virginia—2008

Rev. Dr. Jeffrey Haggray, executive director/minister, D.C. Baptist Convention—2002, 2003, 2005, 2006, 2007

Della Hambrick, SBC home missionary—1989

Rev. Donnell Harris, retired pastor, Montgomery Hills Baptist Church, Silver Spring, Maryland—2001

Rev. Dr. Stan Hastey, executive director, Alliance of Baptists—1988, 1994, 2002, 2003, 2006

Mrs. Hannah Hawkins, founder/director, Children of Mine, Washington, D.C.—2009

Rev. Jack Henry, member, Village Baptist Church—1986 (2), 1987

Baker Hill, SBC missionary to Burkina Faso, Africa—1989

Holly Hollman, general counsel, Baptist Joint Committee for Religious Liberty—2011

Keith Holmes and Mary van Rheenen, CBF field personnel—2013

Molly Houser, SBC missionary to Africa—1993

Rev. Dr. Dan Ivins, pastor, The First Baptist Church in America, Providence, Rhode Island; former pastor, Village Baptist Church, Bowie, Maryland (1974–1984)—1986, 1989, 1994, 2010

Rev. Gary Javens, retired pastor, Clifton Park Baptist Church, Silver Spring, Maryland—2010, 2011, 2012

Rev. Sandi John, pastoral counselor—1988, 1989

Rev. Carmella Jones, missionary, American Baptist Churches—2016

Rev. Dr. James Langley, executive director emeritus, D.C. Baptist Convention—2003, 2009, 2014

Rev. Dr. Denton Lotz, general secretary, Baptist World Alliance—2007

Rev. Dr. C. J. Malloy Jr., retired pastor, FBC Georgetown, Washington, D.C.—2008, 2009 (2), 2010 (3), 2011, 2012 (2), 2013

Rev. Dr. Trisha Miller Manarin, executive coordinator, Mid-Atlantic Cooperative Baptist Fellowship; coordinator, Division on Mission, Evangelism, and Justice, Baptist World Alliance—2017

Elias Maponga, director, Baptist Conference Center, Baptist Convention of Zimbabwe - 2004

Rev. Dr. Earl Martin, retired CBF field personnel—2007

Rev. John Mazvigadza, general secretary, Baptist Convention of Zimbabwe—2006

Dianne and Shane McNary, CBF field personnel—2006

Rev. Starlette McNeill/Thomas, Minister to Empower Congregations, D.C. Baptist Convention; associate pastor, Village Baptist Church, Bowie, Maryland (2013–2017); interim pastor, Village Baptist Church (2018–2019)—2011, 2012, 2013 (3), 2014 (10), 2015 (10), 2016 (9), 2017 (8)

Rev. Dr. Duncan McIntosh, D.C. Baptist Convention; consultant, long-range planning committee, Village Baptist Church—1999, 2000

Paul Montacute, director, Baptist World Aid, Baptist World Alliance—2003

Karen Morrow, CBF field personnel—2006

Rev. Dr. Henry Mugabe, principal, Baptist Theological Seminary of Zimbabwe—2014

Rev. Donald Ndichafah, general secretary, Cameroon Baptist Convention—2012

Rev. Kingsley Perera, general secretary, Sri Lanka Baptist Sangamaya—2005

Rev. David Potter, chaplain, Washington Hospital Center; member, Village Baptist Church—2012 (2), 2013

Rev. Wayne Price, member, Village Baptist Church—1990, 2004, 2010

Mrs. Marilyn Prickett, SBC home missionary, Washington, D.C.—1985

Rev. Dr. Tom Rodgerson, executive director, Centrepointe Counseling—1993, 2004, 2005

Melissa Rogers, general counsel, Baptist Joint Committee for Religious Liberty—1997

Rev. Dr. Ron Rogers, director of missions, Prince George's Baptist Association—1997, 2001

Mrs. Elizabeth Samandi, president, Cameroon Baptist Women's Union—2010, 2012, 2014

Darrell and Kathy Smith, CBF field personnel—2006

Ralph and Tammy Stocks, CBF field personnel—1998 (Ralph Stocks), 2003

Kathie and T Thomas, CBF field personnel—2002

Rev. Jack VandenHengel, executive director, Community Ministry of Prince George's County—1999

Rev. Dr. Daniel Vestal, executive coordinator, Cooperative Baptist Fellowship—2001, 2009

Rev. Dr. Morris Vickers, retired director of missions, Arundel Baptist Association; president, Financial Security Advisors; member, Village Baptist Church—1998 (2), 2000 (2), 2001 (2), 2002, 2003 (2)

Rev. Brent Walker, executive director, Baptist Joint Committee for Religious Liberty—1994, 1996, 2006

Steve Weisman, rabbi, Temple Solel Synagogue, Bowie, MD—2017* (Passover Seder)

**CBF field personnel—2010

Rev. John Woodall, former pastor, Village Baptist Church (1971–1973)—1991

Rev. Phil Wyrick, member, Village Baptist Church; chaplain, U.S. Navy—1991, 1992 (3)

Rev. Silas Yego, presiding bishop, Africa Inland Church, Kenya—2003

*Sunday evening; ** CBF field personnel serving in high security-risk areas

Appendix B

Catalogue of Sermons at Village Baptist Church (1985-2017)

I preached at least 1,496 original Sunday-morning sermons at Village Baptist Church from 1985 until 2017. I say "at least" because some of the sermons I preached over those thirty-three years seem to be missing from my files. I have 1,496 sermons in file folders in my basement. Unfortunately, the sermon manuscripts in my office from 1985 to 1999 were destroyed by the fire that burned the church building in January 2000. In addition, the Sunday bulletin files in the church office for those years were destroyed by the fire. I was able to reconstruct an "almost-complete" catalogue of sermons for 1985–1999 by painstakingly going through every file folder in my basement and retrieving the date, Scripture text, and sermon title for almost every Sunday. In most cases, each file folder contains the bulletin from that Sunday, as well as extensive sermon notes or a complete manuscript. Thus, it was possible to retrieve almost every sermon from those "lost" years. Still, there are some years with blanks on some Sundays, most likely because I was away and there was a guest preacher those days or because the sermon I preached on those "blank" Sundays was lost.

Compiling a sermon catalogue for 2000–2017 was much simpler. There are Sunday bulletin files for those years in the church office. The manuscripts for each of those 791 sermons are in file drawers in my home office, and I have the extensive sermon notes or manuscripts in a separate file folder for each Sunday. In addition, the sermon manuscripts from 2012–2017 are stored electronically on my computer's hard drive. Sermon manuscripts from 2000–2011 are stored electronically on "floppy disks," although many newer computers lack the necessary device to read those disks.

After compiling a sermon catalogue for each year, I analyzed the biblical texts on which those sermons were based. Over the course of thirty-three years, many more sermons were based on passages from the New Testament than from the Old Testament, although some sermons were based on texts from each testament. Not surprisingly, some biblical texts were used repeatedly, especially those related to the Christian year, such as Advent,

Christmas, Epiphany, Easter, Pentecost, and Ascension Sunday. Other sermons connected with secular holidays, such as New Year's Day, the birthday of Martin Luther King Jr., Valentine's Day, Mother's Day, Memorial Day, Father's Day, Independence Day, and Thanksgiving.

Sometimes sermons coordinated with special church events, such as baptisms, infant dedications, deacon ordinations, the commissioning of Sunday school teachers, and annual programs like winter and Lenten Bible studies, Vacation Bible School, Youth Sunday, graduate recognition, the summer mission project, the Thanksgiving offering for world hunger, and the Christmas offering for international mission partnerships. Some sermons were inspired by current events or by personal experiences.

Some sermon series were preached through books of the Bible. For example, in 2000, after the fire, I preached the entire year on the life of Jesus. There were twelve sermons from Mark, sixteen sermons from Luke, and twelve sermons from John, consecutively for forty weeks. One year a sermon series focused on the book of Daniel and another year on the seven churches in the book of Revelation. In many years, the four Sundays of Advent and the Sundays in Lent featured a sermon series. Often, the summer months would be occasion for a sermon series.

In compiling the sermon catalogues, I was chagrined to discover that over the course of thirty-three years, I failed to preach any sermons on a few of the more obscure books of the Bible. I didn't preach a single Sunday-morning sermon on 2 John, 3 John, or Jude. From the Old Testament, I never preached a Sunday-morning sermon based on 2 Chronicles, Hosea (!), Obadiah, Nahum, or Zechariah. I was simply too busy in full-time pastoral ministry to take the time to catalogue my sermons as I was writing and preaching them. Thus, I never noticed the omissions. In the years before the fire (1985–1999), I averaged preaching forty-seven Sunday-morning sermons per year. In the years after the fire (2000–2017), the average dropped to forty-four Sunday-morning sermons per year. The drop was due to two factors. First, I invited more guest preachers in those latter years, even on Sundays when I was present. The intent was to "put a face" on our mission partners by having representatives from those organizations preach a sermon in our church. The second factor, in the last four years of my ministry, was our associate pastor, Rev. Starlette Thomas. I wanted to give her as many preaching opportunities as possible, so she preached whenever I was away and on some Sundays when I was there.

Appendix B

Of the 1,496 sermons, 388 were based on Old Testament texts, and 1,194 were based on New Testament texts. As I said, some sermons were based on both. Of the New Testament sermons, 700 (58.6%) were based on the Gospels. Almost 23% were based on the Pauline epistles. About 8.5% were based on the general epistles, and another 8.5% were based on the book of Acts. The nineteen sermons based on Revelation comprised less than 2% of the total. Clearly, telling the story of Jesus was the major focus of my preaching.

1985	Text	Title
January 6	Gen 8–9	Somewhere Under the Rainbow
January 13	Gen 12:1–5	Begin Again
January 20		
January 27	Heb 13:1–8	Yesterday, Today, and Forever
February 3	Matt 5:1–12	The Secret of Happiness
February 10	Gal 3:26–29	The Great Equalizer
February 17	Acts 8:26–39	Here Is Water
February 24	Mark 14:3–9	Love Is a Spendthrift
March 3	Mark 14:10–21	Broken Hearts
March 10	Mark 14:27–31, 66–72	The Rooster Crowed Twice
March 17	Mark 15:1–15	The People's Choice
March 24	Mark 15:16–25	Burden into Blessing
March 31	Mark 11:1–10, 15, 25–32	King for a Day
April 7	Choir Cantata	
April 14	John 20:1–18	Where Is Jesus?
April 21	Matt 28:16–20	But Some Doubted
April 28	John 14:1–11	The God I Won't Believe In
May 5	Mark 9:33–35; 10:35–45	Lessons from a Checkerboard
May 12	Deut 6:4–9	The Family That Stays Together
May 19	Acts 4:32–5:11	Lies, Flies, Alibis
May 26	Acts 2:1–8, 12–21	Drunk with the Spirit
June 2	John 4:5–30	Every T-shirt Tells a Story

June 9	Ps 103:1–18	Who'll Stop the Rain?
June 16	Rev. Carol Franklin	
June 23	2 Tim 3:14–17	Battle for the Bible (The Book)
June 30	John 8:31–36	Free, Indeed
July 7	1 Cor 15:1–10	Amazing, Grace!
July 14	Acts 9:26–27; 15:36–40	Children of Encouragement
July 21	Deut 30:15–19	Choose Life
July 28	Rom 12:1–2; 1 Pet 2:9–10	Christian Distinctives
August 4	Rom 12:14–21; Matt 5:9	Blessed Are the Peacemakers
August 11	Mark 6:30–44	Lonely Places
August 18	Eph 4:25–32	It's a Mad, Mad World
August 25	Dr. James Dunn	
September 1	John 2:1–11	The Life of the Party
September 8	John 6:1–14	Bread for Life
September 15	James 5:13–26	Does Prayer Work?
September 22	Luke 9:57–62	Hands to the Plow
September 29	Mark 7:24–27	How Firm a Foundation
October 6	1 Cor 1:18–25	Send in the Clowns
October 13	Ps 139:1–12, 23–24	Running Away from God
October 20	Mrs. Marilyn Prickett	
October 27	1 John 4:7–21	Who Cares?
November 3	Rom 7:14–8:2	The War Within
November 10	Gen 1:1–5, 24–28, 31	In His Image
November 17	Isa 40:21–31	God and Your Stress
November 24	Gen 4:1–16	Thanks, but No Thanks
December 1	Isa 7:10–14	God with Us
December 8	Luke 1:26–38	Disturbing the Peace
December 15	Luke 1:39–45	Leaping for Joy
December 22	Luke 2:8–20	Jesus and Santa Claus
December 29	Dr. James Dunn	

1986	Text	Title
January 5	Heb 1:1–4	The End and the Beginning
January 12	Heb 4:14–16	Never Give Up
January 19	Heb 11:1–16	The Roll Call of Faith
January 26	Heb 12:1–2, 12–13	All the Way Home
February 2	Eph 5:15–20	Making the Most of the Time
February 9	John 15:12–17	Love One Another
February 16	John 16:1–44	Rise Again
February 23	John 13:1–17	Dirty Feet
March 2	John 14:1–7	The Way
March 9	John 15:1–11	The Vine
March 16	John 18:1–14	Peace Without Swords
March 23	Choir Cantata	
March 30	John 20:1–10, 19–22	What Next?
April 6	John 19:38–42	Secret Disciples
April 13	Rev. Charles Barnes	
April 20	2 Kgs 5:1–14	Seven Ducks in a Muddy River
April 27	Mark 5:25–34	Weller Than Well
May 4	Gal 6:7–10	Private Lives
May 11	2 Tim 1:1–5	A Mother's Place
May 18	Gen 11:1–9; Acts 2:1–11	Languages of Men and Angels
May 25		
June 1	Mark 9:9–13	Be Careful What You Throw Away
June 8	Mark 10:17–22	Dealing with Success
June 15	Rev. Jack Henry	
June 22	Acts 5:1–11	Ties That Bind
June 29	Mark 8:34–38	The Purpose of Religion
July 6	Luke 4:16–21	Statues of Liberty
July 13	Job 2	Why Me, Lord?
July 20	Ps 14	Do You Believe in God?
July 27	Ps 90:1–12	Halfway Home

August 3	1 Chron 32:1–12	Preparing for Peace
August 10	Ps 51:1–12	Restore the Joy
August 17	Dr. Dan Ivins	
August 24	Gen 3	Don't Blame It on the Snake
August 31	Dr. James Dunn	
September 7	Luke 5:1–11	Gone Fishing
September 14	Acts 16:6–15	Life's Detours
September 21	Rev. James Allcock	
September 28	Phil 3:12–16	Touchdown Jesus
October 5	Matt 21:22	Quick-Fix Religion
October 12	Luke 15:1–3, 11–24	Coming Home
October 19	Luke 15:25–32	The Rest of the Story
October 26	John 3:16	John 3:16
November 2	1 Cor 11:23–26	In Remembrance
November 9	Gen 1:26–28; 2:24; 1 Cor 6:18–7:5	Sex Is Not a Four-Letter Word
November 16	Acts 11:19–26	Signs of Progress
November 23	Luke 16:19–31	My Brother's Keeper?
November 30	Isa 9:1–7	A Prophet's Hope
December 7	Luke 2:1–7	An Innkeeper's Gift
December 14	Luke 2:8–14	An Angel's Joy
December 21	Luke 2:15–20	A Shepherd's Tale
December 28	Rev. Jack Henry	

1987	**Text**	**Title**
January 4		
January 11	Eph 4:1–7, 11–16	The Call of God
January 18	Jas 1:1–8, 12, 16–18	Count It All Joy
January 25	Jas 2:1–9	Rich Man, Poor Man
February 1	Jas 3:1–13	Taming the Tongue
February 8	Jas 5:13–20	A Picture of the Church
February 15	1 Cor 13	The Power of Love

February 22	Rom 8:28–39	Eucatastrophe
March 1	Gal 5:13–25	Fruit of the Spirit
March 8	Matt 21:1–11	Sunday: Day of Triumph?
March 15	Matt 21:12–17	Monday: Day of Principle
March 22	Matt 21:23–27; 22:15–45	Tuesday: Day of Authority
March 29	Matt 26:1–16	Wednesday: Day of Affirmation
April 5	Matt 26:30–56	Thursday: Day of Infamy
April 12	Matt 27:15–31	Friday: Day of Defeat?
April 19	Matt 28:1–10	The Man Who Couldn't Sleep
April 26	Luke 24:36–49	Only the Beginning
May 3	1 Cor 11:17–28	Supper in Three Tenses
May 10	Gen 32:3–8; 33:1–4	Family: God's Idea
May 17	Acts 15:1–20	How to Build a Church
May 24	Acts 1:1–11	The Ends of the Earth
May 31	Youth Sunday	
June 7	2 Tim 1:1–14	Why I Am a Christian
June 14	Rev. Jack Henry	
June 21		
June 28	Matt 5:13–16	Salt and Light
July 5	2 Cor 3:4–6, 12–18	Let Freedom Ring
July 12	Col 1:1–12	Growth in Grace
July 19	Matt 6:25–33	Winning Over Worry
July 26	John 1:1–5, 14, 16–18	Christmas in July?
August 2	2 Pet 1:1–11	Building Christian Character
August 9	Matt 6:9–13	The Lord's Prayer
August 16		
August 23		
August 30	Gen 2:4–9, 15; 3:17–19, 23	Work: Gift or Curse?
September 6	Exod 20:8–11; Mark 2:23–28	Holidays and Holy Days
September 13	Luke 2:14–20	A New Covenant
September 20	Mark 12:41–44	How Much Is Enough?

September 27	Phil 4:10–13	The Secret of Contentment
October 4	Acts 16:25–34	Getting Saved
October 11	Luke 10:25–37	Who Is My Neighbor?
October 18	Matt 6:1–6; 7:1–5; 23:1–3, 23–28	Logs, Specks, Camels, Gnats
October 25	Exod 25:1–8; 40:33–38	The House of the Lord
November 1		
November 8	John 10:1–6, 27–28	Love Lifts Us Where We Belong
November 15	1 Cor 12:4–7	Many Members/One Body
November 22	Lev 23:22, 39–43	Thanks/Giving
November 29	Isa 49:1–6	A Light to the Nations
December 6	Isa 40:1–5	Christmas Peace
December 13	Matt 2:1–12	Christmas Joy
December 20	1 John 4:7–12	Love Came Down at Christmas
December 27	Luke 1:5–23	A Promise Too Good to Believe

1988	**Text**	**Title**
January 3	Matt 2:13–20	Dark Day in Bethlehem
January 10	Mal 1:8–14	Confronting Casual Religion
January 17	Mal 2:10, 13–16	Promises to Keep
January 24	Mal 3:7–12	Robbing God
January 31	1 Cor 3:18–45	Winning
February 7	Acts 8:31–39	More Than Conquerors
February 14	1 Cor 13:4–8a	Making Love Work
February 21	Gen 6:5–8, 7:6–12; 17:21–23	Fortysomething
February 28		
March 6	Num 13:1–3, 25–33	God of the Grasshoppers
March 13	Exod 13:17–18	Live the Journey
March 20	Luke 4:1–13	No Way Out
March 27	Choir Cantata	
April 3	Matt 28:1–8	Surprised by Joy

Appendix B

April 10	Dr. Stan Hastey	
April 17	Luke 4:14–21	Why Go to Church?
April 24	Rom 13:8–10	The Law of Love
May 1	John 15:1–5	Lessons from an Apple Tree
May 8	Deut 5:1–5, 16	A Matter of Honor
May 15	Mark 1:14–20	Making a Christian Commitment
May 22	Acts 2:14, 22–24, 36–41	Come to the Party
May 29	Matt 11:28–30	Rest for the Weary
June 5	Ps 8	A Little Less Than God
June 12	Youth Sunday	
June 19	Rev. Sandi John	
June 26	Matt 11:2–19	A Different Drummer
July 3	Gal 5:1	Christian Freedom
July 10	2 Cor 1:1–11	The God of Comfort
July 17	2 Cor 1:12–22	God's Yes
July 24	2 Cor 4:7–12, 16–18	Earthen Vessels
July 31	2 Cor 5:1–10	Earthly Tents, Heavenly Houses
August 7	2 Cor 5:14–21	A New Creation
August 14	2 Cor 6:1–2	The Acceptable Time
August 21	2 Cor 6:14–7:1	Distinctively Christian
August 28	2 Cor 8:1–7; 9:6–8	A Cheerful Giver
September 4	2 Cor 12:7–10	Life Within Limits
September 11	Luke 12:13–21	Wise Investments
September 18	Jon 1, 2, 3, 4	The Gospel According to Jonah
September 25	Mark 2:1–12	A Hole in the Roof
October 2	Luke 6:17–23	The Sermon on the Plain
October 9	Luke 6:27–31	The Hardest Commandment
October 16	Luke 6:46–49	How Firm a Foundation?
October 23	Eph 2:13–22	A Place for You
October 30	Luke 12:22–31	Don't Worry, Be Happy
November 6	Mark 12:13–17	Caesar and God
November 13	1 Tim 6:6–10, 17–19	Life Which Is Life Indeed

November 20	1 Tim 4:1–5	All Good Gifts
November 27	Phil 2:5–11	Christ-Minded
December 4	Isa 11:1–9	The Peaceable Kingdom
December 11	Matt 2:1–12	Starry Night
December 18	Luke 2:8–20	Christmas Journeys
December 25	John 1:1–5, 14; 1 John 4:7–9	After the Angels

1989	**Text**	**Title**
January 1	Phil 2:1–4	In Full Accord
January 8	John 1:19–29	Prepare the Way
January 15	John 1:35–51	Come and See
January 22	John 2:13–22	Cleaning House
January 29	John 3:1–8	Born Again
February 5	John 4:46–54	The Second Sign
February 12	John 5:1–9	Waiting for an Angel
February 19	John 6:16–21	Walking on Water
February 26	John 8:2–11	A Stone's Throw from Grace
March 5	John 9:1–25	Sight for Sore Eyes
March 12	John 12:1–8	What a Waste!
March 19	Choir Cantata	
March 26	John 14:1–3; 1 Cor 15:51–58	Victory!
April 2	John 20:19–22	Rituals of Belonging
April 9	John 20:24–31	A Question of Faith
April 16	John 21:1–14	The Last Breakfast
April 23	John 21:15–19	A Second Chance
April 30	Acts 1:6–14	The Absence of Christ
May 7	Eph 4:31–5:2	Be Kind
May 14	Prov 23:22–25	Let Your Mother Rejoice
May 21	Prov 22:1–6	Train Up a Child
May 28	Luke 20:22–30	God of the Valleys

Appendix B

June 4	Gen 45:16–28	Packing Your Suitcase: Journey
June 11	Matt 26:26–30	The Table Talks
June 18	Dr. James Dunn	
June 25	Rev. Sandi John	
July 2	Gal 5:1	Being Baptist Means Freedom
July 9	1 Tim 4:7–10	Three Lies
July 16	Luke 9:23–27	Your Cross to Bear
July 23	Matt 18:21–35	Forgiveness Without End
July 30	Dr. Dan Ivins	
August 6	Eccl 6:1–6, 12	What Are We Waiting For?
August 13	Gen 37:2–5, 18–28; 45:4–5; 50:20	Anatomy of a Family
August 20	Mic 6:6–8	Do the Right Thing
August 27	Exod 24:12–18; 32:1–10, 15, 19, 30	Descendants of a Golden Calf
September 3	Ps 34:1–8	Prescription for Happiness
September 10	Acts 1:15–26	Taking Judas's Place
September 17	Acts 2:41–47	Portrait of a Church
September 24	Acts 3:1–10	Power to Walk
October 1	Acts 4:1–12	The Cornerstone
October 8	Acts 6:1–7	A Home to Come Home To
October 15	Acts 6:8–15; 7:54–60	The Power of Commitment
October 22	Mrs. Della Hambrick, World Missions Conference	
October 29	Acts 8:1–8	Take a Sad Song…
November 5	Acts 9:1–19	The Great Turnaround
November 12	Acts 10	Overcoming Prejudice
November 19	Acts 11:27–30	Learning to Share
November 26	Col 3:12–17	Thanks Living
December 3	Matt 1:18–21	What's in a Name?
December 10	Matt 2:1–12	Gifts for a King
December 17	Luke 1:26–37	Message from Another World

December 24	Luke 2:8–16	To Certain Poor Shepherds
December 31	Phil 3:7–14	Back to the Future

1990	**Text**	**Title**
January 7	Acts 2:12–15; 26:24–25	Drunk and Mad
January 14	1 Thess 4:13–18	Good Grief
January 21		
January 28	2 Cor 2:14–17	The Aroma of Christ
February 4	2 Cor 7:4–7	Faith Under Stress
February 11	2 Cor 7:8–12	Healing Broken Relationships
February 18	2 Cor 9:6–15	The Grace of Giving
February 25	2 Cor 13:11–14	The Fellowship of Love
March 4	Rom 3:23; 5:8; 6:23; 10:9	The Gospel According to Romans
March 11	Luke 9:23–24, 28–36, 51	A Glimpse of Glory
March 18	Luke 10:38–42	First Things First
March 25	Luke 14:25–33	Counting the Cost
April 8	Choir Cantata	
April 15		
April 22	Ps 67	Sing Praise to God
April 29	Acts 25:7–10	The Healing Power of Prayer
May 6	Ps 127	Building the Family
May 13	Ps 128	The Happy Family
May 20	Song of Sol 8:6–7; 1 Cor 13:4–7	Two Love Songs
May 27	Eccl 1:2–9, 14; John 3:8	The Answer Blowing in the Wind
June 3	Acts 2:1–8, 43–47	Pentecostal People
June 10	John 6:35, 48–51	The Bread of Life
June 17	2 Sam 18:24–33	A House Is Not a Home
June 24	1 Pet 3:13–18	The Hope That Is in You
July 1	1 Pet 2:13–16	Live Free
July 8	1 Pet 2:22–25	Sins and Misdemeanors
July 15	1 Pet 3:8–12	The Power to Bless

Appendix B

July 22	1 Pet 4:7–11	In the Meantime…
July 29	1 Pet 5:6–11	He Cares for You
August 5	Rom 6:3–4	Newness of Life
August 12		
August 19		
August 26	Philemon	A New Relationship
September 2	2 Thess 3:6–13	Work and Rest
September 9	Rev 1:4–6	Holy Instructions
September 16	1 Sam 1:1–2, 10–11, 19–28	Dedicated to God
September 23	1 Sam 3:1–10	A Word from Our Sponsor
September 30	Dr. James Dunn	
October 7	1 John 1:1–7	What a Fellowship!
October 14	Matt 25:31–46	His World…Our Hands
October 21	Isa 55	Faith in Uncertain Times
October 28	1 Tim 3:1–13	Set Apart for Service
November 4	Matt 28:18–20	Every Christian's Job
November 11	Rom 14:10–19	Walking in Love
November 18	Ps 136	The Steadfast Love of God
November 25	Ps 40:1–3	The Rescuer
December 2	Isa 64:1–8	A Fresh Experience of God
December 9	Mark 1:1–8	Skip Christmas?
December 16	Luke 1:26–32, 46–55	Don't Be Afraid
December 23	1 John 4:8b–10; John 3:16	Home for Christmas
December 30	Rev. Wayne Price	

1991	**Text**	**Title**
January 6	Phil 3:12–14	Off to a Better Start
January 13	Matt 11:28–30	Right to Rest
January 20	Chaplain Phil Wyrick	
January 27	Isa 2:2–4	War and Peace
February 3	Acts 2:42–47	A Sharing Church
February 10	Acts 11:19–26	An Inclusive Church

February 17	Acts 10:34–43	An Evangelistic Church
February 24	Acts 14:1–7	A Growing Church
March 3	John 2:13–25	Tough Love
March 10	John 3:1–15	Something More
March 17	John 12:20–33	The Time Has Come
March 24	Choir Cantata	
March 31	John 20:11–18	The Eighth Day of Creation
April 7	Luke 24:13–35	Hearts Aflame
April 14	1 Cor 15:12–22	The Bottom Line
April 21	Ps 23	Green Pastures
April 28	Deut 18:9–15	Christ and the New Age
May 5	John 15:9–17	Living in Love
May 12	Eph 6:1–4	Positive Parenting
May 19	Acts 2:22–24, 32–33, 36–39	The Gifts of the Holy Spirit
May 26	Gen 1:26–28; Gal 3:26–28	Created Equal
June 2	Gen 1:26–28; Ps 24:1	The Good Earth
June 9	Mark 1:32–39	A Day in the Life
June 16	Mark 5:21–23, 35–43	A Father's Faith
June 23	Mark 6:1–6	The Power to Change
June 30	Lev 25:8–12	Proclaim Liberty
July 7	2 Sam 7:1–17	When God Says "No"
July 14	2 Sam 9	The Kindness of Strangers
July 21	2 Sam 11:1–17	A Matter of Lust
July 28	2 Sam 12:1–14	Punishment and Pardon
August 4	2 Sam 12:15–25	Necessary Losses
August 11		
August 18		
August 25	1 Tim 1:15–17	The Fringe Benefits of Religion
September 1	Mark 6:7–13	Traveling Light
September 8	Matt 7:31–37	Be Opened
September 15	Mark 9:38–41	On Our Side
September 22	Mark 10:2–9	What God Has Joined

Appendix B

September 29	Mark 10:17–31	What Money Cannot Buy
October 6	Jas 2:14–17	Putting Faith to Work
October 13	Rev. John Woodall	
October 20	Prov 6:16–19; 12:22	Telling the Truth
October 27	Exod 19:3–6; 1 Pet 2:9	A New World
November 3	Lev 27:30; 1 Cor 16:1–2	The Tithe Is the Lord's
November 10	Matt 25:14–30	Risk and Security
November 17	Eph 6:18–20	I'll Be Praying for You
November 24	Ps 100	Reasons for Thanksgiving
December 1	Isa 60:1–3	The Light of God
December 8	Jer 3:33–34	A New Covenant
December 15	Zeph 3:14–20	In Our Midst
December 22	Mic 5:2; Luke 2:1–7	Born in Bethlehem
December 29	Luke 2:15–20	Mary's Treasure

1992	**Text**	**Title**
January 5	Luke 3:15–17, 21–22	With Water and the Spirit
January 12	John 2:1–11	The Best Wine
January 19	Chaplain Phil Wyrick	
January 26	Luke 5:1–11	The Rest of Your Life
February 2	Isa 6:1–8	Send Me
February 9	Isa 12	Salvation, Strength, and Song
February 16	Isa 53:1–6	Rejected…Redeemed
February 23	Isa 61:1–7	Good Tidings
March 1	Luke 23:32–34a	Father, Forgive
March 8	John 19:17–27	Family Ties
March 15	Matt 27:45–46	Forsaken?
March 22	John 19:28–29	I Thirst!
March 29	Luke 23:44–46	Into Your Hands
April 5	John 19:28–30	Finished!
April 12	Choir Cantata	
April 19	Luke 23:39–43; 24:1–5	Today, Paradise!

April 26	John 20:19–31	Believing Thomas
May 3	John 21:15–19	Love Is Something You Do
May 10	Mark 10:13–16	Give the Blessing
May 17	1 Cor 13:4–8a	Three Kinds of Love
May 24	Gen 1:26–27; John 15:13	Sanctity of Life
May 31	1 Cor 7:1–9	Family Values
June 7	Gen 1:1–2:3	In the Beginning
June 14	Gen 4:1–10	East of Eden
June 21	Youth Sunday	
June 28	Gen 6:11–22	Saved Through Water
July 5	Chaplain Phil Wyrick	
July 12	Gen 28:10–22	Jacob's Ladder
July 19	Num 22:21–35	An Angel in the Way
July 26	Judg 16:4–22	Samson and Delilah
August 2	1 Sam 17:4–11, 32–51	David and Goliath
August 9	1 Kgs 3:5–28	The Wisdom of Solomon
August 16	Dan 3:8–30	The Fiery Furnace
August 23		
August 30	Dan 6	Daniel in the Lions' Den
September 6	Esth 3:8–11; 4:8–17	For Such a Time as This
September 13	Luke 15:1–7	Joy in Heaven
September 20	Luke 16:1–8	Good Lesson from Bad Example
September 27	Luke 16:19–31	Lazarus at the Gate
October 4	Luke 17:5–10	Faith and Duty
October 11	Luke 17:11–19	Returning to Say Thanks
October 18	Luke 18:1–8	Wearing God Out
October 25	Luke 18:9–14	A Tale of Two Sinners
November 1	Luke 19:1–10	Big Little Man
November 8	Luke 21:1–4	The Widow's Gift
November 15	Luke 12:22–31	First Things First
November 22	1 Thess 5:12–18	Always Give Thanks
November 29	Matt 24:36–44	Christ Is Coming

Appendix B

December 6	Matt 3:1–12	Prepare the Way
December 13	Matt 11:2–11	Misplaced Faith?
December 20	Matt 1:18–25	God with Us
December 27	Chaplain Phil Wyrick	

1993	**Text**	**Title**
January 3		
January 10	Matt 3:13–17	Graceland
January 17	Matt 4:1–11	No Shortcuts
January 24	Matt 4:12–22	Follow Me
January 31	Matt 4:23–25	Love That Heals
February 7	Matt 5:1–12	You Can Be Blessed
February 14		
February 21	Matt 6:9–13	The Lord's Prayer
February 28	Matt 7:1–5	Logs and Specks
March 7	Matt 9:35–38	The Harvest
March 14	John 4:3–30, 39–42	Living Water
March 21	John 9:1–41	Blind No More
March 28	John 11:1–44	Life Before Death
April 4	Baptism/Choir Cantata	
April 11	Matt 28:1–10	Joy in the Journey
April 18	Rom 5:1–8	Rejoicing in Suffering
April 25	Mic 6:6–8	When Religion Gets Sick
May 2	Mrs. Molly Houser	
May 9	Acts 12:1–8, 12–17	Christian Mothers
May 16	Rom 7:14–8:1	The War Within
May 23	Titus 2:11–14	The Pursuit of Happiness
May 30	John 7:30–39; Acts 2:1–4	Filled with the Spirit
June 6	1 Cor 3:16–17; 6:19–20	God's Temple
June 13	1 Cor 11:23–28	A Life Worthy
June 20	Luke 15:11–24	A Father's Love
June 27		

July 4	Matt 19:16–23	Really Free
July 11	1 Kgs 17:1–16	God Will Provide
July 18	1 Kgs 17:17–24	The Final Move
July 25	1 Kgs 18:17–21	God-esteem and Self-esteem
August 1	1 Kgs 18:22–46	And It Rained
August 8	1 Kgs 19:1–12	A Still Small Voice
August 15	2 Kgs 2:1–14	What a Friend
August 22	Rev. Tom Rodgerson	
August 29	Youth Sunday	
September 5	Rev 21:1–4, 22–27	Outside the Gate
September 12	Phil 4:1–7	One in the Spirit
September 19	Rom 1:16–17	Coming to Faith
September 26	Mark 2:21	New Cloth
October 3	Acts 11:25–26	"Christians"
October 10	Col 3:12–14	The People of God
October 17	Col 3:15–17	The Body of Christ
October 24	Luke 11:1–4	Teach Us to Pray
October 31	Luke 11:5–13	Prayer Changes Things
November 7	Eph 4:11–16	Speaking the Truth…in Love
November 14	Col 2:12; 3:1–4	A River Runs Through Us
November 21	Jas 2:14–17	Faith Works
November 28	Matt 1:1–11, 17	The Lineage of Jesus
December 5	Isa 35:1–10	Poems, Prayers, Promises
December 12	Luke 1:26–45	The Problem with Christmas
December 19	Luke 2:1–12	The Flower of the Good Night
December 26	Deacon-led Worship	

1994	**Text**	**Title**
January 2	Matt 2:1–12	A Star
January 9	John 1:9–14	Contradiction from the Start
January 16	Matt 5:14–16	Let Your Light Shine
January 23	Matt 2:13–23	Saved—for a Reason

Appendix B

January 30	Mark 4:35–41	Stilling the Storm
February 6	Matt 14:13–21	Feeding the Five Thousand
February 13	Matt 14:22–33	Walking on Water
February 20	Luke 9:28–36	The Transfiguration
February 27	Luke 10:11–12, 17–20	Seventy Sent Out
March 6	Matt 20:20–28	The Greatest
March 13	Mark 10:46–52	To See Again
March 20	John 11:17–27	The Resurrection and the Life
March 27	Luke 24:1–11	An Idle Tale?
April 3	John 20:19–31	Known by the Scars
April 10	Josh 4:1–7	What Do These Stones Mean?
April 17	Heb 8:6–13	A New Covenant
April 24	1 John 3:11–18	Friendly Fire
May 1	Rev 1:4–6	Jesus's Blood Never Failed Me Yet
May 8	2 Tim 1:1–7	Keepers of the Spring
May 15	1 Cor 8	Christian Freedom
May 22	Acts 2:1–21	Pentecost
May 29	Isa 55:6–13	A Lasting Memorial
June 5	Ps 118:1–24	Carpe Diem—Seize the Day
June 12	Ps 55:1–3, 16–17, 22	Take Time to Pray
June 19	Eph 5:25, 31–6:4	Answer the Call
June 26	1 Chron 15:25–29	Sacred? Dance
July 3	Ps 33:12–22	One Nation: Under God
July 10	Ps 1	Two Ways of Life
July 17	Ps 27	Wait for the Lord!
July 24	Ps 96	Worthy Worship
July 31	Ps 116	God Answers Prayer
August 7	Ps 121	The Lord Will Keep You
August 14	Dr. Stan Hastey	
August 21	Rev. Brent Walker	
August 28	Exod 31:12–18	Why Worship?
September 4	Ps 63:1–7	Personal Worship

September 11	Rev 7:9–12	People of Praise
September 18	Exod 12:21–32	People of the Event
September 25	Deut 16:13–15	People of Celebration
October 2	Heb 13:15–16	People of Service
October 9	Dr. Dan Ivins	
October 16	Prov 14:21, 31; 21:13; 22:9; 31:8–9	Christian Response to Hungry
October 23	Eph 4:26–27	Be Angry, but Don't Sin
October 30	Rom 16:1–2	Phoebe: A Deacon
November 6	2 Cor 9:6–8	She Said It Wasn't Enough
November 13	Phil 2:3–11	Overcoming Pettiness
November 20	2 Cor 7:2–11	Good Guilt
November 27	Isa 9:2–7	Poking Holes in the Darkness
December 4	Mic 5:2–5a; Eph 2:13–17	Peace on Us
December 11	1 John 4:9–16	The Purpose of Christmas
December 18	Luke 2:8–14	Angels Bending Near
December 25	Col 1:15–20	Who Was He?

1995	**Text**	**Title**
January 1	Eccl 3:1–8	A Time for Everything
January 8	Matt 2:1–12	Epiphany
January 15	Dr. Ron Elville	
January 22	Matt 6:19–20	Material World
January 29	Matt 6:5–8	When You Pray
February 5	Luke 5:1–11	Into the Deep
February 12	Matt 14:22–33	Through the Storm
February 19	Matt 16:13–23	Upon *This* Rock?
February 26	Luke 9:28–36	A Mountaintop Experience
March 5	Matt 18:21–22	How Many Times?
March 12	John 13:1–15	Not My Feet!
March 19	Matt 26:31–35	I'll Never Leave You
March 26	John 18:1–12	Do Something!

April 2	Matt 26:56b–58, 69–75	The Rock Crumbles
April 9	Luke 23:33–24	Amazing Grace!/Choir Cantata
April 16	Luke 24:1–12	Journey of Hope
April 23	John 21:1–14	The Last Breakfast
April 30	John 21:15–17	Feed My Sheep
May 7	Acts 1:1–5	Baptized with the Holy Spirit
May 14	Rom 12:9–13	Christian Living
May 21	Col 1:21–29	Mature in Christ
May 28	Luke 24:50–53	Carried Away
June 4	Acts 2:37–42	What Should We Do?
June 11	Deut 5:12–15	Sabbath Time
June 18	Responsive Reading 503	Family Commitments
June 25	Eph 5:21–33	All I Ask of You
July 2	Responsive Reading 719	John Leland: Freedom Preacher
July 9	Jer 17:5–8	Trees and Shrubs
July 16	Rev. Tony Cupit	
July 23	Mark 7:24–30	Wrest a Blessing
July 30	2 Thess 3:6–13	Our Best Bet
August 6	Jas 3:13–18	Seeds of Peace
August 13	Neh 10:28–39	The Danger of Neglect
August 20	Rom 5:1–5	Make Lemonade
August 27	Matt 5:14–16	Let Your Light Shine
September 3	Rom 12:1–2; Eph 4:17–24; 2 Cor 4:16	Conformed? Transformed!
September 10	Eph 4:25, 28	Honest
September 17	Eph 4:26–29, 31–32	Mad
September 24	Eph 4:29–30	Balcony People
October 1	Eph 5:1–2	Imitating God
October 8	Zeph 3:14–20	No Place Like Home
October 15	Deut 15:7–11	Open Your Hand
October 22	Matt 16:24–26	The Nicholas Effect
October 29	John 5:24–29	Eternal Life

November 5	Ps 8:1, 3–9	The Whole World in Our Hands
November 12	Mark 9:14–29	I Believe
November 19	Mark 6:19–21	Treasures in Heaven
November 26	Rev 5	Worthy Worship
December 3	Luke 1:1–25	The Adventure Begins
December 10	Luke 1:26–38	Touched by an Angel
December 17	Luke 1:39–56	Hassle or Joy?
December 24	Luke 1:57–80	The Silence Is Broken
December 31		

1996	**Text**	**Title**
January 7	Matt 2:1–12	The Twelfth Day of Christmas
January 14	Dr. Jere Allen	
January 21	Ps 24:1–6	Reverence for Life
January 28	Rom 8:26–27	Sighs Too Deep for Words
February 4	Exod 2:1–10	Saved by the Belle
February 11	Exod 7:14–24	Let My People Go
February 18	Exod 20:1–17	The Ten Suggestions?
February 25	Exod 16:1–15	In the Wilderness
March 3	Exod 33:17–23	The Backside of God
March 10	Exod 36:1–7	More Than Enough
March 17	1 Tim 6:3–12	Temptation
March 24	1 Cor 1:18, 22–25	A Church Without a Cross
March 31	Bart Webster/Choir Cantata	
April 7	Luke 23:50–24:12	Jesus Is Alive!
April 14	1 Cor 15:1–28	The Message of Hope
April 21	1 John 4:7–21	The Only Failure That Matters
April 28	Col 4:2–6	Making the Most of the Time
May 5	Matt 12:46–50	What Is Family?
May 12	Prov 22:6	Train a Child
May 19	1 Cor 13	A Fresh Look at Love
May 26	Acts 2:1–12	Holy Fire

Appendix B

June 2	Luke 18:15–17	Come as a Child
June 9	Col 3:1–11	New Life in Christ
June 16	Col 3:18–4:1	Promise Keepers
June 23	Gal 6:7–10	God Is Not Mocked
June 30	Col 3:12–15	One in the Spirit
July 7	John 8:31–36	The Cost of Freedom
July 14	Heb 13:1–8	Faith for Changing Times
July 21	Rev 1:9–20	American Pie
July 28	Matt 7:6	Go for the Gold
August 4	Rom 10:12; 1 Cor 12:13; Gal 3:28; Col 3:11	Neither Jew nor Greek
August 11	Prov 15:13, 15; 17:22	A Cheerful Heart
August 18	Rev. Brent Walker	
August 25		
September 1	Col 3:23–24	Back to Work
September 8	Rev 2:1–7	Ephesus: Love Abandoned
September 15	Rev 2:8–11	Smyrna: Trouble Coming
September 22	Rev 2:12–29	Pergamum: Led Astray
September 29	Rev 2:12–29	Thyatira: Jezebel's Folly
October 6	Rev 3:1–6	Sardis: Wake Up
October 13	Rev 3:7–13	Philadelphia: An Open Door
October 20	Rev 3:14–22	Laodicea: Neither Cold nor Hot
October 27	Matt 11:28–30	Come to Me
November 3	1 Thess 4:13–18	Our Christian Hope
November 10	Luke 10:38–42	What Matters Most
November 17	Matt 19:1–12	The 5 "C"s of Marriage
November 24	1 Tim 6:6–10	Contentment
December 1	Luke 1:26–38	The Great Surprise
December 8	Isa 60:1–3; John 1:5	Light in the Darkness
December 15	Phil 2:5–11	He Humbled Himself
December 22	Isa 9:6	Wonderful
December 29	Luke 2:21–32	Go in Peace

1997	Text	Title
January 5	Matt 2:1–15	Bearing Gifts
January 12	Phil 4:10–14	How to Be Unhappy
January 19	Eccl 3:9–14; 9:7	Enough
January 26	Jas 1:19–27	Decaffeinated Religion
February 2	2 Thessalonians	Heaven-O
February 9	Acts 18:12–17	Gallio & Sosthenes
February 16		
February 23	John 13:21–30	It Was Night
March 2	John 13:31–35	A New Commandment
March 9	John 14:15–27	The Advocate
March 16	John 16:25–33	He Stoops to Conquer
March 23	Luke 19:28–38	A Borrowed Burro/Choir Cantata
March 30	John 20:1–10, 19–22	24 Hours of Hope
April 6	John 21:15–17	Feed My Sheep
April 13	John 21:18–22	Follow Me
April 20	Ps 65	Answered Prayer
April 27	Ps 119:97–105	The B-I-B-L-E
May 4	Gen 2:18–25	The Sacred Fire
May 11	Deut 6:1–9; Prov 6:20–23	Teach Your Children Well
May 18	Eph 5:21–33	The Head of the House
May 25	Isa 65:17–25	Peace and Remembrance
June 1	Acts 2:12–21	Visions and Dreams
June 8	1 Cor 11:23–28	Not Perfect
June 15	Eph 6:4	I Wish My Daddy Was a Dog
June 22	Ps 42	Running for Your Life
June 29	Eph 5:1–20	Boycott Disney?
July 6	Rom 13:1–7	The Christian and the State
July 13	2 Tim 3:14–17	John Wycliffe: Scripture Alone
July 20	1 Tim 2:3–6	John Hus: Christ Alone
July 27	Rom 1:16–17	Martin Luther: Faith Alone
August 3	1 Cor 11:17–26	Ulrich Zwingli: Lord's Supper

Appendix B

August 10	Deacon Presentation	
August 17	Melissa Rogers	
August 24	Acts 2:37–39	Anabaptists: Believer's Baptism
August 31	1 Pet 2:4–5, 9	Tyndale: Priesthood Believers
September 7	Matt 4:18–22	Traveling with Jesus
September 14	Gal 3:26–29	The Social Gospel
September 21	Luke 10:30–35; 1 Cor 13	Love—Care
September 28	2 Tim 1:8–14	The Simple Gospel
October 5	Isa 53:4–6	Not My Fault
October 12	Ps 150	Praise the Lord!
October 19	Phil 1:9–11, 27	One Spirit, One Mind
October 26	Ps 66:16–20	The AAA of Prayer
November 2	Phil 2:5–11	W.W.J.D.
November 9	2 Cor 4:6–10	Jars of Clay
November 16	Exod 19:16–19	Sometimes He Comes in Clouds
November 23	Ps 50:1–14, 23	A Sacrifice of Thanksgiving
November 30	Luke 1:39–45, 56	Slow Down for Reflection
December 7	Luke 1:46–55	An Upside-Down Christmas
December 14	Luke 2:1–5	The Inevitable Distractions
December 21	Luke 2:6–18	Whatever the Circumstances
December 28	Luke 2:15–19	Keep Christmas in the Heart

1998	**Text**	**Title**
January 4	Matt 2:1–12	The Gifts of a New Year
January 11	Dr. Morris Vickers	
January 18	Luke 2:41–57	My Father's Business
January 25	Rom 10:9–13	How to Become a Christian
February 1	Luke 15:1–2, 11–32	Come to the Party
February 8	Luke 19:11–27	The King Is Coming!
February 15	Luke 12:13–21	The Rich Fool
February 22	Luke 18:9–14	The Pharisee and the Tax Collector

March 1	Rom 7:14–25	The Problem: Sin
March 8	1 Pet 1:3–9	The Solution: God
March 15	Rom 5:1–11	The Way: Christ
March 22	1 John 1:5–10	The Means: Forgiveness
March 29	Rom 6:1–14	The Result: New Life
April 5	John 13:1–15	The Basin and Towel/Choir Cantata
April 12	Luke 24:1–12	Looking for Jesus
April 19	Matt 27:62–66; 28:11–15	The Last Deception
April 26	Luke 24:36–49	Power from on High
May 3	Matt 28:6–20	Make Disciples
May 10	1 Sam 1:1–28	From God, to God
May 17	Acts 1:1–8	Witnesses
May 24	Acts 1:9–14	Don't Just Stand There
May 31	Acts 2:1–4	Filled with the Spirit
June 7	Acts 2:12–21	Visions and Dreams
June 14	Acts 2:37–42	Communion
June 21	Eph 5:21–33	Mutual Submission
June 28	Acts 2:43–47	Day by Day
July 5	Acts 3:1–10	Independence Day
July 12	Acts 4:1–4	Life After Life
July 19	Acts 4:5–12	The Cornerstone
July 26	Acts 4:13–31	Uneducated and Ordinary
August 2	Acts 4:32–37	One Heart and Soul
August 9	Acts 5:1–11	The Best Policy
August 16	Acts 5:12–16	Healing Power of the Gospel
August 23	Dr. Morris Vickers	
August 30	Dr. James Dunn	
September 6	Ps 34:11–14; Rom 12:18	Dealing with Difficult People
September 13	1 Cor 6:12–20	Glorify God in Your Body
September 20	John 8:2–11	Caught and Forgiven
September 27	Lam 3:19–26	New Every Morning
October 4	Rom 10:13–17	Yes, Jesus Loves Me

Appendix B

October 11	1 Sam 7:1–12	Home Again
October 18	Deut 15:7–11	Hard-Headed and Tight-Fisted
October 25	Amos 5:14–15, 21–24	Justice and Righteousness
November 1	2 Tim 1:8–18	Onesiphorus: Profit Bringer
November 8	Mark 7:14–23	Only Human
November 15	2 Pet 1:3–11	Christian Virtues
November 22	Ps 113	An Attitude of Gratitude
November 29	Isa 9:1–7	Reason for Hope
December 6	Luke 1:26–38	Mary's Story; Ann's Story
December 13	Matt 1:18–25	Joseph's Story
December 20	Luke 2:8–20	The Shepherd's Story
December 27	Luke 2:22–38	Anna's Story

1999	**Text**	**Title**
January 3	Matt 2:1–12	The Fourth Gift of the Magi
January 10	Prov 3:9–10	Honor the Lord
January 17	Maury Sweetin	
January 24	Matt 5:17–20, 33–37	The Truth, the Whole Truth
January 31	Gen 48:8–22	Give the Blessing
February 7	Josh 2:1–14	Rahab's Faith
February 14	Josh 6:1–21	Jericho's Fall
February 21	Rev. Jack VandenHengel	
February 28	Josh 24:14–18	Joshua's Farewell
March 7	Mark 1:29–39	The Lord's Prayers
March 14	Matt 6:5–15	The Lord's Prayer
March 21	Mark 14:13–42	Prayers Before the Cross
March 28	Holy Week Scripture and Song/Choir Cantata	
April 4	John 20:1–18	Life Is Greater Than Death
April 11	Luke 24:13–25	The Breaking of the Bread
April 18	2 Cor 4:5–12	Cracked Pots
April 25	Isa 32:14–20	The Promise of Peace

May 2	Luke 4:1–21	Values, Vision, Mission
May 9	Dan 1:1–21	Food and Faith
May 16	Dan 2	The Statue and the Stone
May 23	Dan 3	Spirit in the Fire
May 30	Dan 4	The Madness of King Neb
June 6	Dan 5	The Writing on the Wall
June 13	Dan 6	Never Compromise
June 20	2 Tim 4:1–8	Finish the Race, Keep the Faith
June 27	Phil 4:8–13	A Simple Life
July 4	Lev 25:8–12	The Blessings of Liberty
July 11	Prov 17:22	A Cheerful Heart
July 18	Prov 1:7; 3:5–7	The Fear of the Lord
July 25	Prov 17:3; 21:2; 28:6, 18	Nothing to Hide
August 1	Matt 5:21–24; 6:12	Your Gift at the Altar
August 8	Acts 17:16–31	Probation Before Judgment
August 15	Matt 8:5–13, 23–27	Where Is Your Faith?
August 22	John 13:34–35; 17:20–26	Unity and Diversity
August 29	Dr. Duncan McIntosh	
September 5	2 Cor 5:16–20	The Ministry of Reconciliation
September 12	John 12:20–26	A Circle Facing Outward
September 19	Heb 10:19–25	The Priority of Worship
September 26	Heb 12:1–2	Recovering Our Spiritual Focus
October 3	Heb 13:1–5, 16	Sacrifices Pleasing to God
October 10	Heb 13:7–8	Renewing the Vision
October 17	Mrs. Ellen Udovich	
October 24	Ps 139:1–18	An Email from God
October 31	Deut 18:9–14	What's with Halloween?
November 7	2 Pet 3:8–13	A Thousand Years Like a Day
November 14	Rom 8:18–25	Saved by Hope
November 21	1 Tim 6:17–19	Rich in Good Works
November 28	Isa 9:6–7	Wonderful Counselor
December 5	Isa 40:1–11	Like a Shepherd

Appendix B

December 12	Isa 7:4; Matt 1:18–23	Emmanuel
December 19	Luke 2:1–11	Savior, Messiah, Lord
December 26	Luke 2:15–21	Jesus!

2000	**Text**	**Title**
January 2	Dr. Jere Allen	
January 9	2 Cor 5:1	[Sunday after the fire]
January 16	Mark 1:1–8	The Beginning of the Good News
January 23	Mark 1:9–14	Jesus Was Baptized
January 30	Mark 1:16–20	Follow Me
February 6	Mark 1:21–28	One with Authority
February 13	Mark 4:1–20	The Sower and the Soils
February 20	Mark 2:1–12	Your Sins Are Forgiven
February 27	Dr. Duncan McIntosh	
March 5	Mark 8:27–30	The Tipping Point
March 12	Mark 8:31–38	The Abundance Mentality
March 19	Dr. Morris Vickers	
March 26	Cindy and Frank Dawson	
April 2	Mark 14:12–25	The Bread and the Cup
April 9	Mark 15:25–39	Who Was Jesus?
April 16	Worship Dance and Adult Choir Cantata	
April 23	Mark 15:41–Mark 16:8+	The Rest of the Story
April 30	Mark 16:9–20	The Unfinished Story
May 7	Luke 1:1–4	Friend of God
May 14	Luke 2:22–40	Dedicated to God
May 21	Luke 2:41–52	Knowing Who You Are
May 28	Luke 3:23–38	Remembrance and Gratitude
June 4	Luke 5:27–39	Eating and Drinking with Jesus
June 11	Luke 7:1–10	Unseen Power
June 18	Luke 7:11–14	Lord of Life
June 25	Luke 7:18–35	Dancing with Jesus

July 2	Luke 7:36–50	Freedom in Christ
July 9	Luke 8:1–3	The Women Disciples
July 16	Luke 9:37–48	The Greatest
July 23	Luke 9:57–62	Fit for the Kingdom
July 30	Luke 10:1–20	The Seventy Sent Solution
August 6	Luke 10:25–37	Go and Do the Same
August 13	Luke 10:38–42	An "ISTJ" Meets Jesus
August 20	Dr. Morris Vickers	
August 27	Dr. Jere Allen	
September 3	Luke 13:10–17	Sabbath Rest
September 10	John 1:35–51	Come and See
September 17	John 2:1–11	The First Sign: Water into Wine
September 24	John 2:13–25	Business as Usual?
October 1	John 3:1–17	Nic at Night
October 8	John 4:1–42	Living Water
October 15	John 4:46–54	Believing Without Seeing
October 22	John 5:1–18	Do You Want to Be Well?
October 29	John 6:1–15	New Math: 5+2=5000+12
November 5	John 6:16–21	Don't Be Afraid
November 12	John 6:25–35	The Bread of Life
November 19	John 9	Now I See
November 26	John 11:1–44	The Resurrection and the Life
December 3	John 1:1–5	Christ Before Christmas
December 10	Responsive Reading 75	The Word Became Flesh
December 17	Matt 1:1–6, 16	A Checkered Family Tree
December 24	Luke 2:1–7	Home for Christmas
December 31	Matt 2:1–12	Home Another Way

2001	**Text**	**Title**
January 7	Ezra 3:1–3, 10–13	The House of the Lord
January 14	Phil 3:10–16	Pressing Toward the Goal
January 21	Amos 5:21–24	Let Justice Roll Like Waters

Appendix B

January 28	Luke 12:22–31	Consider the Ravens
February 4	Eph 4:1–6	United in Christ
February 11	Gen 12:1–7; 15:1–6	Reckless Faith
February 18	Dr. Morris Vickers	
February 25	Matt 5:14–16	Let Your Light Shine
March 4	Matt 16:13–25	Losing Life to Find It
March 11	Matt 17:1–9	A Mountaintop Experience
March 18	Matt 17:22–23; 18:1–5	Downward Mobility
March 25	Matt 18:21–35	The Most Difficult Journey
April 1	Matt 19:16–22	Fools for Christ
April 8	Matt 21:1–9	Your King Is Coming
April 15	Matt 27:50–53; 28:1–10	Easter Earthquakes
April 22	Matt 27:62–66; 28:12–15	The Last Deception
April 29	Matt 28:16–20	The Great Commission
May 6	John 20:24–31	Coming to Believe
May 13	Acts 1:12–14	A Mother's Faith
May 20	Acts 1:1–8	Between Lightning & Thunder
May 27	Luke 24:36–53; Acts 1:9–11	Gone, but Not Gone
June 3	John 14:8–17; 16:5–15; 20:19–22	Receiving the Holy Spirit
June 10	Luke 24:13–35	A Long Night's Journey into Day
June 17	1 Chron 4:9–10	The Prayer of Jabez
June 24	Rom 8:28, 31–39	Master of My Fate
July 1	Rev. Donnell Harris	
July 8	Gen 2–3	Bad Girls of the Bible: Eve
July 15	Gen 19:12–26; Luke 17:28–33	Bad Girls: Lot's Wife
July 22	Gen 39	Bad Girls: Potiphar's Wife
July 29	Josh 2:1–21; 6:22–25	Bad Girls: Rahab
August 5	Judg 16:1–22	Bad Girls: Delilah
August 12	1 Sam 16, 19, 25; 2 Sam 6	Bad Girls: Michal
August 19	1 Kgs 21	Bad Girls: Jezebel

August 26	Luke 7:36–50	Bad Girls: Woman Sinner
September 2	2 Cor 4	Bad Girls: Treasure Jars/Clay
September 9	Dr. Ron Rogers	
September 16	Dr. Morris Vickers	
September 23	Mic 6:8	Justice and Mercy
September 30	Acts 5:27–42	Soul Freedom
October 7	John 14:27; 16:33	The Overcomers
October 14	Jas 2:14–17, 24	Faith Works
October 21	1 Pet 1:3–9	A Living Hope
October 28	2 Tim 4:6–18	Keeping the Faith
November 4	Acts 6:1–7	At Your Service
November 11	Luke 11:1–13	Teach Us to Pray
November 18	Ps 119:97–105	A Lamp, a Light
November 25	Matt 10:1–22	Summoned to Serve
December 2	Luke 1:26–38	Of the Father's Love Begotten
December 9	Dr. Daniel Vestal	
December 16	Luke 1:39–56	Clear as Midnight
December 23	Luke 2:8–20	Go Tell It
December 30	Luke 2:21–38	Simeon's Song

2002	**Text**	**Title**
January 6	Rev 21:1–7	Everything New
January 13	John 8:31–43; 14:1–7	The Crescent or the Cross
January 20	Rom 8:26–39	All Things Work for Good
January 27	Mark 1:32–39	The Source of My Strength
February 3	Mark 14:17–25	Jesus and His Disciples
February 10	Matt 22:34–40; 28:18–20	Gr. Commandment & Commission
February 17	John 3:1–16	Jesus and Nicodemus
February 24	John 4:5–29	Jesus and the Woman at the Well
March 3	Matt 20:20–28	Jesus and the Sons of Zebedee
March 10	Dr. Jeffrey Haggray	
March 17	Dr. Morris Vickers	

March 24	Palm Sunday Passion Story/ Choir Cantata	
March 31	John 20:1–18	I Have Seen the Lord!
April 7	John 21:1–14	Fish for Breakfast?
April 14	Rev. Champion Chasara	
April 21	Matt 6:24; 19:23–26	Who Wants to Be a Millionaire?
April 28	Matt 5:38–48	Perfect?
May 5	Dr. Stan Hastey	
May 12	Matt 10:34–39	Tending the Windmills
May 19	Matt 12:22–32	The Unforgivable Sin
May 26	Matt 6:9–15	Forgive, as Forgiven
June 2	Matt 7:1–6	Specks, Logs, Pearls, Swine
June 9	Matt 18:1–5	Come as a Child
June 16	Matt 18:6–9	Keep the Candle Burning
June 23	Matt 22:1–14	Many Called but Few Chosen
June 30	Rev. Reynold Carr	
July 7	Ps 33:11–16; 1 Pet 2:9–10	One Nation Under God
July 14	1 Pet 3:8–18	The Hope That Is in You
July 21	1 Pet 5:6–11	Cast All Your Cares on Him
July 28	1 Cor 15:12–22, 50–58	Quest for Immortality
August 4	Rom 12:1–2	A Serious Call to a Devout Life
August 11	Eph 4:25–32	An Honest Man
August 18	Josh 24:14–15; Matt 7:24–27	It's Your Choice
August 25	Jas 5:13–16	The Power of Prayer
September 1	Exod 20:8–11; Mark 2:23–3:6	The Most Broken Commandment
September 8	Luke 13:1–5; Deut 4:9	Fallen but Not Forgotten
September 15	Prov 3:5–6	The Serenity Prayer
September 22	Luke 24:13–35	The Back Roads of Life
September 29	Phil 4:10–14	The Contents of Contentment
October 6	Isa 40:1–11, 28–31	Wait for the Lord

October 13	Eph 1:3–14	Were It Not for Grace
October 20	Jas 2:1–17	If Jesus Is Lord
October 27	Ps 27:1–6, 13–14	I Will Not Be Afraid
November 3	Heb 6:1–12	Going on Toward Maturity
November 10	Josh 4:1–7	Another Step in the Journey
November 17	2 Cor 5:16–21	New in Christ
November 24	Matt 25:1–13	Be Prepared
December 1	Hag 2:1–9	Greater Glory
December 8	T and Kathie Thomas	
December 15	Luke 2:13–14	Peace on Earth
December 22	Luke 2:1–7	No Room in the Inn
December 29	Luke 2:8–11	Good News…Great Joy

2003	**Text**	**Title**
January 5	Dr. James Dunn	
January 12	Dr. Stan Hastey	
January 19	Dr. Morris Vickers	
January 26	John 8:2–11	We Reserve the Right…
February 2	Mark 9:14–29	The Big Eight
February 9	Rom 5:1–5; 8:28	When the Sky Is Silent
February 16	snow (services cancelled)	
February 23	Heb 2:1–4	Do You Believe in Miracles?
March 2	Ps 46:1–11	Five Minutes to Midnight
March 9	Prov 13:23; 14:31; 22:16; 29:7; 31:8–9	The Wrong Way
March 16	John 14:1–7	The Only Way
March 23	Ralph and Tammy Stocks	
March 30	Phil 4:4–7	Only a Prayer Away
April 6	1 Cor 1:18, 23–25	It's All about the Cross
April 13	Bell Choir/Choir Cantata	
April 20	John 20:1, 11–18	Echoes in Eternity
April 27	Rev. Champion Chasara	

Appendix B

May 4	1 Pet 1:1–9	Footsteps in the Concrete
May 11	Eph 1:3–14	Your Three Homes
May 18	John 15:1–11	Branches of the Vine
May 25	1 Sam 7:7–12; Acts 10:1–4	Building Our Own Memorials
June 1	Acts 1:1–14	Looking Up Toward Heaven
June 8	Rev. Silas Yego	
June 15	Matt 6:12; Eph 4:32; Col 3:13	Forgive, as Forgiven
June 22	Acts 13:1–4	Sent to Serve
June 29	1 Cor 16:1–4	Autonomous and Cooperative
July 6	Mission Team Report from Appalachia	
July 13	2 Tim 3:14–17	No Creed but the Bible
July 20	Eph 2:4–10	By Grace Saved Through Faith
July 27	Phil 1:1–11	The Fellowship of Kindred Minds
August 3	Dr. Jeffrey Haggray	
August 10	Dr. James Langley	
August 17	Ps 122	Worship: Not a Spectator Sport
August 24	2 Tim 1:8–18	A Matter of Trust
August 31	1 Cor 3:5–9	Digging Clay/Grandchildren
September 7	Eph 4:25–32	A Culture of Kindness
September 14	Ps 46	A Severe Clear
September 21	Mark 6:30–46	Life Without Hurry
September 28	Luke 6:27–36	Love Your Enemies
October 5	Rev. Paul Montacute	
October 12	Gen 28:10–17	Surely the Lord Is in This Place
October 19	2 Cor 9:6–13	Good at Something Good
October 26	Matt 22:34–40; John 13:34–35	Emotional Intelligence
November 2	Luke 9:10–15, 19–24	Butterflies Taste with Feet
November 9	Josh 4:19–24; 5:10–12	The Journey Continues
November 16	2 Cor 4:16–18	Living in the Light of Eternity

November 23	Ps 150	Praise the Lord
November 30	Luke 1:26–38	Nothing Impossible with God
December 7	Luke 1:39–45	Leaping for Joy
December 14	CBF field personnel, high security-risk area	
December 21	Luke 1:46–55	Mary's Song
December 28	Matt 2:1–12	Wise Men Still Seek Him

2004	Text	Title
January 4	Rom 1:1–7	Grace to You
January 11	Rom 6:1–14	Dying and Rising with Christ
January 18	Rom 6:22–23	Slaves to God: Free at Last
January 25	Rom 10:9–13	Confess and Believe
February 1	Matt 6:9–13	The Lord's Prayer
February 8	Rom 13:1–7	Christian Citizenship
February 15	1 Cor 13:4–7, 13	The Greatest Is Love
February 22	Dr. Jere Allen	
February 29	Matt 3:13–4:11	Lenten Journey—Wilderness
March 7	Mark 10:32–34	Lenten Journey—Jerusalem
March 14	John 12:1–11	Lenten Journey—Bethany Road
March 21	Mark 11:1–11	Lenten Journey—Hosanna Road
March 28	Luke 23:24–33	Lenten Journey—Via Dolorosa
April 4	The Passion of Christ/Choir Cantata	
April 11	Luke 24:13–35	Easter Journey—Emmaus Road
April 18	Mark 16:9–20	The Rest of the Story
April 25	Mic 6:6–8; Amos 5:21–24	True Justice
May 2	Rev. Dennis Dhlula and Mr. Elias Maponga	
May 9	Exod 20:12; Deut 5:16	Honor Your Mother
May 16	Rom 1:16; 1 Cor 12:13; Gal 3:28; Col 3:11	One in Christ
May 23	Eccl 3:1–15	A Compass, Not a Clock

Appendix B

May 30	Acts 2:29–39	Power, Peace, Life
June 6	Ps 30	I Hope You Dance
June 13	Phil 1:3–6	Sharing in the Gospel
June 20	Mark 14:36; Rom 8:15; Gal 4:6	Abba Father
June 27	Col 4:7–18	News from Birmingham
July 4	Gal 5:1–6	Christ Has Set Us Free
July 11	1 Tim 4:12–16	Generation to Generation
July 18	Mark 12:28–34	Christian Ethics
July 25	Eph 1:3–14	The Riches of His Grace
August 1	Matt 5:43–48; Luke 13:1–5	The Providence of God
August 8	Rom 16:1–16	The Girls in Rome
August 15	Luke 5:1–11	There's More to Life Than Fish
August 22	Luke 6:30–31; 16:19–31	Beggars at the Gate
August 29	Dr. Tom Rodgerson	
September 5	Rev. Wayne Price	
September 12	Mark 10:17–22	Tough Love
September 19	Rom 8:14–17	The Family of God
September 26	Eph 4:11–16	Spiritual Formation
October 3	1 Tim 3:8–13	Christian Leadership
October 10	Gen 32:3–8; 33:1–11	There's No Place Like Home
October 17	Gen 16:1–11	Domestic Violence/Grace God
October 24	Mark 10:35–45	S.T.S. (Saved to Serve)
October 31	Prov 17:22	A Cheerful Heart
November 7	1 Cor 11:17–28	Communion of the Saints
November 14	2 Cor 5:14–21	New Creations
November 21	Ps 24	Thanks-living
November 28	Mal 3:1–6	Who Can Endure Day of Coming?
December 5	Luke 1:26–38	Nothing Is Impossible with God
December 12	Luke 1:46–49	Holy Is His Name
December 19	Matt 1:18–25	A Change of Plans
December 26	Acts 6:1–10; 7:54–60	The Feast of Stephen

2005	Text	Title
January 2	1 John 4:7–12	Twenty Years
January 9	Linda Salmon (mission trip report)	
January 16	Col 3:11–17	Christ in All
January 23	Luke 4:16–21	Good News to the Poor
January 30	Luke 14:1–14	Dinner with Jesus
February 6	Heb 13:1–2, 16	Hospitality to Strangers
February 13	Matt 25:31–46	The Least of These
February 20	John 1:14–18	Grace Like Rain
February 27	John 16:16–33	Pain into Joy
March 6	John 17:1–3, 20–23	One in Christ
March 13	John 15:12–17	That Little Springtime
March 20	Palm Sunday Litany/Choir Cantata	
March 27	John 20:1–10	By Dawn's Early Light
April 3	John 20:24–29	Known by the Scars
April 10	Rev. Kingsley Perera	
April 17	Matt 6:25–33	Knowing, Doing the Will of God
April 24	Job 1:1, 13–22	When Life Isn't Fair
May 1	Gen 50:15–22	God Intended It for Good
May 8	1 Sam 1:9–18, 20, 24–28	A Godly Mother
May 15	Acts 1:12–14; 2:1–4	Filled with the Spirit
May 22	Gen 25:7–8, 35:28–29; 1 Chron 29:26–28; Job 42:16–17	Old, Full of Days
May 29	Heb 12:1–2	A Cloud of Witnesses
June 5	Matt 5:1–2; 6:5–13	Teach Us to Pray
June 12	1 Pet 2:13–17	God and Country
June 19	Eph 6:1–4	Fathers and Children
June 26	Acts 13:1–3	Traveling Mercies
July 3	Dr. Tom Rodgerson	
July 10	Acts 14:24–28	A Door of Faith

July 17	Matt 6:19–21	Treasure in Heaven
July 24	Rom 8:31–39	Swinging in the Rain
July 31	Dr. Jeffrey Haggray	
August 7	Rev. Jerry Buckner	
August 14	1 John 1:1–7	One Great Fellowship of Love
August 21	2 Cor 5:17–20	The Ministry of Reconciliation
August 28	Ps 119:97–105	The Bible Tells Me So
September 4	John 3:16–17	God So Loved the World
September 11	Col 1:15–20	The Criterion Is Christ
September 18	Matt 22:34–40	The Greatest Commandments
September 25	Matt 28:19–20	The Great Commission
October 2	Matt 6:9–13	The Lord's Prayer
October 9	1 Cor 13:4–8	The Love Chapter
October 16	Matt 25:31–40	The Least of These
October 23	2 Cor 4:16–18	Live Like You Were Dying
October 30	Hab 2:1–4	Righteous Among the Nations
November 6	2 Cor 4:16–5:1	A House Not Made with Hands
November 13	Rev 7:9–12	Every Nation, All Tribes
November 20	Ps 95:1–7a; 1 Thess 5:16–18	Accustomed to Our Blessings
November 27	Luke 1:5–20	Angels in Advent
December 4	Luke 1:26–38	Angels in Advent: Mary
December 11	Rev. Jerry Buckner	
December 18	Matt 1:18–25	Angels in Advent: Joseph
December 25	Luke 2:8–20	Angels in Advent: Shepherds

2006	**Text**	**Title**
January 1	Isa 6:5–7	The Prince of Peace
January 8	2 Cor 8:1–7	A Generous Undertaking
January 15	Ezek 13:1–16	True and False Prophets
January 22	Ezek 37:1–14	The Valley of Dry Bones
January 29	Ezek 47:1–12	The Sacred River
February 5	Gen 18:1–8, 16	Spontaneous Hospitality

February 12	Josh 5:13–15	On the Lord's Side
February 19	Matt 5:14–16	Go Light Your World
February 26	Ps 128	Are We Happy Yet?
March 5	Matt 26:17–30	The Last Passover
March 12	Matt 26:36–46	Go to Dark Gethsemane
March 19	Matt 26:47–56	Betrayed with a Kiss
March 26	Dr. Stan Hastey	
April 2	Matt 27:11–31	Truth on Trial
April 9	Darrell and Kathy Smith	
April 16	Matt 28:1–10	Eucatastrophe
April 23	Matt 28:11–20	Is God Dead?
April 30	Rev. Dennis Dhlula and Rev. Mazvigadza	
May 7	Luke 24:13–35	The Breaking of the Bread
May 14	John 20:1–18	Mary Magdalene and Jesus
May 21	Luke 24:36–49	More Than a Cameo
May 28	Luke 24:50–53	Carried Up into Heaven
June 4	Joel 2:28–32	The Day of the Lord
June 11	Acts 2:43–47	With Glad and Generous Hearts
June 18	Gen 27:1–23, 30–38	A Father's Blessing
June 25	Luke 1:1–4	What Really Happened
July 2	Acts 5:17–32	We Must Obey God
July 9	Acts 6:8–15; 7:54–60	Stephen, Full of Grace
July 16	Acts 8:4–17	Scattered, Proclaim the Word
July 23	Dianne and Shane McNary	
July 30	Acts 9:36–42	Tabitha, Get Up
August 6	Rev. Brent Walker	
August 13	Dr. Jeffrey Haggray	
August 20	Acts 10:1–33	A Change of Heart
August 27	Acts 10:34–48	Baptized with Water and Spirit
September 3	Acts 11:1–18	America's Favorite Pastime
September 10	Acts 11:19–26	First Called "Christians"

Appendix B

September 17	Acts 12:1–11	The Great Escape
September 24	Acts 12:18–24	How the Mighty Have Fallen
October 1	Acts 15:1–11	An Unfinished Life
October 8	Jer 31:31–34	A New Covenant
October 15	Deut 15:1–15	Church's Challenge: Realism
October 22	Acts 11:27–30	Church's Challenge: Relief
October 29	Exod 23:10–11; Lev 19:9–10	Church's Challenge: Rehabilitation
November 5	Rom 16:1–2	Deacons of the Church
November 12	Amos 5:21–24; Mic 6:8	Church's Challenge: Justice
November 19	2 Cor 6:14–7:1	We Are All Pilgrims
November 26	2 Thess 2:13–17	Eternal Comfort, Good Hope
December 3	Karen Morrow	
December 10	Luke 1:26–38	Mary—Servant of the Lord
December 17	Matt 1:18–25	Joseph—A Righteous Man
December 24	Luke 2:8–20	To Certain Poor Shepherds
December 31	Luke 2:21	What's in a Name?

2007	**Text**	**Title**
January 7	Matt 2:1–12	Epiphany
January 14	Matt 4:18–22	Following Jesus
January 21	Matt 6:25–34	What, Me Worry?
January 28	Matt 6:19–21	Treasures in Heaven
February 4	Mark 10:17–22	What Do You Lack?
February 11	John 2:1–11	The First Sign: Water into Wine
February 18	John 4:46–54	The Second Sign: Long Distance
February 25	John 5:1–9	Take Your Mat and Walk
March 4	John 6:1–15	Five Loaves and Two Fish
March 11	John 6:16–21	When the Wind Blows
March 18	John 9:1–7	Was Blind, but Now I See
March 25	John 11:1–44	The Ultimate Gift

April 1	Remembrance of Holy Week/Choir Cantata	
April 8	John 20:1–18	One More Day
April 15	John 20:24–31	Life in His Name
April 22	Matt 5:21–26; 7:12	Reverence for Life
April 29	John 14:1–7	The Way
May 6	John 6:47–68	The Bread of Life
May 13	1 Cor 7:12–16	Christian Influence
May 20	Acts 1:1–14	Unlikely Angels
May 27	John 14:15–21, 25–27	With You in Spirit
June 3	Ps 118:21–24	This Is the Day
June 10	1 Cor 11:17–28	Come to the Table
June 17	John 14:8–14	Show Us the Father
June 24	Eph 4:25–32	Happily Ever After
July 1	Dr. Earl Martin	
July 8	Mark 1:4–11	Truth in Advertising
July 15	2 Tim 3:14–17	People of the Book
July 22	1 Pet 2:4–5, 9–10	A Priest at Every Elbow
July 29	Gal 5:1, 13–14	A Generous Orthodoxy
August 5	Dr. Jeffrey Haggray	
August 12	Dr. Denton Lotz	
August 19	Katherine and Rolf Buehler	
August 26	Acts 6:1–7	Crisis in the Church
September 2	Phil 4:8–9	An Honorable Life
September 9	Exod 24:12–18; 31:18	Take Two Tablets
September 16	Exod 20:1–3; Matt 22:34–40	First Things First
September 23	Exod 20:4–6; 32:1–20	American Idols
September 30	Exod 20:7; Matt 5:33–37; Jas 5:12	Integrity
October 7	Exod 20:8–11; Matt 12:1–14	Remember the Sabbath

October 14	Exod 20:12; Matt 12:46–50	Family Ties
October 21	Exod 20:13; Matt 5:21–24	Life Belongs to God
October 28	Exod 20:14; Matt 5:27–32	Marriage Is for Keeps
November 4	Exod 20:15–16; Rom 13:8–10	Trustworthy
November 11	Exod 20:17; Luke 12:13–15, 32–34	Contentment
November 18	Mission trip to Knoxville/China	
November 25	Col 3:16–17	Psalms, Hymns, Spiritual Songs
December 2	Matt 1:18–25	Infant Holy
December 9	Luke 2:1–7	Infant Lowly
December 16	Luke 2:8–14	Saw the Glory
December 23	Luke 2:15–20	Thus Rejoicing
December 30	Luke 2:21–35	No Regrets

2008	**Text**	**Title**
January 6	Matt 2:1–12	Gifts for a King
January 13	Ps 24:1–5	The Earth Is the Lord's
January 20	Luke 10:25–37	Love Your Neighbor
January 27	Luke 4:14–30	You Can't Go Home Again
February 3	Rev. Jerry Buckner	
February 10	Mark 14:3–9	The Little People of the Passion
February 17	Luke 22:7–13	Making a Place for Jesus
February 24	John 18:1–12	Malchus
March 2	Matt 27:15–26	Died in My Place
March 9	Luke 23:32–43	With Me in Paradise
March 16	Mark 15:16–20, 33–39	This Was God's Son!
March 23	Luke 24:1–11	They Did Not Believe Them!
March 30	John 19:38–42	Going Public
April 6	John 21:1–14	Breakfast with Jesus
April 13	John 21:15–19	Do You Love Me?

April 20	Luke 19:1–10	A Wee Little Man
April 27	Luke 2:22–40	Holy to the Lord
May 4	John 1:19–29	Pie Jesus
May 11	Acts 2:1–4, 14, 17–18, 21, 38	One in the Spirit
May 18	John 4:1–29	Telling My Whole Life
May 25	Luke 3:23–24, 38	Do You Know Who You Are?
June 1	Ps 139:1–18	The World Is Too Much with Us
June 8	Ps 40:1–3	Waiting Patiently for the Lord
June 15	Ps 103:1–18	A Father Has Compassion
June 22	Ps 8	A Little Lower Than God
June 29	Ps 27	My Light and My Salvation
July 6	Ps 46	Our Refuge
July 13	Ps 42	Longing for God
July 20	Ps 92	Steadfast Love
July 27	Rev. Jerry Buckner	
August 3	Rev. Jerry Buckner	
August 10	Ps 122	The Glad House
August 17	Rev. Elizabeth Evans Hagan	
August 24	Ps 51:1–17	A Clean Heart
August 31	Ps 90	Teach Us to Count Our Days
September 7	Matt 5:1–12	Happy or Blessed?
September 14	Matt 5:17–26	The Higher Law
September 21	Matt 5:27–37	'Til Death Shall Part Us
September 28	Matt 5:38–48	Perfect in Love
October 5	Matt 6:5–13	Forgive Us Our Debts
October 12	Matt 6:25–33	Life in the Kingdom
October 19	Matt 7:1–11	Judgment and Discernment
October 26	Rev. Dr. C. J. Malloy Jr.	
November 2	Rev. Bonnie Dixon	
November 9	Matt 7:12–14	Golden Rule and Narrow Way
November 16	Matt 7:15–21	You Will Know Them by Fruits

November 23	Lev 23:9–14, 22	An Offering to the Lord
November 30	Isa 9:2–7	All I Want for Christmas: Hope
December 7	Isa 40:1–11	All I Want for Christmas: Peace
December 14	Isa 52:7–10	All I Want for Christmas: Joy
December 21	John 1:1–5, 14, 16–18; 3:16	All I Want for Christmas: Love
December 28	Luke 2:8–20	All I Want for Christmas: Jesus

2009	**Text**	**Title**
January 4	Matt 2:1–12	Lead, Kindly Light
January 11	Matt 2:13–18	Rachel Weeping for Children
January 18	Matt 2:14–15, 19–22	Out of Egypt
January 25	Matt 3:1–12	The First Baptist
February 1	Matt 3:13–17	Beloved
February 8	Rev. Dr. C. J. Malloy Jr.	
February 15	Matt 14:1–12	A Person of Character
February 22	Matt 14:12–17	The Sign of the Fish
March 1	Matt 4:18–22	Gone Fishing
March 8	Luke 5:1–11	What a Catch!
March 15	Matt 14:13–21	5,000 Fed
March 22	Matt 17:22–27	Somebody's Got to Pay
March 29	Rev. Dr. Daniel Vestal	
April 5	Dramatic Reading from Matthew/Choir Cantata	
April 12	Luke 24:1–12	The Third Day
April 19	John 20:24–31	Doubt & Faith
April 26	Acts 11:19–26	Five Kinds of Christians
May 3	Luke 16:1–9	Asset Management
May 10	2 Tim 1:1–5	Thanks for Your Help
May 17	Luke 10:29–37	The Compassionate Samaritan
May 24	Acts 1:6–9	Last Will and Testament
May 31	John 3:16	Speaking in Tongues
June 7	1 John 4:7–12	Three Levels of Love

June 14	Rom 12:1–2	Countercultural Christianity
June 21	Youth Sunday	
June 28	Heb 13:1–5	The Grass Is Always Greener
July 5	Job 1:13–21; 2:9–13	Blessed Be the Name of the Lord
July 12	Mark 10:13–16	Come as a Child
July 19	Mark 10:17–22	Do the Right Thing
July 26	Mark 10:23–27	The Geography of Greed
August 2	Matt 9:10–13; 11:16–19	The Life of the Party
August 9	Mark 9:33–37	From the Inside
August 16	John 6:60–69	The Book That Understands Me
August 23	Rev. Dr. C. J. Malloy Jr.	
August 30	Rev. Dr. James Langley	
September 6	Acts 11:27–30	One Great Fellowship
September 13	Luke 6:12–16	Twelve…and Counting
September 20	John 1:35–42; Mark 1:16–18	Andrew: The First Follower
September 27	Matt 16:13–25	Simon Peter: The Rock?
October 4	John 1:43–46	Philip: Come and See
October 11	John 1:43–51	Nathaniel: Principle, Prejudice
October 18	John 20:19–29	Thomas: From Doubt to Faith
October 25	Matt 9:9–13; Luke 6:12–16	Matthew & Simon: Enemy Friend
November 1	John 14:15–24	Thaddaeus/Judas (not Iscariot)
November 8	John 13:21–30	Judas Iscariot: The Traitor
November 15	Mark 10:35–45	James & James: Greater, Lesser
November 22	Mrs. Hannah Hawkins	
November 29	John 19:25b–27	John: The Beloved
December 6	Mark 3:13–19a	The Twelve: Like Us
December 13	Youth Musical/Choir Cantata	
December 20	Luke 2:1–7	Real Spectacle of Christmas
December 27	Luke 2:22–38	Child of Destiny

Appendix B

2010	**Text**	**Title**
January 3	Rev. Wayne Price	
January 10	Matt 2:1–12	The Journey
January 17	Matt 5:10–12	Persecuted for Righteousness
January 24	Luke 13:1–5, 34–35	The Blame Game
January 31	John 14:1–6	So What's the Difference?
February 7	Matt 22:17–21	Tax, Tip, or Tithe?
February 14	Rev. Dr. C. J. Malloy Jr.	
February 21	Rev. Neville Callam	
February 28	Rom 10:14–17	Faith Comes by Hearing
March 7	Matt 26:26–30	The Miracle of Forgiveness
March 14	Matt 26:31–46	Long Obedience, Same Direction
March 21	Matt 27:27–31, 45–50	The Crucified God
March 28	Jesus Walked, Died, Lives!/ Choir Cantata	
April 4	John 20:1–18; 1 Cor 15:3b–7	Jesus Is Alive
April 11	Rom 6:1–11	Dying and Rising with Christ
April 18	Luke 15:1–10	Lost and Found
April 25	Luke 15:11–24	Two Lost Sons: Younger
May 2	Luke 15:25–32	Two Lost Sons: Older Brother
May 9	Luke 15:11–13, 17–20, 25, 28, 31–32	The Prodigal Father
May 16	Rom 16:1–7, 16	Co-workers in Christ
May 23	Acts 2:1–8, 14–21	Get Up and Go
May 30	John 15:12–17	No Greater Love
June 6	Mark 8:1–9	A Picnic with Jesus
June 13	Acts 6:1–7	Waiting Tables
June 20	Youth Sunday	
June 27	Acts 16:6–10	Village to Village
July 4	Gal 3:27–28; 5:1	Liberty and Equality
July 11	Eph 4:1–6	Generic Christianity

July 18	1 Cor 1:1–3	Called to Be Saints
July 25	Lam 3:1–24	The Steadfast Love of the Lord
August 1	Rev. Gary Javens	
August 8	Rev. Dr. C. J. Malloy Jr.	
August 15	Rev 3:1–13	Hear the Spirit
August 22	Luke 7:1–10	Under Authority
August 29	Mrs. Elizabeth Samandi	
September 5	John 4:46–54	The Fever Left Him
September 12	Gen 12:1–9	Father of a Nation
September 19	Gen 17:1–8, 15–22	A Covenant with God
September 26	Gen 21:1–3; 22:1–14	The Lord Will Provide
October 3	Rev. Dr. C. J. Malloy Jr.	
October 10	Exod 3:1–15	Holy Ground
October 17	Exod 14:10–31	What Are You Afraid Of?
October 24	Exod 19:16–20; 20:1–17	Moses Spoke with God
October 31	Deut 31:1–2, 7–8, 14–15, 23	Faith for Changing Times
November 7	1 Sam 16:1, 6–13	The Lord Looks on the Heart
November 14	1 Sam 17:24–37	Facing the Giants
November 21	1 Sam 18:6–12; 24:1–7	Overcoming Evil with Good
November 28	2 Sam 7:1–17	The House of David
December 5	CBF field personnel, high security-risk area	
December 12	Luke 2:8–14	Angels Bending Near
December 19	Children/Youth Musical/Choir Cantata	
December 26	Rev. Dr. Dan Ivins	

2011	**Text**	**Title**
January 2	Matt 2:13–23	Stars and Dreams
January 9	1 Kgs 17:1–16	Elijah the Tishbite
January 16	1 Kgs 17:17–24	Back to Life

Appendix B

January 23	1 Kgs 18:1–2, 17–40	Showdown at Mount Carmel
January 30	Luke 2:41–51	What on Earth Am I Here For?
February 6	Rev. Dr. C. J. Malloy Jr.	
February 13	1 Kgs 19:1–16	The Sound of Silence
February 20	1 Kgs 21:1–10, 17–19, 27–29	Justice for Naboth
February 27	2 Kgs 2:1–14	Taken Up in Glory
March 6	Mark 1:1–11	The Beginning of the Good News
March 13	Matt 4:1–11	No Shortcuts
March 20	Luke 9:18–27	The Road Home
March 27	John 14:1–7	Where Do You Get Your Truth?
April 3	Mark 14:12–16, 22–25	The Lord's Supper
April 10	Mark 14:32–52	All of Them Deserted Him
April 17	Messiah Foretold and Fulfilled/Choir Cantata	
April 24	Matt 28:1–10	Death Be Not Proud
May 1	1 Cor 15:12–22	Alive in Christ
May 8	Matt 20:20–28	When Heroes Fall
May 15	Jas 1:9–17	Million-Dollar Rooms
May 22	Jas 1:19–27	Doers of the Word
May 29	Jas 2:8–17	Living Faith
June 5	Jas 3	A Tongue Is a Fire
June 12	Jas 4:1–10	Grace to the Humble
June 19	Youth Sunday	
June 26	Katherine and Rolf Buehler	
July 3	Jas 2:1–8	A More Perfect Union
July 10	Jas 4:13–17	Making the Most of the Time
July 17	Jas 5:1–11	Justice and Mercy
July 24	Jas 5:12	Been Through the Water
July 31	Jas 5:13–16	Pray for One Another
August 7	Eph 2:11–22	No Longer Strangers
August 14	Rev 3:7–8, 20	An Open Door

August 21	Gal 3:23–29	Freedom in Christ
August 28	Col 3:12–17	Where Healing Begins
September 4	Rev. Starlette McNeill	
September 11	1 Pet 1:3–9	Black Swans and Love of God
September 18	1 Pet 2:4–5, 9–10	A Holy Priesthood
September 25	1 Pet 2:13–17	Honor the Emperor
October 2	Rev. Gary Javens	
October 9	1 Pet 3:8–9	No Place Like Home
October 16	1 Pet 3:13–18	The Hope That Is in You
October 23	1 Pet 4:1–8	Live by the Will of God
October 30	1 Pet 4:9–11	Hospitality
November 6	1 Pet 4:12–19	Sharing Christ's Sufferings
November 13	1 Pet 5:1–5	S.T.S. (Saved to Serve)
November 20	1 Pet 5:6–11	A Glass-Half-Full Day
November 27	Luke 1:26–38	Mary: Hope
December 4	Matt 1:18–25	Joseph: Peace
December 11	Luke 2:8–20	Shepherds: Joy
December 18	Love Has Come/Choir Cantata	
December 25	Col 1:1–2, 11–19	The Fullness of God

2012	**Text**	**Title**
January 1	2 Pet 3:8–18	Now and Eternity
January 8	Matt 2:1–12	Gifts for a King
January 15	Amos 5:21–24	Justice and Righteousness
January 22	Luke 2:22–40	Presented to the Lord
January 29	Rom 12:1–2	Transformed, Not Conformed
February 5	Luke 3:1–17	A Voice Crying in the Wilderness
February 12	Luke 3:21–22	The Father's Blessing
February 19	Rev. Dr. C. J. Malloy Jr.	
February 26	Luke 4:1–13	Tempted
March 4	Luke 4:14–21	Good News to the Poor

Appendix B

March 11	Luke 5:1–11	A Greater Purpose in Life
March 18	Luke 5:17–26	Stand Up and Walk
March 25	Luke 5:27–35	Eating and Drinking with Sinners
April 1	The Passion Story/Choir Cantata	
April 8	Luke 24:1–11	Heaven Is for Real
April 15	Luke 24:36–49	What's the Least I Can Believe?
April 22	2 Thess 3:6–13	The Dignity of Work
April 29	1 Tim 1:1–2, 12–17	Clean
May 6	1 Cor 11:23–28	Examine Yourselves
May 13	Eph 5:21–6:4	Subject to One Another
May 20	Acts 1:1–14	Now What?
May 27	Acts 2:1–4	Filled with the Spirit
June 3	Gal 5:16–25	Fruit of the Spirit
June 10	1 Pet 3:7–11	The Test
June 17	Youth Sunday	
June 24	Rev. Gary Javens	
July 1	David Potter	
July 8	1 Tim 3:1–7	A Noble Task/Rev. Starlette McNeill
July 15	Gen 1:1–5, 24–28, 31	The Image of God
July 22	Gen 2:4b–9, 15–25	Not Good to Be Alone
July 29	Gen 3:1–24	In Adam's Fall We Sinned All
August 5	Gen 4:1–16	My Brother's Keeper
August 12	Gen 6:5–22; 7:6–10	Saved Through the Water
August 19	Gen 11:1–9	Babel On
August 26	Rev. Dr. C. J. Malloy Jr.	
September 2	Gen 11:27–12:4	Travelers on a Journey
September 9	Gen 12:4–9	Worship Is a Verb
September 16	Gen 12:10–20	Looking Out for #1
September 23	Gen 13:1–18	No Strife Between Us
September 30	Gen 14:10–20	A Tenth to the Lord
October 7	Gen 17:15–22	How Old Is Too Old?

October 14	Gen 17:1–8	An Everlasting Covenant
October 21	Gen 18:1–15; Heb 13:2	Hospitality to Strangers
October 28	Gen 21:1–7	Your Place in the Family
November 4	Rom 1:1–7	Called to Be Saints
November 11	Rom 16:1–2	A Deacon of the Church
November 18	Rev. David Potter	
November 25	Heb 11:13–16	We Are All Pilgrims
December 2	Luke 1:26–35	Proof of Heaven
December 9	Luke 1:39–56	The Things That Make for Peace
December 16	Shepherds or Magi/Choir Cantata	
December 23	Luke 2:1–7	No Place for Them
December 30	Luke 2:8–20	After Christmas

2013	**Text**	**Title**
January 6	Matt 2:1–12	The Journey
January 13	Matt 2:13–18	Rachel Weeping for Children
January 20	Matt 2:19–23	Follow Your Dream
January 27	Matt 3:1–6, 13–17	Water and the Spirit
February 3	Matt 4:1–11	Temptation
February 10	Matt 4:18–22	Following Jesus
February 17	Rev. Starlette McNeill	
February 24	Matt 4:23–25	The Ministry of Jesus
March 3	Matt 16:13–23	Rock or Stumbling Block?
March 10	Matt 16:24–28	Take Up Your Cross
March 17	Mark 15:15–24	Wrong Place at the Wrong Time
March 24	Palm Sunday Worship/ Choir Cantata	
March 31	John 20:11–18a	Surprise and Expectation
April 7	Luke 24:13–35	Breaking of the Bread
April 14	Eph 5:10–20	You Only Live Once
April 21	Ps 90	The Days of Our Life

April 28	Ps 42	Hope in God
May 5	Ps 128	Find Your Blue Zone
May 12	Col 3:12–4:1	Clothe Yourselves with Love
May 19	Acts 2:1–4, 37–39	The Gift of the Holy Spirit
May 26	Heb 12:1–2	A Cloud of Witnesses
June 2	1 Pet 3:8–17	The Hope That Is in You
June 9	Gen 9:8–17	Under the Rainbow
June 16	Keith Holmes and Mary van Rheenen	
June 23	Col 1:24–29	Mature in Christ
June 30	Rev. David Potter	
July 7	Gal 5:13–25	Freedom in Christ
July 14	Acts 17:16–28	No Longer Unknown
July 21	Mic 6:6–8	What the Lord Requires
July 28	Prov 19:1–17	Kind to the Poor
August 4	Ps 119:105; 2 Tim 2:15; 3:14–17	Rightly Dividing Word of Truth
August 11	Rom 12:14–21	Live Peaceably
August 18	Mark 2:13–17	Just as I Am
August 25	Rev. Starlette McNeill	
September 1	Rev. Dr. C. J. Malloy Jr.	
September 8	John 1:1–18	Who Is Jesus?
September 15	Matt 3:13–17	Jesus Is Baptized
September 22	Matt 4:18–22	Jesus Said: Follow Me
September 29	Luke 7:36–50	Friend of Sinners
October 6	Mark 2:23–28	Jesus and the Sabbath
October 13	John 2:1–11	Keep the Party Going
October 20	Luke 11:5–13	Never Give Up
October 27	Mark 5:1–20	Jesus Casts Out Demons
November 3	Matt 26:26–29	A Thanksgiving Feast
November 10	Ps 119:105	When Life Goes Dark
November 17	Luke 19:1–10	Happy, Happy, Happy

November 24	Ps 86:1–11	Help, Thanks, Wow!
December 1	Luke 1:5–17	Hope
December 8	Luke 1:26–38	Peace
December 15	Rev. Starlette McNeill/Choir Cantata	
December 22	Luke 2:1–7	Person of the Year
December 29	Luke 2:8–20	To Certain Poor Shepherds

2014	**Text**	**Title**
January 5	Matt 2:1–12	A Ruler to Shepherd
January 12	Matt 2:13–18	Tragedy and Consolation
January 19	Rev. Starlette McNeill	
January 26	1 Cor 6:12, 19–20	Temple of the Holy Spirit
February 2	2 Cor 5:14–17	A New Creation
February 9	1 John 2:15–17	What Money Cannot Buy
February 16	Rev. Starlette McNeill	
February 23	Matt 5:1–12	The Pursuit of Happiness
March 2	Luke 12:35–48	And the Oscar Goes To…
March 9	Mark 1:16–20	The Sign of the Fish
March 16	Mark 8:27–35	Jesus, the Christ
March 23	Rev. Starlette McNeill/Youth Sunday	
March 30	Matt 3:13–17; 17:1–8	Son of God
April 6	John 4:39–42	The Savior of the World
April 13	Rev. Starlette McNeill/Choir Cantata	
April 20	Matt 28:1–10	The Game Changer
April 27	Luke 24:13–35	The Walk to Emmaus
May 4	John 21:15–19	The Power of Words
May 11	Matt 12:46–50	The Family of Jesus
May 18	Jas 5:13–16	The Power of Prayer
May 25	Matt 25:14–30	The Crime of Living Cautiously
June 1	Ps 118:1–24	Carpe Diem

Appendix B

June 8	Acts 2:1–4, 14–21	Pentecost Power
June 15	Luke 2:41–52	My Father's House
June 22	Phil 1:1–6	Sharing in the Gospel
June 29	Rev. Starlette McNeill	
July 6	Gal 4:21–5:1	For Freedom Christ Set Us Free
July 13	Ps 96	Worship the Lord
July 20	Rev. Dr. Henry Mugabe	
July 27	Mic 6:8	Justice and Kindness
August 3	Rev. Starlette McNeill	
August 10	Rev. Starlette McNeill	
August 17	Jer 31:31	A New Covenant
August 24	Rom 12:9–21	Overcome Evil with Good
August 31	Exod 33:17–23; John 1:17–18	No One Has Ever Seen God
September 7	Luke 8:4–15	We Were Made to Thrive
September 14	Luke 16:19–31	The Rich Man and Lazarus
September 21	Luke 18:9–14	Now I See
September 28	Luke 11:5–13	Don't Give Up
October 5	Rev. Starlette McNeill	
October 12	Luke 15:11–32	There's No Place Like Home
October 19	Luke 12:13–21	Rich Toward God
October 26	Luke 13:1–9	A Tree Without Fruit
November 2	Luke 14:1–14	Places of Honor
November 9	Luke 14:25–33	Counting the Cost
November 16	Luke 16:1–13	Does Dishonesty Pay?
November 23	Luke 10:25–37	Help Somebody!
November 30	Luke 18:1–8	When He Comes
December 7	Isa 40:1–5	Prepare the Way
December 14	Rev. Starlette McNeill/Choir Cantata	
December 21	Luke 2:8–14	Savior, Messiah, Lord
December 28	Rev. Starlette McNeill	

2015	**Text**	**Title**
January 4	Rom 1:8–17	Not Ashamed of the Gospel
January 11	John 1:19–34	The Lamb of God
January 18	John 2:1–11	Ordinary to Extraordinary
January 25	John 2:13–22	Religious Extremism
February 1	John 3:1–16	Born Again
February 8	John 4:1–14	Living Water
February 15	Rev. Starlette McNeill	
February 22	John 4:46–54	Your Son Will Live
March 1	John 5:1–9a	Power Within
March 8	John 6:1–15	5,000 Fed
March 15	John 9:1–11	Now I See
March 22	Youth Sunday	
March 29	Rev. Starlette McNeill/Choir Cantata	
April 5	John 20:1–10	The Tomb Is Empty
April 12	John 20:11–18a	He Calls You by Name
April 19	John 20:19–25	Fear and Doubt
April 26	John 20:24–29	Beyond Doubt
May 3	John 21:1–14	Breakfast with Jesus
May 10	John 19:25b–30	Here Is Your Mother
May 17	Acts 1:1–9	You Will Receive Power
May 24	Acts 2:1–4, 12–17, 21	Supernatural High
May 31	1 Pet 3:13–18	Advice to Graduates
June 7	Exod 19:1–6	On Eagles' Wings
June 14	Exod 19:16–20; 20:18–21	Smoke on the Mountain
June 21	Rev. Starlette McNeill	
June 28	Exod 20:1–17	The Ten Words
July 5	Exod 24:12–18; 31:18	A Covenant with God
July 12	Exod 32:1–20	A Broken Covenant
July 19	Rev. Starlette McNeill	
July 26	Rev. Starlette McNeill	

August 2	Rev. Starlette McNeill	
August 9	John 10:1–10	Jesus Christ, the Door
August 16	John 17:1, 20–23	One in the Spirit
August 23	1 John 4:7–8	Love One Another
August 30	1 John 4:9–12	If We Love, God Lives in Us
September 6	Prov 22:1–6	A Good Name
September 13	Ps 119:105–112	The Bible Tells Me So
September 20	Rom 16:1–2	Servant Leaders
September 27	Rev. Starlette McNeill	
October 4	Rev. Dr. Pam Durso	
October 11	Phil 1:1–6	The Story of Village
October 18	2 Cor 9:6–15	God's Indescribable Gift
October 25	Rev. Starlette McNeill	
November 1	1 Cor 1:1–3	Called to Be Saints
November 8	Acts 6:1–7	Chosen to Serve
November 15	John 1:1–5, 14	Light in the Darkness
November 22	Phil 4:4–7	With Thanksgiving
November 29	Acts 1:6–14	Mary, Did You Know?
December 6	Luke 8:19–21	The Family of Jesus
December 13	Rev. Starlette McNeill/Choir Cantata	
December 20	Luke 2:22–35	Mary, Soul-Pierced
December 27	Rev. Starlette McNeill	

2016	**Text**	**Title**
January 3	Matt 2:1–12	Take Me to the King
January 10	Matt 2:13–18	Massacre of the Innocents
January 17	Gal 3:27–29	One in Christ Jesus
January 24	Blizzard 2016 (services cancelled)	
January 31	Rom 8:26–28	All Things Work Together
February 7	2 Cor 12:7b–9	Mercies in Disguise

February 14	Rev. Starlette McNeill	
February 21	Matt 22:34–40	The Greatest Commandments
February 28	Matt 26:14–16	30 Pieces of Silver
March 6	Matt 26:20–29	This Is My Body; This Is My Blood
March 13	Matt 26:6–13	In Remembrance of Her
March 20	Matt 21:1–11	Your King Is Coming/Choir Cantata
March 27	Matt 28:1–10	Raised from the Dead
April 3	Matt 28:11–15	They Took the Money
April 10	Rev. Starlette McNeill	
April 17	Matt 28:18–20	With You Always
April 24	Matt 18:21–35	How Many Times?
May 1	1 Pet 1:3–9	The Outcome of Your Faith
May 8	Ruth 1:1–17	Most Influential
May 15	Acts 2:1–4, 37–42	The Birthday of the Church
May 22	1 John 4:7–12	The Birthday of Village Church
May 29	Heb 12:1–2	The Race Before Us
June 5	John 7:37–39	Living Water
June 12	1 Cor 11:17–28	We're in This Together
June 19	Youth Sunday	
June 26	Rev. Dr. Otniel Bunaciu	
July 3	Gal 5:1, 13–14	Freedom in Christ
July 10	1 Cor 13:4–7, 13	The Greatest Gift
July 17	Isa 56:1; 57:1–2, 18–21	Justice and Peace
July 24	Rev. Starlette McNeill	
July 31	Gen 3:1–8	Crashing Without Burning
August 7	Gen 12:1–3, 10–20	A Test of Faith
August 14	Num 20:2–12; Deut 34:1–12	The Promised Land
August 21	2 Sam 11:2–15, 26–27	Bad Things Done by Good People
August 28	Rev. Starlette McNeill	
September 4	Rev. Starlette McNeill	

Appendix B

September 11	Rom 15:22–29	Like Faith and Order
September 18	Matt 20:20–28	Called to Serve
September 25	John 15:9–11	Jesus, Man of Joy
October 2	Rev. Starlette McNeill	
October 9	1 Pet 2:9–10	Come from Away
October 16	Ps 90:1–12; Jas 4:13–17	Counting Our Days
October 23	Rev. Dr. Bruce Gourley	
October 30	Acts 6:1–7	Waiting on Tables
November 6	Ps 91	The Election
November 13	Ps 92:1–4	Good to Give Thanks
November 20	Rev. Starlette McNeill	
November 27	Luke 1:5–14, 18–20, 24–25	What the Lord Has Done
December 4	Rev. Carmella Jones	
December 11	Rev. Starlette McNeill/Choir Cantata	
December 18	Rev. Starlette McNeill	
December 25	Luke 2:7–20	Song of the Angels Is Stilled

2017	**Text**	**Title**
January 1	Luke 2:22–24, 36–38	Anna's Praise
January 8	Matt 2:1–12	Gifts for a King
January 15	Luke 2:22–32	A Light for Revelation
January 22	Luke 3:1–3, 21–22	Jesus Is Baptized
January 29	Luke 3:23a; 4:1–13	Jesus Is Tempted
February 5	Luke 4:14–21	The Mission Statement of Jesus
February 12	Rev. Starlette McNeill	
February 19	Luke 4:22–30	Jesus, the Troublemaker
February 26	Luke 4:31–37	Authority and Power
March 5	Luke 4:38–44	Never Done
March 12	Luke 5:1–11	A New Career
March 19	Luke 5:12–16	Clean!
March 26	Luke 5:17–26	Forgiven; Healed!

April 2	Luke 5:27–32	Following Jesus
April 9	Rev. Starlette McNeill/Choir Cantata	
April 16	Luke 24:1–12	Death Was Arrested
April 23	Rev. Starlette McNeill	
April 30	Rom 6:3–5	Newness of Life
May 7	Jas 1:2–9	You Raise Me Up
May 14	John 19:25b–27	Mary, the Mother of Jesus
May 21	Rev. Starlette McNeill/Youth Sunday	
May 28	1 Thess 4:13–14	Grieving with Hope
June 4	1 Cor 12:4–11; Gal 5:22–25	Gifts and Fruit
June 11	Phil 3:7–14	The Magnificent Obsession
June 18	Luke 11:9–13	The Heavenly Father
June 25	Rev 21:1–7	When Death Was Arrested
July 2	Gen 2:18–25	Mutual Empowerment
July 9	Gen 30:1–13	The Handmaid's Tale
July 16	Heb 10:19–25	Provoke One Another
July 23	Rev. Dr. Trisha Miller Manarin	
July 30	Exod 32:1–8, 19–30	On God's Side
August 6	Mic 6:8	The Good Life
August 13	Ps 90:1–2, 9–17	Grow Old Along with Me
August 20	Amos 5:18–24	The Day of the Lord
August 27	Rev. Starlette McNeill	
September 3	2 Tim 3:10–17	Back to School
September 10	Heb 13:1–8	No H8
September 17	Rom 16:1–16	A Deacon of the Church
September 24	Matt 5:43–48	The Sun Rises and the Rains Fall
October 1	Rev. Starlette Thomas	
October 8	Ps 24:1–5	The Earth Is the Lord's
October 15	Matt 20:20–28	But to Serve

Appendix B

October 22	Matt 18:21–22	77 Times
October 29	Rom 1:16–17	Live by Faith
November 5	Ps 46	God Is Our Refuge
November 12	Rev. Starlette Thomas	
November 19	Ps 107:1–9	His Steadfast Love
November 26	Phil 1:2–6	I Thank God for You
December 3	Isa 7:14; 9:6; Matt 1:18–23	What's in a Name?
December 10	Rev. Starlette Thomas/Choir Cantata	
December 17	Luke 2:1–7	An Uncertain Journey
December 24	Luke 2:8–20	The Singing of Angels
December 31	John 1:14–18	God's Love Made Visible

Appendix C

January, Winter, Summer, and Lenten Bible Studies (1986-2017)

Pastor's Sunday School Class (2000-2017)

Although I did not aspire to be a preacher, I always enjoyed studying the Bible. In college and in seminary, one of my "guilty pleasures" was taking biblical courses as electives. At Baylor I was enthralled by Dr. Bob Patterson's introduction to the Old Testament. For the first time, all the stories of the Old Testament began to fit together. Patterson's explanation of the "JEPD" theory of how the Pentateuch was put together was a revelation to me. I began to see there was a lot more to the Bible than I had been taught in Sunday school.

In seminary I took as many biblical courses as my schedule would allow. Two of my favorites were the Gospel of John, taught by Dr. Alan Culpepper, and the parables of Jesus, taught by Dr. Peter Rhea Jones. Textbooks and commentaries for those and other "Bible classes" became the core of my theological library.

The spring of my last year at Southern Seminary, a group of us went to Churchill Downs in Louisville to experience some horse races. I was not a betting man, but I put down two dollars on a trifecta with the intention, if I did score a big payout, of using the winnings to buy a used set of *The Interpreter's Bible*, the commentary series edited by Dr. George Buttrick. I didn't win, but eventually I was able to buy the set, along with *The Interpreter's Dictionary of the Bible*, also edited by Dr. Buttrick. I also bought a used set of *The Broadman Bible Commentary* since some of the volumes were written by my seminary professors.

In the fire that destroyed our church building in 2000, my entire library was destroyed, except for one Bible I had taken home the night before. Over the following years my library was rebuilt with donations from other ministers and through purchases of new commentary sets and other reference books. Dr. Earl Martin, retired Cooperative Baptist Fellowship field personnel, gave me his set of *The Interpreter's Dictionary of the Bible.* John Mitchell, a member of our church who went to law school after seminary, gave me his set of *The Interpreter's Bible.* My home church in Fort Worth, Broadway Baptist, gave me a new set of *The Anchor Bible Dictionary.*

Among the most valued additions I was able to purchase were *The New Interpreter's Bible* commentary set, *The New Interpreter's Dictionary of the Bible,* the *Interpretation* commentary series, and the *Smyth & Helwys Bible Commentary* series. Having access to good commentaries and reference books was essential to sermon preparation and Bible teaching. Even though many resources are available online, I still prefer a book I can hold in my hands, mark up, and read slowly and thoughtfully.

I did not begin teaching Sunday school until 2000, after our church building burned. Before that, I used the Sunday school hour to go over my sermon in my office. But after our building was destroyed, we were meeting at the Bowie Alliance Church. I had access to the pastor's study, but it didn't feel right to stay in there while everyone else was in Sunday school. So I proposed a new pastor's Sunday school class that would meet up the street at our rented temporary church offices. The class would be a basic Bible study, verse by verse, book by book, open to any adults who might be interested in such an approach. By this time, after fifteen years of preaching Sunday after Sunday, I no longer felt the need to go over my sermon again during the Sunday school hour. Plus, I always did plenty of that the night before. Saturday nights are not a carefree time for pastors. For me, Saturday nights were a time to focus intently and intensely on what I would be saying Sunday morning.

The pastor's Sunday school class continued after we occupied the rebuilt church building in late 2002. The class included some members with very little Bible knowledge or Sunday school experience. The basic verse-by-verse, book-by-book approach helped them feel less intimidated by their lack of Bible knowledge. We would read a few verses, pause for questions and comments, and then move on to the next few verses. I continued this approach for the rest of my ministry at Village. Eventually the class included members who did have Bible class experience, but it was still open to anyone.

I also led a Sunday evening Bible study for four to eight weeks every winter, from 1986 through 2017. It began as a January Bible study, then became a winter Bible study, then transitioned into a Lenten Bible study. I would select a Bible book or topic, sometimes with a supplementary study book available for purchase by participants. If we were studying a book of the Bible, often I would preach from that book on Sunday mornings. In 1988 I offered a Sunday evening Bible study throughout the summer. We used as our resource book, *Introducing the New Testament*, by John Drane.

To be honest about it, I enjoyed teaching more than preaching. The creativity required to write a sermon, and then the oral skills required to deliver it, was certainly demanding. But the interaction from teaching gave more immediate feedback. Teaching Sunday school and the various evening Bible studies came more naturally to me than preaching. Teaching was basically the overflow from my personal Bible study. Preaching was more difficult, even if rewarding in a different way.

A pastor's job involves many dimensions—preaching, teaching, pastoral care, church administration, evangelizing, ministering, writing, socializing, fellowshipping, fundraising, visioning, conducting baptisms and infant dedications and weddings and funerals, and so much more. I was better at some of those roles than others. But teaching had a special place in my heart, right along with reading and studying the Bible. And to think, doing what I loved could help others too!

January Bible Studies (1986-1990)

January 1986—Hebrews; Friday nights in homes; Sunday morning sermons on Hebrews

January 1987—James; Sunday nights in homes; Sunday morning sermons on James

January 1988—Malachi; Sunday nights at church; Sunday morning sermons on Malachi

January–February 1989—John; Sunday nights at church; Sunday morning sermons on John

February 1990—2 Corinthians; Sunday nights at church; Sunday morning sermons on 2 Corinthians

Summer Bible Study (1988)

June–August 1988—Sunday nights at church; *Introducing the New Testament* (Drane)

Winter Bible Studies (1991-2007)

February 1991—Acts; Sunday nights at church; Sunday morning sermons on Acts

February 1992—Isaiah; Sunday nights at church; Sunday morning sermons on Isaiah

February 1993—Sermon on the Mount; Sunday nights at church; Sunday morning sermons on Matthew 5–7

January–March 1994—The Life of Christ; Sunday nights at church; Sunday morning sermons on the Gospels; study book, *Immanuel: Reflections on the Life of Christ* (Card)

February–March 1995—Genesis; Sunday nights at church

February 1996—Exodus; Sunday nights at church; Sunday morning sermons on Exodus

January–February 1997—Revelation; Sunday nights at church

February 1998—Parables of Jesus in Luke; Sunday nights at church; Sunday morning sermons on Luke

February 1999—Joshua; Sunday nights at church; Sunday morning sermons on Joshua

February 2000—Mark; Sunday nights at home of Leslie and Pete Parreco; Sunday morning sermons on Mark

February 2001—Luke; Sunday nights at home of Leslie and Pete Parreco

February 2002—The Life of Paul; Sunday nights at home of Leslie and Pete Parreco

February 2003—*1 & 2 Samuel* (Dant); Sunday nights at church

January 2004—*Romans* (Olson); Sunday nights at church, Sunday morning sermons on Romans

January 2005—*John—The Son of Zebedee* (Culpepper); Sunday nights at church

January 2006—Ezekiel; Sunday nights at church; Sunday morning sermons on Ezekiel

January 2007—*Matthew* (Sayles); Sunday nights at church; Sunday morning sermons on Matthew

Lenten Bible Studies (2008-2017)

Lent 2008—The Passion of Jesus; Sunday nights at church with dinner

Lent 2009—*Timeless Witness: Classic Christian Literature* (Lane); Sunday nights at church with dinner

Lent 2010—The Sermon on the Mount; Sunday nights at church with dinner

Lent 2011—*The Many Gospels of Jesus* (Comfort/Driesbach); Sunday nights at church with dinner

Lent 2012—*The Jesus of the Bible* (Miller); Sunday nights at church with dinner

Lent 2013—*Jesus, the Final Days* (N.T. Wright/Evans); Sunday nights at church with dinner

Lent 2014—*Discovering Jesus* (Barclay); Sunday nights at church with dinner

Lent 2015—*John* (Kostenberger); Sunday nights at church with dinner

Lent 2016—*Matthew* (Wilkins); Sunday nights at church with dinner, Sunday morning sermons on Matthew

Lent 2017—*Exodus* (Goldingay); Sunday nights at church with dinner; Passover Seder

www.ingramcontent.com/pod-product-compliance
Lightning Source LLC
Chambersburg PA
CBHW051117160426
43195CB00014B/2248